YALE LECTURES ON THE SUNDAY-SCHOOL

Yale Divinity School
Feb. 29th. 1888

Rev. Henry Clay Trumbull D.D.;

    Dear Sir,

        The Faculty of the Seminary desire to offer to you their cordial thanks for the Course of Lectures on the Lyman Beecher Foundation, which you have recently given in this Institution. We beg leave to express the hope that these instructive and interesting discourses may soon be given to the public.

        Timothy Dwight
        Geo. E. Day.
        Samuel Harris
        George P. Fisher
        Lewis O. Brastow
        John E. Russell
        George B. Stevens

YALE LECTURES ON THE SUNDAY-SCHOOL

THE

SUNDAY-SCHOOL

ITS ORIGIN, MISSION, METHODS, AND AUXILIARIES

———

The *By* Lyman Beecher Lectures

Before Yale Divinity School

for 1888

———

By H. CLAY TRUMBULL

Editor of The Sunday School Times, Author of Kadesh Barnea,
The Blood Covenant, Teaching and Teachers, etc.

———

90

PHILADELPHIA

JOHN D. WATTLES, Publisher

1888

PREFACE.

These Lectures are, in their present form, an immediate result of a special and unexpected call from the Faculty of Yale Divinity School. Yet they are in reality the growth of years; and because of this fact their practical value ought to be the greater.

It is just thirty years ago, on the day of this writing, that I entered the Sunday-school field as the field of my chosen life-work. Already I had been interested in this work from my very start in the Christian life; but now I was led to give myself to the promoting of its interests, to the abandonment of all other occupations. To this decision I was influenced by my belief that the Sunday-school is an agency approved of God for the evangelizing and the religious training of the race; and that it is peculiarly and pre-eminently adapted to the needs of our American communities. Hardly had I entered my new field, however, when I was met by the criticism, or the objection, that the Sunday-school is in rivalry with the mission of the family on the one hand, and of the ministry on the other, and that at the best it is a poor substitute for either.

These criticisms at once turned me to the careful study of the agency in the prosecution of which I had enlisted. My belief in the value of the agency was a cause, and not a result, of my being engaged in it. If there was

v

a better agency available in the plans of God, I wanted to change my course accordingly. And so it was that I entered upon a critical examination of the teachings of the Bible and of outside history, in order to learn more surely what was God's chiefest provision for the ingathering and for the religious upbringing of the children of men. The more I studied the more I found, in the teachings of Scripture and of history, which was at variance with traditional practices and views, but which must be accepted by him who would follow God's word and the leadings of sound reason. I came to realize, as never before, that the Sunday-school of to-day substantially represents God's chosen agency, from of old, for the evangelizing and for the instruction of those whom his Church is set to reach and to rear; and in this new conviction I gained steadily in devotedness to the work which I now deemed God's work pre-eminently.

Just here I may properly cite the testimony, in this direction, of one whose opinion will be recognized as worth so many times more than my own. The Rev. Dr. Horace Bushnell was good enough to have a kind and generous personal interest in me from the beginning of my Christian life. After the years of my army chaplaincy (which alone was my connection with the ordained ministry) he repeatedly urged me to devote myself to the labors of the pulpit and of the pastorate; but I was confident that the Sunday-school field was where God would have me labor, and so there I remained. As the years passed by, Dr. Bushnell's estimate of the idea which is back of the Sunday-school was much enlarged, and he had a new sense of its relative importance. Meeting me one day not long before his death, Dr. Bushnell said: "Trumbull, you knew better than I did where the Lord wanted you. I honestly thought the pulpit was a bigger place for you, and I tried to get you into it. But now I've come to see that the work you are in is the greatest work in the world." And after a moment's pause he added, "Sometimes I think it's the *only* work there is in the world." And many another has come, in these later years, to see this truth as this great thinker saw it.

When I had been called to the editorial advocacy and exposition of the Sunday-school, my gathered material for the showing of the historic development of the modern Sunday-school was laid aside; and I thought it would never be put into any permanent form. But the summons from Yale to deliver a series of lectures on the Sunday-school and its Auxiliaries, as the Lyman Beecher Lecturer for 1888, was a providential call to the taking up and the systematizing and the completing of this material; and the volume herewith is an outcome of that summons.

Both in my earlier and in my later investigations, I have been materially aided by specialists in one field and another of research. Among these helpers to whom I am particularly indebted, I mention gratefully Professor Dr. J. A. Broadus, of the Southern Baptist Theological Seminary, Louisville, Kentucky; Professor Dr. M. B. Riddle, of the Western (Presbyterian) Theological Seminary, Allegheny, Pennsylvania; Professor Dr. J. Rendel Harris, of Haverford College; the Rev. Dr. E. T. Bartlett, Dean of the Episcopal Divinity School, and Professor Dr. J. F. Garrison, of the same institution; Professor Dr. W. J. Mann, of the Lutheran Theological Seminary; the Rev. Dr. A. Spaeth, President of the Lutheran General Council; Professor Dr. R. E. Thompson, of the University of Pennsylvania, and the Rev. Dr. Morris Jastrow, of Philadelphia; also my colleague in editorial work, Professor Dr. H. V. Hilprecht, and my brother, Dr. J. Hammond Trumbull, of Hartford, Connecticut. In the collecting and verifying of all the Talmudic citations, I have had valuable assistance from Dr. Jacob Mayer, a careful rabbinical scholar. In my huntings for books of reference I have received special assistance from the Rev. Joseph H. Dulles, of Princeton, New Jersey; Mr. James MacAlister, of Philadelphia; and Mr. Benjamin Clarke, of the London Sunday School Union. In searching out and verifying references generally, as well as in the preparation of the bibliographical and topical indexes, I acknowledge important aid from the Rev. E. M. Fergusson. The mention of these names is an indication of the number of skilled workers who have contributed to whatever of thoroughness or of accuracy there is in the volume as it stands.

The hearty welcome which these Lectures received from those before whom they were delivered, justifies the belief that they will be found to have a value to those who read them in their present form. They are printed substantially as delivered, with the addition of foot-notes, in proof of the correctness of their position.

H. CLAY TRUMBULL.

PHILADELPHIA, *September* 1, 1888.

CONTENTS.

LECTURE III.

THE SUNDAY-SCHOOL: ITS MODERN REVIVAL
AND EXPANSION.

LECTURE IV.

THE SUNDAY-SCHOOL: ITS INFLUENCE ON
THE FAMILY.

LECTURE VIII.

THE SUNDAY-SCHOOL: ITS AUXILIARY TRAINING AGENCIES.

LECTURE IX.

PREACHING TO CHILDREN: ITS IMPORTANCE AND ITS DIFFICULTIES.

LECTURE X.

PREACHING TO CHILDREN: ITS PRINCIPLES
AND ITS METHODS.

INDEXES.

LECTURE I.

THE SUNDAY–SCHOOL: ITS JEWISH ORIGIN AND
ITS CHRISTIAN ADOPTION.

I.

THE SUNDAY-SCHOOL: ITS JEWISH ORIGIN AND ITS CHRISTIAN ADOPTION.

Definition of a Sunday-school.—Rabbinical Traditions of its Primeval Prominence.—Old Testament Light on its Pathway.—Its Mentions in Ancient History.—Its Prominence in the Synagogue Plans.—Its Primal Curriculum.—Its Essential Methods of Working.—Its Fundamental Importance in the Jewish Economy.—Jesus as a Scholar in the Sunday-school.—As a Teacher there.—His Methods of Teaching.—His Command to Start Sunday-schools Everywhere.—Apostolic Sunday-school Work.—Sunday-schools as the Basis of the Christian Church.

The Sunday-school: Its Origin, Mission, Methods, and Auxiliaries; this is the subject of a series of lectures which I am to deliver here at the invitation of the honored Faculty of Yale Divinity School. And, as preliminary to an intelligent discussion of the theme, it is important to arrive at a definition of the term "Sunday-school," as that term is to be understood and employed in this discussion.

A Sunday-school is an agency of the Church, by which the Word of God is taught interlocutorily, or catechetically, to children and other learners clustered in groups or classes under separate teachers; all these groups or classes being associated under a common head. Herein the Sunday-school is differentiated from the catechismal

3

general service, from the expository Bible lecture, from the children's meeting, and from any school for secular instruction on the first day of the week. Its source of authority is God's Church; its subject-matter of study is the Bible; its form of teaching includes a free use of question and answer; its membership includes children; its arrangement is by groups clustering severally around individual teachers, as component portions of a unified whole. Any one of these particulars lacking, a school held on Sunday fails of being specifically a Sunday-school. All of these particulars being found, a gathering is substantially a Sunday-school, on whatever day of the week it assembles, or by whatsoever name it be called.

That the Sunday-school in its essential characteristics, as thus defined, was a prominent feature in the economy of the Jewish Church, and that it was included as an integral factor of the Christian Church in the declared plans of the divine Founder of that church, would seem to be evident in the light of the plain facts of history— sacred and secular. It is to those facts that I invite fresh attention just here.

The origin of the Sunday-school, or of this catechetical Bible-school, like the origin of the synagogue, is not fixed with accuracy in Jewish history. Traditions ot both these religious agencies run far back of the trust-worthy records; but even these traditions have a certain value, as indicative of the earlier existence of the insti-tutions about which they are found already clustering, (with a deeply rooted popular confidence in their verity,) when the institutions themselves have their first distinct record. Hence the multiplied traditions of the promi-nence and the power of the synagogue Bible-school in the earlier ages of the world's story, which are to be found recorded in the Talmud and the Targums, are of interest as giving an air of antiquity to that agency of instruction when first it appears in unmistakable plainness as an established historical fact, surrounded by many myths and legends of its primeval honor and usefulness.

The Rabbis tell us that Methuselah was a teacher of the Mishna, before the Flood;[1] that, after the Deluge, Shem and Eber had a House of Instruction where the Halacha was studied;[2] that Abraham was a student of the Torah when he was three years old,[3] and that he was afterward under the teaching of Melchizedek in matters concerning the priesthood;[4] that young Jacob as a good boy did go to the Bible-school, while Esau as a bad boy did not;[5] that Dinah the daughter of Jacob came to grief[6] through playing truant from the Bible-school while her brothers were in attendance there;[7] that among the pupils of Moses in his great Bible-school were his father-in-law Jethro and young Joshua, and that the latter was preferred above the sons of Moses, as his successor, because of his greater zeal and fidelity in the Bible-school exercises;[8] that the victory of Deborah and Barak reopened the schools for Bible study, which had been closed by the Canaanites;[9] that Samuel conducted Bible-schools which were continued to the days of Elisha and

---

[1] Yalqut on Gen., 12 *a.* See, also, Delitzsch-Weber's *Syst. der Altsynag. Paläst. Theol.*, p. 34.

[2] Targ. Jon. on Gen. 22: 19; 24: 62. Bereshith Rabba, ch. 84; comp. ch. 56 and ch. 63.   [3] Bereshith Rabba, ch. 95.

[4] Bereshith Rabba, ch. 43. Yalqut on Gen., 19 *c.*   [5] Bereshith Rabba, ch. 63.
[6] Gen. 34: 1 ff.   [7] Qoheleth Rabba, 93 *a.*
[8] Yalqut on Exod., 76 *a ;* on Josh., 3 *a.* Comp. also Berakhoth, 63 *b.*
[9] Targ. Jon. on Judg. 5: 2.

beyond;[1] that wicked King Ahaz had the Bible-schools for children closed in order to exterminate the religion of Moses; that good King Hezekiah, on the other hand, not only fostered the Bible-school system,[2] but personally bore his own children to receive instruction in one of these schools;[3] and finally that the prophecy of Haggai concerning the greater glory of the second temple[4] had reference to the Bible teaching which was to be carried on there, and which, by means of the synagogues and Bible-schools, was to be extended near and far.[5] All this is mere fanciful tradition, it is true; but even as tradition it has an interest through what it shows of the estimation in which the Bible-school was held by the Rabbis, at the time of the recording of these steadily gathering traditions concerning its ancient place and power.

In the line of gleams of light from the Old Testament text on this pathway of rabbinical tradition, we find, in Genesis,[6] a reference to Abraham's three hundred and eighteen instructed[7] retainers. In the Chronicles, we see

---

[1] Targ. Jon. on 1 Sam. 19: 18 f.

[2] 2 Chron. 28: 24; 29: 3. See Rashi, *in loco;* also Molitor's *Philos. d. Gesch.*, Part I., p. 155.

[3] Berakhoth, 10 *a, b.* Menorath Ha-maor, iii., 2, 2.   [4] Hag. 2: 9.

[5] Comp. Shir Rabba on Cant. 7: 12, 13; Yalqut, *in loco;* Erubin, 21 *a.*

[6] Gen. 14: 14.

[7] The Hebrew word (*chaneekh*) translated in our English Bible "trained," includes in its meaning the idea of a training in religion as well as in a use of weapons; and its use in this place would presuppose a process of school instruction under Abraham's oversight. (Comp. Gesenius's *Thesaurus*, s. v., with citation from Kimchi; Fleischer, in Levy's *Neuhebr. Lex.*, s. v.; Wellhausen's *Skizz. und Vorarb.*, Heft 3, p. 154; Dillmann's *Comm. z. Gen.*, in loco; Buxtorf's *Lex. Heb. et Chald.*, s. v.; Schaff-Lange's *Comm.*, in loco, with citation from Wordsworth: "Abram had trained them in spiritual things in the service of God, as well as in fidelity to himself; see chap. 18: 19; 24: 12-49.") Junius and Tremellius, in the Genevan Bible of 1630, say that

that when Jehoshaphat was working reforms in his land, the princes and the priests and the Levites "taught in Judah, having the book of the law of the Lord with them; and they went about throughout all the cities of Judah, and taught among the people."[1] In Nehemiah[2] we have a completer exhibit of actual methods of Bible instruction, in the record of a great open-air Bible-school in Jerusalem, after the return of the Jews from captivity. Ezra was the superintendent in this school. His assisting teachers are mentioned by name. The opening prayer, the responsive service, and the details of class teaching, are all described, as if in illustration of the custom in such a gathering then, and thenceforward, in the Holy Land.

Coming down to a time when we have contemporaneous records to aid us, at a point where the Bible narrative is lacking in fullness of detail, we find Josephus claiming that, from the days of Moses, it was a custom of the Jews to assemble in their synagogues every Sabbath, not only to hear the law, but "to *learn* it accurately," and that so thorough is this instruction of the young in the teachings of the law, that, as he expresses it, " if any one of us [Jews] should be questioned concerning the laws, he would more easily repeat all than his own name."[3] This certainly is evidence that these weekly gatherings

these servants of Abram were "instructed concerning the right of this expedition, and concerning religious knowledge." Payne Smith (Ellicott's *O. T. Comm.*, at Gen. 4: 17) points out that " in old times the ideas of training and dedication were closely allied, because teaching generally took the form of initiation into sacred rites, and one so initiated [or trained] was regarded as a consecrated person."

[1] 2 Chron. 17: 7-9.　　　　　　　　　　　　　　[2] Neh. 8: 1-8.

[3] *Contra Ap.*, ii., 17, 18. Comp. i., 12; *Antiq.*, iv., 8, 12.

for Bible study were not a very new thing in the days of
Josephus. We find Philo, also, who even antedates Josephus, affirming that the synagogues of the Jews were
really " houses of instruction," and that with the help of
these agencies the Jews were, " by their parents, tutors,
and teachers," instructed in the knowledge of the law
"from their earliest youth," so that " they bear the image
of the law in their souls."[1] Moreover, with all the unhis-
toric character of the Talmud and the other rabbinical
writings, there are given in them many items of information concerning the times of their compiling, and the
times just before, which are not to be passed over lightly
in an investigation like this. Competent and careful scholars of this literature have brought out facts which justify
the statements which I now make in this connection.

According to the Rabbis it was about 80–70 B. C. that
Simon ben Shetach, as president of the Sanhedrin, established — or, as some would claim, he re-established—a
system of religious schools in conjunction with the local
synagogues throughout Palestine, making attendance at
them obligatory.[2] Whatever question there may be as to
the personality of this Simon ben Shetach, there would
seem to be good reason for believing that this special
work which is ascribed to him was wrought by some
person or persons as early as the date to which he is
assigned. " Eighty years before Christ," says Deutsch,
" schools flourished throughout the length and breadth

---

[1] *Vita Mosis*, i., 27 (Mang. II., 168). *Legat. ad Caium*, §§ 16, 31 (Mang.
II., 562, 577).

[2] Jerus. Kethuboth, viii., 11. Ginsburg, art. " Education," in Alexander-
Kitto's *Cyc. of Bib. Lit.* Schürer's *Hist. of the Jewish People*, Div. II.,
Vol. II., § 27, p. 49. Hamburger's *Real-Encyc.*, II., 672 (note 1), 1102.

of the land;—education had been made compulsory;"[1] and this statement represents the modern view of Jewish scholars generally. Additional honor in this line is again ascribed by the Rabbis to Joshua ben Gamla (that is, Jesus the son of Gamaliel), who was high-priest about 63–65 A. D., and of whom Josephus makes frequent mention. He is said to have "enacted that teachers should be appointed in every province and in every town, and [that] children of six or seven years old [should be] brought to them."[2] This is believed by many to have been a re-enacting of laws of an earlier date, which had fallen into neglect in the progress of time. Certain it is that, at the latest, in the second century after Christ, the records of the Mishna assume the existence of elementary religious schools in connection with the synagogues; not as recently established, but as a well-known institution.[3]

Thus, from the evidence of Philo and of Josephus, and from the incidental proofs furnished in the assumed state of things according to the earliest records of the Talmud, we have every reason to believe, and none to doubt, that a system of Bible-schools in connection with the synagogues of Palestine was a recognized feature of the Jewish economy at the beginning of the Christian era. Describing the influences which were about a Jewish child at this period, Edersheim says: "There can be no reasonable doubt that at that time such schools existed throughout the land."[4] Schürer, who is little

---

[1] *Literary Remains*, p. 23. Comp. Jost's *Allg. Gesch. d. Israel. Volk.*, Vol. II., p. 13, note.

[2] Schürer's *Hist.*, Div. II., Vol. II., § 27, p. 49; also Vol. I., § 23, p. 201.

[3] *Ibid.*, Vol. II., § 27, p. 49.

[4] *Life and Times of Jesus the Messiah*, I., 230. Comp. *Sketches of Jewish Social Life*, p. 118.

inclined to give weight to mere tradition, or to accept any point which will bear challenging, says that while the education of Jewish children in the teachings of the law "was, in the first place, the duty and task of parents, it appears that, even in the age of Christ, care was taken for the instruction of youth by the erection of schools on the part of the community."[1]

Ginsburg finds added proof of the growth in prominence and favor of these elementary Bible-schools at an earlier date than our era, in their impress upon the Hebrew language of the times. "So popular did these schools [which are ascribed to Simon ben Shetach] become," he says, "that whilst in the pre-exile period

---

[1] *Hist.*, Div. II., Vol. II., § 27, pp. 48-50. Reuss (*Geschichte der Heiligen Schriften Alten Test.*, p. 677) says of the Pharisees in the days of Christ: "The most powerful lever of their activity was the *school.*" Geikie (*Life and Words of Christ*, I., 172) says: "It cannot be doubted that boys' schools were already general in the time of Christ." Merrill (*Galilee in the Time of Christ*, p. 91) in combating the claim that there was at that time in Palestine any system of popular education, in our modern understanding of the term "education," says: "The only schools were those connected with the synagogues. The only school-book was the Hebrew Scriptures. A synagogue presupposed a school, just as in our country a church presupposes a Sunday-school. Church and district-school [the New England term for a neighborhood public school] is not a parallel to the Jewish system of things, but church and Sunday-school is." While these pages are being put in type, I see, for the first time, Stapfer's *Palestine in the Time of Christ*, in which again the suggestion is made of a likeness of the ancient Jewish schools to the modern Sunday-schools. "What means of instruction," he asks (p. 142), "were there at Nazareth between the years 4 B. C. and 10 A. D., that is to say, in the time of the Lord's boyhood? Was there already a free school, or class for the townspeople's children, taught by the chazzān? This seems to us extremely likely, though we have no positive proof. Perhaps on the Sabbath day there was a catechising, or what we should now call a Sunday-school." These repeated references, by writers from widely different standpoints, to this correspondence of the synagogue schools with the Sunday-school, give proof that the idea is in no sense a forced one from the mind of a Sunday-school specialist.

the very name of *schools* did not exist, we now find in a very short time no less than eleven different expressions for 'school.'"[1] These expressions include such meanings as "house of instruction," "house of learning," "house of the book," "house of the teacher," "house of the master," "the seat" (where the disciples sat at the feet of the master, or teacher), "an array" (where the disciples were arranged according to their seniority and acquirements), and "the vineyard" (the place of refreshing and of fruitfulness).

That the elementary schools of this Jewish system of public education were Bible-schools, corresponding quite closely in their essential features with our modern Sunday-schools, is a demonstrable fact. Indeed, the chief value of the synagogues themselves, in the estimation of the Jews, was as a means of promoting the study and teaching of the law. "The main object of these Sabbath-day assemblages in the synagogue," says Schürer, "was not public worship in its stricter sense; that is, not devotion, but religious instruction, and this for an Israelite was, above all, *instruction in the law.*"[2] And of the *schools* connected with the synagogues, Schürer says: "The subject of instruction . . . was as good as exclusively the law; for only its inculcation in the youthful mind, and not the means of general education, was the aim of all this zeal

---

[1] *Cyc. of Bib. Lit.*, art. "Education." Comp. Deutsch's *Literary Remains*, p. 23 f.

[2] *Hist.*, Div. II., Vol. II., § 27, p. 54. As illustrative of a common error at this point, Cohen (cited by Geikie, in *Life and Words of Christ*, I., 566, Notes) claims that while there might have been *schools* in Jerusalem, there could not have been any *synagogues* there, "since public worship could be held there, nowhere but in the Temple." In fact, the synagogues were nowhere places for public worship, in its then understood sense, while the Temple yet stood,

for the instruction of youth. And indeed the earliest instruction was in the reading and inculcation of the *text of Scripture.*" [1]

From five to ten years of age, the Jewish child was to study in these schools the Bible text only.[2] It was not until after a five years' course in the plain teachings of the Bible itself, that he was to venture into the bewildering maze of what corresponded with our modern catechisms and commentaries and lesson-helps generally; a custom which is not without its valuable suggestion for religious teachers of children in our day. And it is a noteworthy fact that the Jewish child's first Bible-school lessons were in Leviticus,[3] rather than in Genesis or Exodus. An arrangement of that sort would provoke no little adverse comment, if it were proposed by an International Lesson Committee of to-day; all of which goes to show that it is not an easy matter to satisfy everybody in the arranging of a Sunday-school curriculum. From ten to fifteen years of age, the Jewish child's school studies were in the substance of the Mishna, or the yet unwritten Mosaic traditions, with their rabbinical commentaries, while still he included the Bible text in his studies. After that age, the youth was privileged to share in those endless discussions of the Rabbis over the details of the Mishna teaching, which later made up the Gemara, or the " completion " of rabbinical exegesis and eisegesis.[4]

---

[1] *Hist.*, Div. II., Vol. II., § 27, p. 50.

[2] Buxtorf's *Synag. Jud.*, p. 140 f.   Taylor's *Sayings of the Jewish Fathers*, p. III.   Comp. Ginsburg, in *Cyc. of Bib. Lit.*, art. " Education ; " Edersheim's *Life and Times*, I., 232 ; Hamburger's *Real-Encyc.*, I., 340 ; and Strack, in Herzog's *Real-Encyc.*, IX., 389.   [3] Wayyiqra Rabba, ch. 7.

[4] See proofs of all this in Hamburger, Herzog, Edersheim, and Ginsburg, as above.   See, also, Van Gelder's *Die Volkssch. d. Jüd. Alterth.*, p. 10 f.

Care was taken that the text-books and lesson-helps in these Bible-schools were ample and trustworthy.[1] A library was attached to every school-house,[2] where copies of the Holy Scripture were kept available. Although it was deemed unlawful to make copies of small portions of any of the books of Scripture, an " exception was made of certain sections which were copied for the instruction of children."[3] These selections included the historic record from the Creation to the Flood; the first nine chapters of Leviticus, and the first ten chapters of Numbers;[4] together with the Shema,[5] which, strictly speaking, was Deuteronomy 6: 4-9, but which frequently embraced also Deuteronomy 11: 13-21 and Numbers 15: 37-41, and the Hallel (Psalms 113-118, 136).[6] This seems to have been the origin of the Sunday-school lesson-leaf, with its " fragmentary," or " scrappy," portions of the Bible, which is now vexing so many pious minds as a dangerous modern innovation. It was first authorized by the Sanhedrin Uniform Lesson Committee, two thousand years or so ago. Attention was also given to the fitness of the instruction from these lesson-leaves; " that the lessons taught . . . should be in harmony with the capacities and inclinations of the children; practical, few at a time, but weighty."[7]

The location and surroundings of the Bible-schools

---

[1] Pesachim, 112 *a.*

[2] Jerus. Megilla, iii., 1. Edersheim's *Life and Times*, I., 233.

[3] Edersheim, as above.

[4] Jerus. Megilla, as above. See, also, Sopherim, v., 1, p. 25 *b;* Gittin, 60 *a;* cited by Edersheim, as above. Comp. Ginsburg, in *The Bible Educator*, I., 47.

[5] See Schürer's *Hist.*, Div. II., Vol. II., § 27, pp. 77, 84 f.

[6] Farrar's *Life and Work of St. Paul*, I., 43.

[7] Ginsburg, in *Cyc. of Bib. Lit.*, art. " Education." See, also, Berakhoth, 63 *a;* Qiddushin, 82 *b;* Wayyiqra Rabba, ch. 3.

were deemed not unimportant. Ordinarily they were in the synagogue building, or in a building attached to it;[1] but in any event they must not be in a too crowded quarter, nor near an insecure crossing-place of a river.[2] School hours were limited, and they were variously proportioned according to different seasons of the year.[3] Neither health nor safety for the scholars might be disregarded with impunity. One teacher must be secured for every twenty to twenty-five children on an average, within the particular school limits.[4]

In addition to these elementary Bible-schools, which

[1] See Vitringa, *De Synag. Vet.*, pp. 133-135; also Hamburger's *Real-Encyc.*, II., 1103.   [2] Pesachim, 112 *a*.   Baba Bathra, 21 *a*.
[3] Edersheim's *Life and Times*, I., 232.

[4] See Marcus's *Paedag. d. Israel. Volk.*, II., 48. Maimonides (*Yad Hachazaqa*, I., 2) summarizes the rabbinical requirements on the school question, as follows: "1. Teachers of children must be appointed in every province, every district, and every city. The inhabitants of a city, in which the children are not sent to a teacher, are to be interdicted until they engage a teacher; and if they persist in their refusal, the city itself is to be put under the interdict; for the world exists only by the breath from the lips of school children. 2. The child has to be sent to school, according to its physical strength and constitution, at its sixth or seventh year, but not under six years of age. . . . The teacher must instruct them all day and a part of the night, to accustom them to learn day and night. No vacations are granted to the children, except the afternoon preceding the Sabbath, or the Holiday, and the holidays themselves. On the Sabbath nothing new must be learned, but rehearsing is permitted. Not even spare hours shall be given them to assist in the building of the holy temple. 3. A teacher, who goes out and leaves the children by themselves, or who stays with them and does some other work, or is lazy in his teaching, is included in the curse pronounced over him 'that does the work of the Lord negligently' (Jer. 48: 10); therefore, only a God-fearing and conscientious man is to be engaged as teacher. 4. Neither an unmarried man shall be teacher (on account of the visits of the mothers of the children), nor women (on account of the fathers, etc.). 5. There must be one teacher for every twenty-five children. For a number of above forty an assistant is necessary; and for a yet greater number, two assistants. 6. It is allowable to send a child to another teacher, if the latter's care and zeal justify it; but only

were provided for in every community, there were more advanced Bible-schools in connection with every local synagogue;[1] as also, in some cases, in the houses of the Rabbis.[2] It was in these synagogue Bible-schools that the Jewish religious training agency found its more peculiar likeness to our best modern church Sunday-schools. The outside Bible-schools were as the primary department, and the synagogue Bible-schools as the main department of the religious school system. The regular Sabbath services of the synagogue included a forenoon service of worship and an afternoon service of interlocutory Bible-study for young and old together, with an intermission between for dinner; a plan quite similar to that which prevails in many of our best organized city churches to-day.[3] The forenoon service was known as the Beth-ha-Sepher, the House of the Book; and the afternoon service as the Beth-ha-Midrash, the House of the Searching, or Study.[4] The study-room was ordinarily the upper room[5] (not the basement room, as in some of our modern churches); and the school service held there was not infrequently spoken of as " the syna-

when teacher and child live in the same place and no river divides between their houses. Under no consideration can a child be brought into another city, or over a river (even in the same city) except the river be safely bridged over."

[1] Jerus. Kethuboth, xiii., 1. Lightfoot's *Horae Hebraicae,* I., 78. See, also, Vitringa, *De Synag. Vet.,* p. 133 ff., and Schürer's *Hist.,* Div. II., Vol. I., § 25, p. 325; Vol. II., § 27, p. 53.

[2] Lightfoot's *Hor. Heb.,* IV., 15; also Hausrath's *Hist. of N. T. Times,* I., 90.

[3] Lightfoot's *Hor. Heb.,* II., 96; IV., 123.

[4] Jerus. Kethuboth, xiii., 1 (the latter is here called Beth-Talmud). Lightfoot's *Hor. Heb.,* I., 78. See, also, Megilla, 28 *b,* cited in *Hor. Heb.,* IV., 280.

[5] Jerus. Shabbath, i., 2. Lightfoot's *Hor. Heb.,* II., 96; IV., 14 f. Comp. Succa, 45 *a.*

gogue,"[1] inasmuch as it was a proper department of the synagogue.

So important was the Bible-studying service, in the estimation of the Rabbis, that the saying arose: "The righteous go from the synagogue to the school;"[2] or, as we might have it in modern parlance: "The good man goes from the church to the Sunday-school." It was even suggested that this is the idea in Psalm 84: 7: "They go from strength to strength [from one source of strength to another source of strength; and so], every one of them appeareth before God in Zion." He who went from the house of the book (the house of reading or the house of prayer) to the house of study, was said to be worthy of the presence of the Shekinah.[3] And the duty of bringing the children from the one service to the other was explicitly enjoined by the Rabbis.[4] One of the services was not enough by itself (whichever it was), without the other to complement it.

The sessions of the elementary Bible-schools were daily, except on the Sabbath.[5] The sessions of the synagogue Bible-schools, like the synagogue services, were on Mon-

---

[1] Lightfoot's *Hor. Heb.*, II., 96. Vitringa, *De Synag. Vet.*, p. 133 f. Taylor's *Sayings of the Jewish Fathers*, p. 65, note 27. Simon's *L'Educ. et l'Instr.*, p. 31. Sepp's *Das Leben Jesu Christi*, I., 173. Hirsch's *Aus d. rabb. Schull.*, p. 8. That the custom of looking upon the place of social worship and the place of study as one and the same place was a common one among the Jews, is indicated in the survival of the term "school," in designation of the synagogue by Portuguese and German Jews. The same term is similarly employed in Italy, as witnesses the designation in Leghorn of the synagogue street, as *Via della Scuola*.

[2] "From the place of prayer to the place of study." Cited in the Qabbalistic book Zohar.   [3] Midrash Tehillim on Psa. 84: 7.

[4] Baba Bathra, 21 *a*.   Hamburger's *Real-Encyc.*, II., 1103.

[5] Comp. Qiddushin, 30 *a*.   Ginsburg, in *Cyc. of Bib. Lit.*, art. "Education."

day and Thursday, as well as on the Sabbath, in order that the country people, when they came into town to do their marketing, might have the privileges of religious instruction.[1] For the same reason, sessions of these Bible-schools were also, at times, held in some open square, or by the wayside.[2] Tri-weekly services of the synagogues, and tri-weekly sessions of the accompanying schools, have, indeed, been continued down to modern times in some of the more strict and orthodox Jewish communities.

Synagogues, with their accompanying Bible-schools, were found in all the towns and villages of Palestine, and in many Gentile cities beyond, where any considerable number of Jews had their temporary home.[3] In some Palestinian cities these training agencies were multiplied. Thus, for example, there were at least thirteen synagogues and schools in Tiberias;[4] and in Jerusalem there were, according to one authority, four hundred and sixty, and according to another, four hundred and eighty.[5] This would give a larger number of Sunday-schools to Jerusalem twenty centuries ago, than are to be found to-day in Boston, or in New York, or in Chicago. But the Sunday-school statistics of that day were not even so trustworthy

---

[1] Jerus. Megilla, iv., 1; comp. i., 1-3. Schürer's *Hist.*, Div. II., Vol. II., § 27, p. 83. See, also, Baba Qamma, 82 *a;* Lightfoot's *Hor. Heb.*, II., 93; Schürer, in Riehm's *Handwörterbuch des Biblischen Altertums*, II., 1594 *b;* and Jost's *Allg. Gesch. d. Israel. Volk.*, II., 76.

[2] Edersheim's *Life and Times*, I., 231.

[3] Acts 9: 2, 20; 13: 5, 14, 15, 43; 14: 1; 15: 21; 17: 1, 17; 18: 4, 7, 8, 17, 26; 22: 19; 24: 12; 26: 11.

[4] Berakhoth, 30 *b.* Lightfoot's *Hor. Heb.*, I., 158.

[5] Jerus. Kethuboth, xiii., 1. Jerus. Megilla, iii., 1. Lightfoot's *Hor. Heb.*, I., 78.

2

as those of the present time; and it is probable that the numbers here given are to be taken symbolically, or gematrially,[1] rather than literally;[2] although Ginsburg[3] deems these figures not "at all exaggerated." At all events, they go to show that the Sunday-school agency was at that time not an insignificant one in the great Jewish metropolis.

In the ordinary conduct of these synagogue Bible-schools, at a later period, and presumably from an early date, the Rabbi (or the superintendent, as we should call him) occupied a seat on a platform, or on cushions, which raised him above the level of the school-room floor. His *chabērim*, or colleagues, or assisting teachers (assistant superintendents as they were in some cases), were seated a little lower than himself, although still above the floor; frequently in a semicircle at his right hand and his left.[4] The pupils were seated cross-legged, in Oriental fashion, on the floor; literally at the feet of their teachers.[5]   In

[1] See Farrar's *Early Days of Christianity*, Bk. V., chap. 28, § 5.

[2] Lightfoot's *Hor. Heb.*, I., 78.

[3] In *Cyc. of Bib. Lit.*, art. "Synagogue."

[4] See Godwyn's *Moses and Aaron*, p. 30 f.

[5] Joses ben Joezer said, "Let your house be a meeting-house for the wise; and powder thyself in the dust of their feet, and drink their words with thirstiness" (Pirqe Aboth, i., 4). Vitringa understands this as meaning that the pupils should drop themselves on the ground which the teachers covered with the dust of their feet (*De Synag. Vet.*, p. 168 f.). It is claimed that before the days of Gamaliel the pupils *stood* before their teachers in reverence for the law; but that afterward they sat (Gemara Megilla, 21 a; Vitringa, p. 166). This claim, however, is shown by Vitringa, and by Lightfoot (*Hor. Heb.*, III., 46-48), to be not justified by the facts. Comp. Luke 10: 39; Acts 22: 3. In Sanhedrin, 5, it is said, "In Bitter there were three teachers, in Yabneh four, of whom one, R. Shimeon, spoke also in the presence of the other three, but seated on the floor;" meaning that while yet a pupil he was permitted at times to teach. R. Eliezer (Megilla, 19) said, "I never

the larger schools there were, in addition to the *chabērim*, or colleagues, assistants known as *amoraim*, or speakers, or repeaters; corresponding somewhat to monitors in the English school system. The truth to be taught by these speakers was whispered in their ears by the Rabbi, to be spoken out by them in a loud tone of voice. And here is the force of the expression, "What ye hear in the ear, proclaim upon the housetops." [1] In the more primitive and elementary schools, the pupils sat on the ground in a semicircle, facing their sitting teacher.[2]

Although the traditional law, with its expositions by the fathers, rather than the simple text of the Bible, was the more immediate subject of study, or of discussion, in the Beth-ha-Midrash, the Bible text was supposed to be the primary basis of the "searching" here, as it had been the exclusive theme of study in the elementary schools which preceded this. And the Beth-ha-Midrash included the young, as well as older persons, among its pupils.[3]

passed over the heads of the holy nation;" that is, over the heads of the pupils that sit on the floor of the Beth-ha-Midrash. See note on this subject in Taylor's *Sayings of the Jewish Fathers*, p. 28 f.

[1] Matt. 10: 27.

[2] Maimonides (cited by Vitringa, p. 166) says that "the teacher sits at the head, while the disciples surround him in front, like a wreath, so that all of them can see the teacher, and hear his words. And the teacher is not sitting on a seat and his disciples on the ground; but either all sit on the ground, or all sit on seats." Comp. Isa. 30: 20, "Thine eyes shall see thy teacher" (R. V., marg.). Again, in Shir Rabba (on Cant. 6: 11, l. c.), referring to the pomegranates in the vineyard, it is said: "These are the children that are seated, and occupy themselves with the Torah, who sit in rows like the grains of the pomegranate." For a description of the Oriental schools of to-day, see Lane's *The Modern Egyptians*, Vol. I., pp. 73-78; Ebers's *Egypt*, II., 64-71; Loftie's *A Ride in Egypt*, pp. 182-194; Jessup's *Syrian Home Life*, p. 48 f.

[3] Berakhoth, 17 *a*. Lightfoot's *Hor. Heb.*, II., 95. Comp. gloss in Shabbath, 115 *a*, cited by Lightfoot, III., 101; and Hamburger's *Real-Encyc.*, II., 676, 1104.

In addition to the opening and closing exercises of worship which always had their place in these Bible-schools,[1] the method of instruction was almost entirely interlocutory and catechetical. The idea of attempting to instruct passive hearers by the teacher's continuous discourse does not seem to have entered the acute Jewish mind. That was a later seduction of the Adversary. On this point the evidence is overwhelming; and it is important that it be recognized accordingly, in view of its practical bearing on the whole system of Jewish and Christian Bible-school teaching.

Vitringa says: " It was the teacher's [part] to listen; and the pupil's [part] to question;"[2] not the teacher's part to lecture and the scholar's part merely to hear. Again Vitringa says: "The mode of teaching [that is, one of the modes of teaching] was this: the colleagues (wise men and students) raised a question on this or that subject, while the teacher answered it fully through an interpreter [speaking it low to an *amora*, who would repeat it aloud to the colleagues]; or again [as another mode of teaching] the teacher himself began the discussion of a theme raised by him."[3] And whether it was the teacher, or a colleague, or a pupil, who began the discussion, it was by the pupil's share in the questioning that the pupil's chief gain as a pupil was made. In Pirqe Aboth, or the Sayings of the Fathers, a tractate of the Mishna, it is declared that in order to make the Torah his own possession, a student must not only listen to it attentively, but must have a part in its discussion, and must ask and answer questions concerning it, and must

---

[1] Berakhoth, 16 *b*, 17 *a*.   [2] *De Synag. Vet.*, p. 168.   [3] *Ibid.*, p. 157.

repeat over what he has heard.[1]   Lightfoot cites Maimonides as saying, that in a city where there are not two wise
men, one capable of instructing, and the other competent
to hear, and to ask and answer questions, there cannot be
a true sanhedrin, " although there were a thousand Israel-
ites in that city."[2]   In other words, there can be no school
without a teacher, and no teaching without questioning.

Says Ginsburg:[3] "The mode or manner in which
instruction was communicated [in these Jewish Bible-
schools] was chiefly catechetical.   After the master [the
teacher] had delivered his dicta or theme, the disciples
[the scholars] in turn asked different questions, which he
frequently answered by parables or counter questions. . . .
Sometimes the teacher introduced the subject by simply
asking a question connected with the theme he proposed
to propound [as his lesson for the day]; the replies given
by the different disciples [or scholars] constituted the discussion, which the master at last terminated by declaring
which of the answers was the most appropriate.   Thus
Rabbi Jochanan ben Zakkai . . . on one occasion wanted
to inform his disciples what was the most desirable thing
for man to get.   He then asked them, 'What is the best
thing for man to possess?'   One replied, 'A kind nature;' another, 'A good companion;' another, 'A good
neighbor;' another, 'The power to foresee consequences;'
whilst Rabbi Eleazer said, 'A good heart.'   Whereupon
Rabbi Jochanan remarked, 'I prefer Rabbi Eleazer's answer to yours; for in it all your answers are comprehended.'"[4]   "All was life, movement, debate," in these

[1] Pirqe Aboth, vi., 6. Comp. Taylor's *Sayings of the Jewish Fathers*, p.
115 f., and Marcus's *Paedag.*, II., 42.   [2] *Hor. Heb.*, III., 48.
  [3] In *Cyc. of Bib. Lit.*, art. " Education."   [4] Pirqe Aboth, ii., 9-12.

Bible - schools, says Deutsch;[1] "question was met by counter-question, answers were given wrapped up in allegories or parables; the inquirer was led to deduce the questionable point for himself by analogy."

Many indications are given in the Talmud of the fundamental importance attached to this interlocutory, or catechetical, method of Bible teaching, as in contrast with passive hearing. Referring to the words in Jeremiah 23: 29, "Is not my word like as fire? saith the Lord," Rabbi Ishmael is cited as saying: "As the fire does not continue to burn on *one* piece of wood, so also the words of the Torah cannot prosper with him who has and studies them for himself" [2]—all by himself. Again, in answer to the question, "Why is the Torah like wood?"—or a tree (as declared of Wisdom in Proverbs 3: 18, "She is a tree of life to them that lay hold on her"), it is said, from Rabbi Nachman ben Yitschaq: "As a small piece of wood [when lighted] kindles the greater, so the little ones among the disciples of the wise kindle the greater ones and sharpen their wits."[3] And one who was himself a superintending Rabbi testified: "Much I have learned from my teachers; more from my colleagues; but most of all from my scholars."[4] Again it is declared by a Rabbi: "The Torah is acquired only by companionship" (through co-work between two).[5] "Berooriah, the celebrated wife of Rabbi Meir, met one of her husband's pupils who studied silently. She, watching him, said, 'That which is designed for all [the members of the body] must be secured by expression, or it will not be secured in the heart.'"[6] Of another pupil it is

[1] *Literary Remains*, p. 24 f.   [2] Taanith, 7 *a*.   [3] *Ibid.*

[4] *Ibid.;* also Makkoth, 10 *a*.   [5] Berakhoth, 63 *b*.   [6] Erubin, 54 *b*.

said that, not studying aloud, he forgot in three years all he had learned in the school.[1] And Rabbi Joshua ben Levi affirmed: "He who teaches without having the lesson repeated [back to him] aloud is like one who sows and does not reap."[2]

A responsibility was recognized as resting on the Jewish teacher, not only to *try* to teach, but to teach. Until he had actually taught his scholar, his work was practically a failure, or at the best an incompleted purpose. Rabba Raba said: "If a lesson is not understood by a pupil, the trouble is not so much with the pupil as with the teacher, who fails to make the lesson clear to that scholar."[3] Here is a recognition of the fundamental truth that teaching a thing is not merely telling that thing, but is causing another to know that thing. It was said of Rabba Preda, "He was ready to repeat his teaching a hundred times to his scholars, if that were necessary to their understanding of it."[4]

Such prominence, indeed, was given to repetition, or to reviewing, in the synagogue Bible-schools, that, according to one rule, "On a Sabbath only things previously learned should be repeated, nothing new being introduced at such a time."[5] This would seem to make the Sabbath the review season, or the re-enforcement season for the entire

---

[1] Menorath Ha-maor, iv., 1, 5.

[2] Sanhedrin, 99 *a*. In many Jewish schools, as in Oriental schools, to-day, the pupils, while studying, rock their heads and bodies backwards and for-wards, not only as a help to memory, but (as it is claimed) in illustration of the spirit of David when he said (Psa. 35: 10), "All my bones shall say, Lord, who is like unto thee?"

[3] Taanith, 8. Hamburger's *Real-Encyc.*, II., 672. Comp. Qoheleth Rabba on Eccl. 10: 15.   [4] Erubin, 54 *b*. Hamburger, *ibid.*

[5] Yore Dea, 245; cited in Hamburger's *Real-Encyc.*, II., 674.

week's Bible-study. And so possessed were the scholars supposed to be with a living interest in their lessons when they came to the Bible-school, that a proverbial caution of the Rabbis was: " At the coming in of the teacher the scholars shall not overwhelm him with questions;"[1] or, as we should express it, " Don't all speak at once! "

The ability and readiness to ask questions fittingly, as well as to answer them correctly, were indeed deemed an indispensable qualification of a Jewish teacher. No power of continuous discourse on his part was a substitute for that. Of the seven talmudic requisites of an educated man, five of them bear directly on this point. He will not be in haste to reply; he will ask only fitting questions; he will give suitable answers; he will answer the first thing first, and the last thing last; and he will candidly confess the limits of his knowledge.[2] It is even asserted by the Rabbis that there are to be Bible-schools in heaven;[3] and that "just as questions are asked and answered in the schools below, so questions are asked and answered in the schools above;"[4] which is only another way of asserting that neither on earth nor in heaven can there be any real teaching which does not secure real learning; that, while a man can preach whether any one heeds him or not, he cannot teach unless some one learns.

"Special attention was given to the culture of the memory," in the training of Jewish children, "since for-

[1] Shabbath, 3 *a.* See, also, Tosephta Sanhedrin, ch. iv.; cited by Marcus, *Paedag.*, II., 50.

[2] Pirqe Aboth, v., 10. See, also, Taylor's *Sayings of the Jewish Fathers*, p. 100 f., with note giving the comments of R. Obadiah of Sforno.

[3] Qoheleth Rabba on Eccl. 8 : 10.

[4] Qabbalist R. Menaḥem Reqanati, in *Comm. on Exod.*, ch. 18.

getfulness might prove as fatal in its consequences as ignorance or neglect of the law."[1] Even where words were to be memorized in their literalness, the Jewish scholar was not left to study by himself, nor was the teacher contented with a single repetition of the truth he would have learned. Iteration and reiteration on the teacher's part, and responding repetitions on the part of the scholar, were insisted on.[2]

An illustration of the approved method in this line is given in the talmudic account of the way in which Moses conducted his school for the original teaching of the Torah and the Mishna:[3] "Moses repaired to his tent, followed by Aaron, to whom he communicated the received law and its interpretation. Aaron then rose and removed to Moses' right side; whereupon Aaron's sons, Eleazar and Ithamar, entered, and received the same communication from Moses, after which they took their seats respectively on either side of Moses and Aaron. Then the seventy elders came, and Moses taught them in the same way as he had taught Aaron and his sons. Finally all the people entered—or every one who had a desire for the knowledge of the Lord—and Moses made them also acquainted with these teachings of the Lord. In this way Aaron had heard the law from Moses' lips four times, his sons three times, the elders twice, and the people once. Then Moses rose from among them, and Aaron repeated aloud what he had [now] heard four

---

[1] Pirqe Aboth, iii., 12. Chagiga, 9 *a.* Qiddushin, 50 *b.* See, also, Edersheim's *Life and Times*, I., 230.

[2] It has been claimed, indeed, that if every copy of the Talmud were destroyed, " any twelve learned Rabbis would be able to restore it verbatim from memory." (Gfrörer's *Jahrh. d. Heils*, I., 170; cited in Edersheim's *Sketches of Jewish Social Life*, p. 129, note.)   [3] Erubin, 54 *b.*

times, and he left the tent.   Then Aaron's sons, who had
by this time heard the law four times (three times by
Moses and once by their father), repeated it aloud to the
audience, and they left.   Thereupon the seventy elders,
who also by this time had heard the same teachings four
times, repeated it to the people.   The people now had
heard it four times also—once from Moses, once from
Aaron, once from Aaron's sons, and finally from the
elders.   Thus instructed, they also left the tent, teaching
each other what [of the written law] they had learned, and
writing it down [for *they*, also, must repeat it in order
to make it their own].   The interpretation [of the law
as distinct from the written law itself] they imprinted on
their minds, and delivered it orally to their children; and
these again to theirs."   And thus it was that the simplest
form of teaching by means of memorizing was conducted
among the Jews.

It was not that these catechetical Bible-schools were
merely incidental to the Jewish life and polity; they were
reckoned a very part of the religious system itself, essential to the stability and perpetuity of the national existence
and character.   Many a talmudic proverbial saying might
be cited in illustration of this truth.   Thus, for example:
" The world continues to exist, only by the breath of the
children of the schools." [1]   " The children must not be

---

[1] Shabbath, fol. 119 *b*.   Geikie (*The Life and Words of Christ*, Vol. I., p.
565, Notes) calls attention to the fact that Dukes (in *Rabbinische Blumenlese*,
104) explains this as referring to " the innocence of young children," rather
than to the importance of their education.   But, even with that meaning, it is
clear that the innocent children are, by this talmudic saying, reckoned as sure
to be in the schools of the nation.   Moreover, Maimonides (cited in note 1,
p. 14, *ante*) explicitly applies this talmudic saying to the importance of the
children's education.   See, also, on this point, Van Gelder's *Die Volkssch. d.
Jüd. Alterth.*, p. 3.

detained from the schools, even though it were to help rebuild the temple."[1] " The true guardians of the city are the teachers."[2] " If you would destroy the Jews you must destroy their schools."[3] "He who learns the Torah and does not teach it, is like a [fragrant] myrtle in the desert, where there is no one to enjoy it."[4] " He who teacheth a child is like one who writeth with ink on clean paper; but he who teacheth old persons is like one who writeth with ink on blotted paper."[5] " He who teaches the Torah to the child of his fellow-man, is to be looked upon, in a scriptural point of view, as though he had begotten him."[6] " He who refuses a pupil one lesson has, as it were, robbed him of his parental inheritance."[7] " He who teaches the child of his fellow-man shall occupy a prominent place among the saints above."[8] This last aphorism would seem to be a paraphrase of the promise in Daniel,[9] which, in its marginal reading, is : " The teachers shall shine as the brightness of the firmament; and they that turn many to righteousness, as the stars, forever and ever."

A Bath-Qol (a very voice of God) said to the Jews : " Dearer to me is the breath of the school-children, than the fragrance of the sacrifices on the smoking altar."[10]

---

[1] Shabbath, 120.   [2] Jerus. Chagiga, vii., 7.

[3] Bereshith Rabba, ch. 65.   Hamburger's *Real-Encyc.* II., 1102 f.

[4] Rosh Ha-shana, 23 *a*.   Comp. Buxtorf's *Syn. Jud.*, p. 139.

[5] This maxim, which has come to be the common property of Jewish and Christian educators alike, would seem to be a talmudic rendering of the words of Saul of Tarsus, the pupil of Gamaliel.   It is given in Pirqe Aboth (iv., 27) as ascribed to Elisha ben Abooyah, the great apostate, who is called in the rabbinical writings *achēr*, that is, " the other one," after Jesus of Nazareth, who is spoken of in those writings as *otho ha-eesh*, " that man."

[6] Sanhedrin, 19.   [7] Cheleq, 91.   [8] Shabbath, 33.   [9] Dan. 12 : 3.

[10] Qoheleth Rabba on Eccl. 9: 7.   Hamburger's *Real-Encyc.*, II., 1103.

And the Rabbis, commenting on the words in the psalm of David, "Touch not my anointed ones, and do my prophets no harm,"[1] explained that the Lord's "anointed ones" are the school-children, and his "prophets" are their teachers.[2]   God himself is even represented by the Rabbis as teaching little children.   "What is God doing in the fourth part of the day [the last quarter of the day]?" asks R. Acha.   And the answer is: "He sits and teaches children the Torah, as it is said in Isaiah 28 : 9, 'Whom will he teach knowledge? and whom will he make to understand the message? them that are weaned from the milk, and drawn from the breasts.'"[3]   To live in a community where there was no Bible-school was forbidden to the godly Jew.[4]   "A village without a school for children ought to be destroyed," said a talmudic authority;[5] and it was even said, after the destruction of Jerusalem, that that disaster came because the schools there—many as they were—were neglected.[6]

And this was the Bible-school system of the Jews in Palestine, at the time that Jesus of Nazareth was born into that land, to be brought up there as a Jew.   Bible teaching was to begin at home.[7]   At from five to seven years of age, at the latest, the child was to find his place in the church Bible-school.[8]   He was there to memorize

---

[1] Psa. 105: 15; 1 Chron. 16: 22.

[2] Kethuboth, 103.   Shabbath, 119.   See, also, Yalqut on Psa. 105: 15.

[3] Yalqut on Isa., 47 *a*.   [4] Sanhedrin, 17 *b*.   [5] Shabbath, 120.   [6] *Ibid.*

[7] "Passing over the Old Testament period, we may take it that, in the days of Christ, home teaching ordinarily began when the child was about three years old" (Edersheim's *Sketches of Jewish Social Life*, p. 129).

[8] Five years of age was the time for an exceptionally healthy and vigorous Jewish child to begin his school study (Pirqe Aboth, v., 24); but with the average child six years of age was counted young enough.   "There is both

the words of Scripture, and he was at the same time to
come to an understanding of its meaning through the
process of familiar questioning and answering. Later,
he was to be a member of the synagogue Bible-school;
to share there the benefits of that interlocutory teaching which was the only process which the Jews deemed
worthy of the name of teaching. So far the facts would
seem to be fairly established.

Referring to the elementary Bible-schools, such as have
been here outlined, Edersheim says:[1] "We do not even
know quite certainly whether the school-system had, at
that time, extended to far-off Nazareth; nor whether
the order and method which have been described were
universally observed at that time. In all probability,
however, there was such a school at Nazareth; and, if
so, the Child-Saviour would conform to the general practice of attendance. We may thus, still with deepest
reverence, think of him as learning his earliest earthly
[Bible-school] lesson from the Book of Leviticus."

In the one glimpse that is given us of the childhood of
our Lord,[2] he is seen in one of the more advanced Bible-
schools of his day, within the temple limits, at the age of
twelve years, having a part in its ordinary exercises, in
accordance with the customs of that time. "There were
occasions," says Edersheim,[3] "on which the temple became virtually, though not formally, a Beth-ha-Midrash.

common sense and sound experience in this talmudical saying (Kethuboth,
50 [3]), ' If you set your child to regular study before it is six years old, you
shall always have to run after, and yet never get hold of, it.' This chiefly has
reference to the irreparable injury to health caused by such early strain upon
the mind " (Edersheim, as above, p. 105).

[1] *Life and Times*, I., 233. [2] Luke 2: 42-47. [3] *Life and Times*, I., 247.

For we read in the Talmud that the members of the temple Sanhedrin, who on ordinary days sat as a court of appeal, from the close of the morning to the time of the evening sacrifice, were wont on Sabbaths and *feast-days* to come out upon ' the terrace' of the temple, and there to teach. In such popular instruction the utmost latitude of questioning would be given. It is in this audience, which sat on the ground, surrounding and mingling with the doctors [the teachers] . . . that we must seek [at this time] the child Jesus."

There he was, as the evangelist gives the record, " sitting in the midst of the teachers, both hearing them, and asking them questions." [1] It was not that his presence

[1] Luke 2: 46. This simple incident in the Bible story has been a fruitful theme of discussion among commentators. It has been claimed by some that the child Jesus here took his place as a teacher among teachers, or at least assumed some other position than that of a mere learner (comp. Lightfoot's *Hor. Heb.*, III., 48 ; Bishop Taylor's *Life of Christ*, p. 156 ; Bengel's *Gnomon*, in loco ; Strauss's *New Life of Jesus*, II., 98 f. ; De Wette's *Handb. z. N. T.*, in loco ; Lange's *Life of Jesus*, I., 322 f. ; Ewald's *Hist. of Israel*, VI., 187 f. ; Sepp's *Das Leben Jesu Christi*, I., 185 ; Ellicott's *Life of Christ*, p. 95). Others have seen in the narrative only the record of a young learner's method in a Jewish Bible-school (comp. Origen's *Opera Omnia*, Tom. V., p. 158 ; Wetstein's *N. T. Graec.*, in loco ; Rosenmüller's *Alte u. Neue Morgenland*, VI., 46 ; Neander's *Life of Jesus Christ*, p. 30 f. ; Olshausen's *Bib. Comm.*, in loco ; Meyer's *N. T. Comm.*, in loco ; Alford's *Greek Test.*, in loco ; Stier's *Words of the Lord Jesus*, I., 19 ; Van Oosterzee in Schaff-Lange's *Bib. Comm.*, in loco ; Andrews's *Life of Our Lord*, p. 102 ; Keim's *Hist. of Jesus of Nazara*, II., 133 ; Farrar's *Life of Christ*, I., 74-77 ; Geikie's *Life and Words of Christ*, I., 226-228 ; Plumptre, in Ellicott's *New Test. Comm. for Eng. Readers*, in loco). In explanation of the supposed contradiction in the Holy Child's being only a learner, while yet he is singled out as in some way in the midst of the teachers, perhaps no more satisfactory suggestion has been made than that which Godet proffers (*Comm. on Luke*, in loco): " The expression ' seated in the midst of the doctors ' proves, no doubt, that the child was for the time occupying a place of honor. . . . Jesus had given some remarkable answer, or put some original question ; and, as is the case when a particularly intelligent pupil presents himself, he had attracted, for a moment, all the interest of his

there was exceptional, nor yet that his bearing a part in the ordinary exercises of study was to be wondered at. So far he was simply in the line of a Jewish youth's privileges and duty.[1] But that which *was* remarkable in the case of the Holy Child was his marvelous knowledge in the realm of God's Word, as compared with the knowledge of the teachers surrounding him. "All that heard him were amazed at his understanding and his answers."[2] And so important did he himself deem this exercise, that he asked his anxious mother why she had sought him anywhere else than just there, during his stay in the holy city as a child.

teachers. There is nothing in the narrative, when rightly understood, that savors in the least of an apotheosis of Jesus." This is practically the view of Weiss (*Life of Christ*, I., 276) and of Edersheim (*Life and Times*, I., 247 f.).

[1] Josephus (*Vita*, ch. 2) claims to have been often called on by the high-priests and elders to give his opinion on points of the law, when he was about fourteen years old. This is commonly spoken of as a proof of his egotism ; but the egotism is in his boasting of a fact which was by no means unique, as he seems to have counted it. See a reference to the enkindling power of young-sters among Rabbis at p. 22, *ante*. The Rabbis had a saying (Bammidbar Rab-ba, 14) that " the word of God out of the mouth of a youngster is to be received as from the mouth of a wise man, yea, as from the mouth of an assembly of wise men, yea, from the very Sanhedrin, yea, as from the mouth of Moses, yea, as from the mouth of the blessed God himself." Even in modern times a bright youngster has attracted special prominence by his skill in question-answering. Dr. Rawley, the biographer of Lord Bacon, tells of the promi-nence thus accorded to his hero. " Rawley's story introduces us to a child of singular gravity and adroitness, the future Chancellor and courtier. The Queen ' delighted much then to confer with him, and to prove him with ques-tions ; unto whom he delivered himself with that gravity and maturity above his years, that Her Majesty would often term him ' The young Lord Keeper.' Being asked by the Queen how old he was, he answered with much discretion, being then but a boy, that he was two years younger than Her Majesty's happy reign, with which answer the Queen was much taken." (William Aldis Wright's Preface to Bacon's *Advancement of Learning*, p. vi. f.).

[2] Luke 2 : 47.

After this, when our Lord had entered upon his public ministry, he is spoken of again and again as *teaching* in the synagogues, as distinct from his *preaching* there. If, indeed, we were wholly unfamiliar with the arrangement and customs of the Jewish synagogues in that day, we might be at a loss as to the difference between these two exercises of "teaching" and "preaching" within the limits of the same sacred structure. But knowing what we do, it would seem fair to infer that our Lord bore a part in the morning service of worship and preaching in the synagogue, and in the afternoon service of worship and teaching in the same synagogue; in other words, that he, according to the custom of the godly Jew, went from the synagogue to the Bible-school.

The evangelist Matthew, who peculiarly wrote from the Jewish stand-point said, in terms which all Jews would understand, that "Jesus went about in all Galilee, teaching in their synagogues, and preaching the gospel of the kingdom;"[1] teaching by that form of instruction which admitted of free interlocutory play between teacher and taught, and preaching by the distinct heralding of a message from God. And again, by the same evangelist the record stands: "Jesus went about all the cities and the villages, teaching in their synagogues, and preaching the gospel of the kingdom."[2] Mark and Luke, also, repeatedly distinguish between the "preaching" and the "teaching" of our Lord.[3] He is, moreover, represented in all the Gospels as pursuing this work of "teaching," wherever he might be; by the wayside,[4] by the

---

[1] Matt. 4 : 23.   [2] Matt. 9 : 35; also 11 : 1.
[3] Mark 1 : 14, 21, 22, 39; Luke 20 : 1.
[4] Mark 6 : 6, 34; 10 : 1; Luke 13 : 22; John 4 : 1-42.

sea,[1] in the private house,[2] or in the temple court,[3] as well as in the synagogue,[4]—teaching the Jews by that familiar interlocutory and inter-colloquial method with which the Jews were so familiar.

John the Baptist is always represented as *preaching*,[5] never as *teaching*.   Even when he gave particular instruction in the line of personal duty, to the soldiers, to the publicans, and to the Jewish people, he is spoken of as a preacher.[6]   But Jesus is represented as a teacher of truth, in addition to his mission as a preacher of righteousness. Thus, for example, when he was at Jerusalem at the feast of the tabernacles, it is recorded of him: " When it was now the midst of the feast Jesus went up into the temple, and taught [sat as the teacher of a gathered class of pupils].   The Jews therefore marveled, saying, How knoweth this man letters, having never learned? [having never been the pupil of a well-known Rabbi]."[7]   No such question as this seems to have been asked concerning John the Baptist; for he was only a preacher.   It was appropriate concerning Jesus, because he now occupied the place of a teacher, questioning his pupils and answering their questions.

We cannot suppose that all of the questions asked of or by our Lord, in the progress of his manifold teaching, are recorded in the Gospel narratives preserved to us.   If

---

[1] Mark 2 : 13 ; 4 : 1, 2.

[2] Matt. 13 : 36 ; 17 : 25 ; Mark 9 : 33-50 ; Luke 7 : 36-50 ; 10 : 38-42 ; 19 : 5-27.

[3] Matt. 21 : 23 to 22 : 46 ; Mark 12 : 35 ; 14 : 49 ; Luke 19 : 47 ; 21 : 37 ; John 7 : 14, 28 ; 8 : 2, 20.

[4] Matt. 13 : 54 ; Mark 6 : 2 ; Luke 4 : 15, 31-33 ; 6 : 6 ; 13 : 10 ; John 6 : 59 ; 18 : 20.

[5] Matt. 3 : 1-12 ; Mark 1 : 1-8 ; Luke 3 : 1-9.

[6] Luke 3 : 10-18.   [7] John 7 : 14, 15.

that had been attempted, " I suppose that even the world itself would not contain the books." [1] But there is no lack of evidence that questioning and counter-questioning entered freely into his ordinary teaching processes.

Observe, for example, the record of our Lord's latest exercises of teaching in the temple court, as it is found in Matthew's Gospel.[2] " When he was come into the temple, the chief priests and the elders of the people came unto him as he was teaching, and said, [taking their part in the exercise by this question,] By what authority doest thou these things? and who gave thee this authority? And Jesus answered and said unto them, [in accordance with a very common method of response in Jewish Bible-school teaching,] I also will ask you one [counter] question, which if ye tell me, I likewise will tell you by what authority I do these things. The baptism of John, whence was it? from heaven or from men? And [at that question] they [the questioning priests and elders] reasoned with themselves, saying, If we shall say, From heaven; he will say unto us, Why then did ye not believe him? But if we shall say, From men; we fear the multitude; for all hold John as a prophet. And they answered Jesus, and said, We know not. He also [then] said unto them, Neither tell I you by what authority I do these things."

But our Lord's questionings were not merely, as might seem from this illustration so far, for the purpose of avoiding a profitless discussion with his enemies. On this occasion, he immediately followed up his silenced opposers with the parable of the two sons directed to

---

[1] John 21 : 25.   [2] Matt. 21 : 23 to 23 : 39.

work in their father's vineyard; prefacing it with the rhetorical question, "But what think ye?" and then asking, categorically, "Whether of the twain did the will of his father?" Another parable, also, was then applied by the questions, "When therefore the lord of the vineyard shall come, what will he do unto those husbandmen?" and "Did ye never read in the Scriptures?" Group after group of his nominal scholars joined in this questioning, and was met according to the spirit of the particular inquiry. Interrupted at this point for the day, the teaching exercise was resumed on the following day. It was begun with a parable spoken by our Lord. At that point the Pharisees came to him with their wily question, "Is it lawful to give tribute unto Cæsar, or not?" Calling for a specimen of the tribute money, our Lord asked, "Whose is this image and superscription?" and when they answered "Cæsar's," he added, "Render therefore unto Cæsar the things that are Cæsar's; and unto God the things that are God's." It was then the Sadducees' turn, with their knotty question about the marriage relation after the resurrection. The question our Lord met directly with an affirmation of absolute truth; but he followed this with an instructive question concerning the text of the Mosaic Scriptures, which the Sadducees held to be true and conclusive: "As touching the resurrection of the dead, have ye not read that which was spoken unto you by God, saying, I am the God of Abraham, and the God of Isaac, and the God of Jacob? God is not the God of the dead, but of the living."

And so the record of the questioning and the answering in that series of teaching exercises goes on, concerning the law and concerning the Messiah, until it concludes with the declaration, "And no man was able to answer him a word, neither durst any man from that day forth ask him any more questions." Can there be any reasonable doubt, in view of such an illustration as this, of the Jewish method of interlocutory teaching employed by our Lord, that when our Lord is referred to as "teaching," as distinct from his "preaching," we are to understand that the term "teaching" applied to the method of his instruction, as well as to its substance?

Obviously, it is in the light of well-known Jewish customs, rather than only in the light of classic Greek or of modern English, that we are to interpret the terms "teach" and "teaching," in the narrative of our Saviour's life-course. It is in the same light, also, that we must read the Great Commission, as it stands in its one undisputed authentic form, at the close of the Gospel of the Kingdom:[1] "Go ye therefore, and make disciples [scholars][2] of all the nations, baptizing them into the name of the Father and of the Son and of the Holy Ghost: teaching[3] them to observe all things whatsoever I commanded you: and lo, I am with you alway, even unto the end of the world." As the Jews would have understood that charge,

---

[1] Matt. 28 : 19, 20.

[2] According to the Talmud (Pirqe Aboth, I., 1), one of the three fundamental duties of the fathers in Israel, as communicated by God to Moses, by Moses to Joshua, by Joshua to the elders, by the elders to the prophets, and by the prophets to the men of the Great Synagogue, was to "raise up many scholars," or to secure and to train many pupils. Hence, to a Jew, the command of our Lord to go and make scholars of, or from among, all the Gentiles, had a distinct and well-defined meaning.

[3] "This teaching," says Alford, (*Greek Test.*, in loco,) "is not merely the *kērugma* of the gospel—not mere proclamation of the good news—but the whole catechetical office of the Church upon and in the baptized. . . . The command is to the Universal Church—to be performed, in the nature of things, by her *ministers* and *teachers*."

and as we have every reason to suppose that our Lord meant it, the direction therein is, to organize Bible-schools everywhere as the very basis, the initial form, of the Christian Church. Grouping scholars—the child and the child-like—in classes, under skilled teachers, for the study of the Word of God by means of an interlocutory co-work between teacher and scholars; that is the starting-point of Christ's Church, as he founded it. Whatever else is added, these features must not be lacking.

And it would seem that this was the way in which the Great Commission was understood by the Apostles and their immediate successors. We find little said in explicit description of the sanctuary services of the Apostolic Church; partly, doubtless, because so generally the well-known synagogue services were simply adapted to the necessities of the new organization. Schaff sums up the whole case at this point, when he says concisely: "As the Christian Church rests historically on the Jewish Church, so Christian worship and the congregational organization rest on that of the synagogue, and cannot be well understood without it."[1] Fisher says, with like explicitness: "The synagogue served as a model in the organization of churches."[2] It would be strange, passing strange, if the Christian Church, while retaining the other main features of the synagogue, had ignored its very chiefest feature, the Bible-school service; especially as the Great Commission laid pre-eminent emphasis on the work therein included. Nor is there reason for serious question just here. There are many indications in the Book of Acts and in the Epistles that "teaching,"

[1] Schaff's *Hist. of the Christian Church*, I., 456.
[2] Fisher's *Hist. of the Christian Church*, p. 35.

after the pattern of the synagogue Bible-schools, was a
recognized agency for the extension of the Christian
Church, and for the upbuilding in the new faith of those
who were won to Christ from the Jewish fold or from the
Gentile world.

It is said of "Peter and the apostles"[1] in Jerusalem, that, "every day, in the temple and at home, they
ceased not to teach and to preach Jesus as the Christ."[2]
These apostles were Jews before they were Christians,
and it was as Jews that they had learned how to teach.
That they realized the distinction between "teaching"
and "preaching," is evidenced in their frequent antitheti-
cal use of the one term over against the other. "Paul
and Barnabas," again, "tarried in Antioch, teaching and
preaching the word of the Lord, with many others also."[3]
The *truth* taught by these Christian teachers was very
different from that which had been there taught as truth
before; but the *method* of the teaching was in all probability the same.

Paul had been a scholar in the Beth-ha-Midrash of
Gamaliel.[4] He was skilled in the teaching processes of
the best Jewish Bible-schools. As he and Silas journeyed,
"they came to Thessalonica, where was a synagogue of
the Jews: and Paul, as his custom was, went in unto
them, and for three Sabbath days [or for three weeks,
including the Mondays and Thursdays between Sabbaths,
he] reasoned with them from the Scriptures [discussed
with them out of the Scriptures in Jewish teaching fash-
ion], opening and alleging, that it behooved the Christ to
suffer, and to rise again from the dead."[5] At Berea,

[1] Acts 5 : 29.   [2] Acts 5 : 42.   [3] Acts 15 : 35.
          [4] Acts 22 : 3.   [5] Acts 17 : 1-3.

again, Paul did a similar work; and the record stands of his Berean hearers, that "these were more noble than those in Thessalonica, in that they received the word with all readiness of mind, examining [for themselves] the Scriptures daily, whether these things were so. Many of them therefore [as might be supposed] believed," including "Greek women of honorable estate, and of men, not a few." [1] At Athens, Paul "reasoned [or discussed, in Bible-school manner] in the synagogue with the Jews and the [other] devout persons;" and he did the same thing "in the market-place every day with them that met with him;" [2] using the interlocutory or the intercolloquial method of teaching and learning, which was the essence of the Jewish educational system.

The Beth-ha-Midrash gatherings, and the Beth-ha-Midrash methods, seem to have been the fresh starting-points of the Christian Church in all the earlier apostolic work under the requirements and the authority of the Great Commission. At Corinth, Paul seems to have begun his labors by having a share in the Beth-ha-Midrash exercises of the synagogue. "And he reasoned in the synagogue every Sabbath, and persuaded [or sought to persuade] Jews and Greeks." When, however, he made bold to preach the gospel there, "testifying to the Jews that Jesus was the Christ," a breach was made between him and them, and he went out, carrying with him the ruler of the synagogue, and started a new Bible-school in "the house of a certain man named Titus Justus, . . . whose house joined hard to the synagogue." There he continued "a year and six months, teaching the word of God among them." [3]

[1] Acts 17 : 11, 12.   [2] Acts 17 : 17.   [3] Acts 18 : 1-11.

At Ephesus, after a three months' trial of "reasoning [with] and persuading [or of trying to persuade the Jews in the synagogue school] as to the things concerning the kingdom of God," Paul, as at Corinth, went out from the synagogue school, taking with him the Christian scholars; and he gathered the nucleus of a Christian Bible-school in connection with a daily exercise "in the school of Tyrannus," which "continued for the space of two years."[1] Again, for two whole years Paul was similarly occupied. "in his own hired dwelling" in Rome; "preaching the kingdom of God, and teaching the things [the 'all things' commanded of Christ] concerning the Lord Jesus Christ."[2] That was the way in which our Lord had enjoined it upon his disciples to extend and to upbuild his Church; by making scholars of those who would be learners, and by teaching them that which they had need to know; and that was the way in which the disciples carried on the work which had been committed to them by our Lord.

Incidental references to "instruction,"[3] as a well-under-

---

[1] Acts 19 : 1-10.   [2] Acts 28 : 30, 31.

[3] The word *katēcheo* (to instruct catechetically) has as one of its meanings—both in its earlier and in its later use—the idea of a sound resounding, or of a sound given back again. Our word "echo" is from this root. So, again, is our word "catechising" in its modern signification of teaching by form of question and answer. (On this point see Thayer's *Greek-Eng. Lex. of N. T.;* Liddell and Scott's *Greek-Eng. Lex.;* Schleusner's *Lex. Græco-Lat. in Nov. Test.*, s. v.; with references to Homer, Hesiod, Lucian, etc.). Whether, as has been often claimed by critical commentators from the days of Melanchthon down, this word, in its primitive meaning, properly suggests a process of teaching which secures an answer back from a sounding question, or whether that idea is an outgrowth of its later uses, it certainly would seem clear that the term *katēcheo*, as used in the New Testament, refers to a method of explicit and systematic teaching with which the Jewish Christians were familiar; while, as has been shown, the only method of such teaching which we know of as in use by the Jews at this time and earlier, was by means of question and answer.

stood process of technical Christian teaching, are made by Luke in connection with the warm-hearted convert Theophilus,[1] and of the eloquent and zealous preacher Apollos.[2] "Teachers"[3] are named among the recognized workers of the Christian Church; and their office work of "teaching"[4] is given prominence in its place. It is even named as an essential qualification of a bishop, that he shall be "apt to teach."[5] And "children"[6]—as those to whom our Lord gave prominence—are specifically included in the number of those to whom the apostolic epistles were sent as a fresh basis and outline of instruction. Hence there is sound reason for supposing that the best lessons of the Jewish Church, and the specific injunctions of the divine Founder of the Christian Church, concerning the church care of children, and the systematic study of the Scriptures through the process of interlocutory instruction, were borne in mind, and were put in practice by the divinely guided leaders of the Apostolic Church.

That it was the Bible itself, the inspired text of the

In other words, the form of catechetical instruction in use by the Jews, and again by the first Jewish Christians, is fairly to be recognized as the interlocutory form, whether the New Testament word employed for its designation would in itself give proof of this fact, or not.

[1] Luke 1:4. Dr. Schaff (Schaff-Lange's *Comm.*, in loco) says, at this point: "Literally, 'catechised,' 'catechetically taught'—*katēchēthēs*. The specific word should have been retained here and elsewhere, instead of the more indefinite *instruct* or *teach*. Catechising is a primitive and most important institution of the Church, and a preparatory school for full membership. Archbishop Usher says: 'The neglect of catechising is the frustrating of the whole work of the ministry.'" (Comp. also Meyer's *Comm.*; Plumptre, in Ellicott's *N. T. Comm.*; and Farrar, in the *Cambridge Bible for Schools*,—all *in loco*.) [2] Acts 18:25.

[3] Acts 13:1; 1 Cor. 12:28, 29; Eph. 4:11. [4] Rom. 12:7; Col. 1:28; 3:16. [5] 1 Tim. 3:2.

[6] Eph. 6:1; Col. 3:20; 2 John 1.

sacred writings, that was to be the subject-matter of
teaching and of study from childhood to maturity in the
church Bible-school, is pointed out by Paul, in his counsel
to the young bishop of Ephesus concerning the training
work to which he was set of God. "Every scripture inspired of God is also profitable for teaching, for reproof, for
correction, for instruction which is in righteousness: that
the man of God may be complete, furnished completely
unto every good work."[1] The word here rendered "instruction" is not *katechesis*, as in some of the cases noted.
"It is, in the Greek," as a modern church historian has
pointed out,[2] "*paideia*, from *pais*, a child, and signifies
an education begun in childhood; or, if we may fall
back upon the case of Timothy,[3] in the days of lisp-
ing infancy. Those who have encountered Xenophon's
Cyropædia, or the education of Cyrus from his boyhood, will recognize and catch in a moment the word's
signification. Christianity, in its comprehensive plan for
a human existence, is a *Christo-pedia*, is intended [is
divinely intended] to begin with a child's first dawnings
of reason and conscience; and to go on with him, step by
step, till he learns, and by Heaven's grace fulfills, all his
Christian responsibilities, till he is made, not worthy,
indeed, but, to use scriptural language, meet for the inheritance of the saints in light. And the church, with its
chief teacher in the pulpit, and its subordinate teachers
in the Bible-class and the Sunday-school, is to be the
grand instrumentality for keeping God's truth alive and

[1] 2 Tim. 3: 16, 17.

[2] Dr. T. W. Coit, in "History of Catechising" in *The Sunday School Times*,
April 19, 1879. Comp. "The Office of Catechising," *ibid.*, July 5, 1879.

[3] 2 Tim. 3: 15.

predominant in the human mind, and bringing that truth forth to victory for the salvation of the soul."

And now let us look back and see what we have ascertained in the course of our investigations so far. From the days of Abraham, systematic "instruction" had its place in the plans of the chosen people of God. From the days of Moses, the Jewish Church had a measure of responsibility for the religious training of the young. From the days of Ezra, the Bible-school was a recognized agency, among the Jewish people, for the study and teaching of God's Word. In the days of Jesus of Nazareth, there was, in the land of his birth and sojourn, a system of Bible-schools, corresponding quite closely in their general features with our modern Sunday-schools. The elementary or primary schools in this system gave chief prominence to the study of the Bible text. The advanced or senior schools in this system were a department of the synagogue; and in them Bible commentaries, in addition to the Bible text, were a subject of familiar study. The elementary schools were for children only. The senior schools had a place for children as well as for adults. In all the schools the arrangement was that of scholars grouped under a special teacher; and the process of teaching was by form of question and answer. Our Lord seems to have been a scholar in schools of this character; and again he was a teacher in such schools. In founding his Church, he made Bible-school work its basis. His disciples recognized the scope and details of his plan, and they prosecuted their labors of evangelizing and of edifying accordingly. The Bible-school was the starting-point of the Christian Church; and it was by means of

Bible-school methods that the Christian Church was first
extended and upbuilded.

And thus it is that we find in the history and the traditions of the biblical age, the Jewish origin and the
Christian adoption of the distinguishing characteristics
of that agency of religious teaching which is known in
our day as the Sunday-school.

LECTURE II.

THE SUNDAY–SCHOOL: SEVENTEEN CENTURIES
OF ITS VARYING PROGRESS.

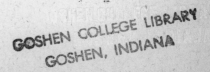

II.

THE SUNDAY-SCHOOL: SEVENTEEN CENTURIES OF ITS VARYING PROGRESS.

Christian Beginnings in Gentile Communities.— Questions and An-
swers in Catechumenical Instruction.—Questions and Answers
in Pulpit Preaching.— Methods of Teaching in Alexandria.—
Evangelizing by Mission - schools. — Ritualism Overshadows
Bible Study.— The Dark Ages a Consequence.— Gleams of
Light in Darkness.— Revival of Schools in the Reformation.—
Catechisms Multiplied.— Romish Recognition of the School
Idea.—Catechisms as a Barrier to Catechetical Teaching.— A
Lesson from New England.— Superiority of Teaching over
Preaching in the Training Process.— A New Decline of the
Bible-school Agency.

So long as the Christian Church found its new centres
of evangelizing in Jewish communities, the character of
its sanctuary services and the methods of its training
work were, as a matter of course, largely conformed to
the plan and practices of the Jewish synagogue.[1] Its
Bible-schools were based on the synagogue-school foun-

---

[1] " It must in the first place be remembered that the original members of
the Christian brotherhood were Jews, and were in no haste to abandon the
religious customs of their nation. Christ had come 'not to destroy the law
but to fulfil,' and the example of the Master strongly inculcated respect for
the ancient forms. . . . We should naturally, therefore, be prepared to find
in Jewish forms the starting-point of the development of those adopted by the
Christians " (G. Baldwin Brown's *From Schola to Cathedral*, p. 5 f.).

dation, as seems evident from the indications already pointed out in the Book of Acts and in the Epistles.[1] But when the Church gained a foot-hold in purely Gentile communities, and extended its membership among those who had known nothing of Jewish training methods, it necessarily varied its system of instruction, adapting the details of that system to the peculiar needs of its new fields.[2]

For a long time Christianity had no one land and people which it controlled religiously, as the Jewish Church had had; hence it was unable to enforce a uniform church-school system in all communities alike, with carefully graded instruction from the primary class to the divinity school. The best that it could yet do was to provide, in every local church gathering, for the catechetical instruction of the young, including the children of believers, and all other children who could be brought under its care; and then to establish, at certain large centres, schools for the more thorough instruction in the "all things" which the fully furnished Christian had need to know. And just this it did do, as ecclesiastical history makes clear. Meanwhile individual Christians were forward and active in efforts to reach and to teach the young whenever and wherever they might do so. For this reason they were always ready to be teachers in any school where they might, by the teaching process, impress the truth of God on impressible minds and hearts. "The Apostolic Church," says Baron Bunsen, "made

---

[1] See pp. 37-41, *ante.*

[2] Hatch, in *The Organization of the Early Christian Churches* (Bampton Lectures for 1880) makes clear these two propositions (p. 208): "1. That the development of the organization of the Christian churches was gradual. 2. That the elements of which that organization were composed were already existing in human society."

the school the connecting link between herself and the world."[1] Tertullian's counsels concerning the relation of Christian teachers to heathen literature,[2] while engaged in the work of popular instruction, are illustrative of this truth.

It was because of the power already obviously gained over the popular mind by Christian teachers, through this catechetical teaching-process, in the schools of the Roman Empire, that Julian the Apostate, in the fourth century, "determined to take the control of education into the hands of the state;" and that he issued his formal edict, designed to shut out all Christian teachers from those schools. The Emperor realized that the continuous life of Christianity pivoted on the *school* idea,—on the inter-locutory teaching of the young,—and that, if he could put an end to this line of Christian work, he could hope to check the permanent progress of Christianity. As Bishop Lancelot Andrewes, two centuries ago, said of this plan of Julian's: "If he had not been as a cloud that soon pass-eth away, it might have been feared that in a short time he had overshadowed true religion."[3] Or again, as more recently Bishop John Wordsworth has said: "If Julian had lived, and this edict could really have been put into force for any time, it must have been a very dangerous instrument for the injury of the faith."[4] In other words, God's method of extending and upbuilding his Church

[1] *Hippolytus and His Age*, II., 105.

[2] Tertullian's "On Idolatry," ch. x., in *The Ante-Nicene Fathers*, III., 66 f.

[3] *The Pattern of Catechistical Doctrine*, p. 7.

[4] Art. "Julianus–Emperor," in Smith's *Dict. of Christian Biog.* Comp. Schaff's *Hist. of the Christian Church*, III., 53 f., and Fisher's *Hist. of the Christian Church*, p. 91.

4

was the one effective method, his enemies themselves being judges.

Our Lord had taught that children and the child-like were to be the foremost object of his people's care, and that interlocutory teaching was the method by which his cause should be promoted and extended in the world. His followers recognized the importance of this twofold truth; and from the beginning they gave a chief place, in the work of evangelizing, to efforts among children and the child-like; and interlocutory teaching was the method by which they made the truths of the gospel effective upon the minds of those reached by them. Within a century after the apostolic age, Celsus, a prominent and powerful opponent of Christianity, charged Christians with extending their numbers and propagating their views by getting hold of children privately in homes and schools, and influencing them by conversations with them, without the knowledge of their parents or teachers, and thus leading them away from the religion of their parents. In replying to this charge of Celsus, Origen did not deny the main facts of the case as stated by Celsus; but he insisted that the children thus reached by Christians out of Pagan homes were benefited by the lessons imparted to them, and that if their parents were wise and well disposed they would recognize this as the truth.[1]

Not by great sermonizers swaying the minds of adult unbelievers, but by individual teachers reaching and teaching children and the child-like individually, were the triumphs of early Christianity mainly won. "It is a remarkable fact," says Schaff, "that after the days of the

---

[1] Origen's "Against Celsus," Bk. iii., chs. 55-58; in *The Ante-Nicene Fathers,* IV., 486 f.

Apostles no names of great missionaries are mentioned till the opening of the Middle Ages. . . . There were no missionary societies, no missionary institutions, no organized efforts in the Ante-Nicene age; and yet in less than three hundred years from the death of St. John the whole population of the Roman empire, which then represented the civilized world, was nominally Christianized." [1] And this was because the divinely approved plan of the child-reaching and the child-teaching methods of Christian activity were adhered to by the immediate successors of the apostles of our Lord.

The catechetical instruction of the Early Church, which finds mention in the New Testament record,[2] grew in prominence and in obvious importance until the very church edifices were constructed with a view to the accommodation of its subjects.[3] Meanwhile the foremost minds in the Church at large were gladly devoted to the work of catechising; great preachers as well as great teachers being willing to leave all other work, if necessary, in order to exercise the function of the catechist.[4]

---

[1] Schaff's *Hist. of the Christian Church*, II., 19 f.

[2] Luke 1: 4; Acts 18: 25. See notes, pp. 40, 41, *ante.*

[3] See art. "Catechumen," in *Encyc. Brit.;* also Bingham's *Antiquities of the Christian Church*, Bk. viii., chs. 3-7. "For the Church," says Bingham, "ever since she first divided her catechumens and penitents into distinct orders and classes, had also distinct places in the church for them." "The . . . probable numbers of the members of a congregation likely to be in the condition of catechumens," says the *Encyclopædia Britannica*, "may serve to explain in some degree the architectural arrangements still to be seen in some churches of the early centuries [as, for example] . . . the church of St. Ambrose at Milan, and that of St. Clement at Rome, and some others." Thus it would seem that the providing accommodations for the Sunday-school membership in the church-building has the sanction of high antiquity.

[4] See De Pressensé's *Christian Life and Practice in the Early Church,*

It is true—and it is strange that it is true—that there has been some question whether the catechetical instruction of the Early Church included, as an essential feature, the interlocutory method of teaching. And as an often used argument against the probability of the prevalence of this method, the unbroken form of the few catechumenical discourses preserved to us is pointed out.[1] But, apart from the fact that effective elementary teaching by continuous discourse to passive hearers is, and always has been, and ever must be, practically impossible, there is evidence from various sources that the early Christian Fathers no more attempted this false method than did the Jewish Rabbis before them. Nor, indeed, does the form of the early catechetical discourses, any more than a similar form in our modern school text-books, preclude the idea that free questioning on the substance of the text was deemed indispensable as a means of testing and fixing the learner's knowledge of its meaning. The absence of set questions and answers in the text of the catechetical discourses simply shows that the interlocutory teaching of the early catechumens was by means of no mere perfunctory questioning with memorized rote answers in reply.

The fact that the religious teaching of the Jews, through whom the Christians received their religion, was mainly by the approved means of question and answer, renders it most improbable that a less effective method of teaching was adopted by the best Christian instructors without

Bk. I., ch. 1, § 1; also Proudfit's " Catechetical Instruction before the Reformation," in *Home, the School, and the Church*, IV., 47.

[1] See, *e. g.*, Von Zezschwitz's art. " Katechetik," in Herzog's *Real-Encyc.;* also Mayer's *Gesch. d. Katechumenats u. d. Katechese*, pp. 6, 255, 269, 300.

any good reason for the change. It is even pretty clear that the preaching, or sermonizing, or homilizing, of the first two or three Christian centuries, was largely in the nature of interlocutory conferences between the preacher and his congregation.[1] Paniel, in his elaborate "Pragmatic History of Christian Oratory and Preaching," throws light on this point. Calling attention to the fact that in the earlier centuries "the public edifying discoursing in an intelligible tongue was still quite generally called *didaskalia*,"[2] he says: "The didaskalia was from the beginning nothing else than a mode of instruction which arose from the familiar colloquy of the members of the congregation; taking its material from the Gospel narratives, from the Messianic prophecies of the Old Testament, and from the stories of the life and death of the apostles, of their disciples, and of the martyrs."[3] Its immediate method was the formal dialogue. Its material was suited to the occasion and the hearers.[4] "As religious questions were put

---

[1] See Broadus's *Lectures on the History of Preaching*, p. 46. The very term "homily," applied to the early Christian discourses, would seem to indicate an interlocutory conference between the preacher and his people. *Homilia* means "companionship," "intercourse," "communion." See Thayer's *Greek-Eng. Lex. of N. T.*, s. v.

[2] *Pragmat. Gesch. d. Christl. Beredsamkeit u. d. Homiletik*, p. 79. "The right to teach, however, was not confined to the presbyters or official persons, but depended generally on *charisma tēs didaskalias* [the grace, or gift, of teaching]; and in virtue of this *charisma* [gift] the work of teaching belonged also to ordinary members of the church, 1 Cor. 14: 26. This, however, did not preclude the possibility of an official obligation to teach (not a monopoly) being laid upon individual members of the church who were qualified to teach; and so those called to this duty became the *didaskaloi* of the Church" (Beck's *Pastoral Theology of the New Testament*, p. 25 f.).

[3] *Pragmat. Gesch. d. Christl. Beredsamkeit u. d. Homiletik*, p. 135.

[4] The inspired description of the gathering on the day of Pentecost, when the Christian Church, as such, had its forming (Acts 2: 1-40) illustrates this

to him, or as the edifying conversation of members of the congregation turned the thought to a particular theme, the preacher entered into explanations and contemplatings, dwelling more fully on one point, and more briefly on another. A methodic development of his own course of thought could be brought out only so far as the characteristics of his hearers, and as the questions or objections raised by them, made this possible. The preacher himself was only *one* of the speakers; even though he was the principal one. The others were the co-speakers, who prompted the chief speaker to his speaking, and who retained the right to interrupt him at any time. Even when the ministry was transferred to a designated class of persons, this right of joining in conversation with the preacher [as he discoursed] was not wholly surrendered by the congregation." [1]

In illustration of this latter claim, Paniel points out [2] that "Macarius's homilies show most clearly the intercourse which existed between the preacher and his hearers in the early Christian times. In this regard they are real

method. Peter was the chief speaker among the disciples, but by no means the only one. From the time that they "all . . . began to speak with other tongues," until the repentant Jews interrupted Peter with their question to him and to "the rest of the apostles, 'Brethren, what shall we do?'" the occasion would seem to have been a conference, rather than a congregation of passive hearers sitting before a sermonizer. Yet here is where we find the record of what is known as "Peter's Sermon." Justin Martyr's familiar description ("Apology," i., 67, in *The Ante-Nicene Fathers*, I., 185 f.) of the ordinary Sunday services of the Christians in his day [the middle of the second century] is quite consistent with this view of the case. After the reading of the Scriptures by some of their number, the chief one among them, he says, "verbally *instructs* and *exhorts*" in the line of the Bible lessons; thus conforming to the New Testament plan of "teaching and preaching."

[1] *Pragmat. Gesch. d. Christl. Beredsamkeit u. d. Homiletik*, p. 135.

[2] *Ibid.*, p. 400.

'homilies;' yea, they, together with some similar sermons by Ephraem Syrus, by Isaias Abbas, and by Marcus Asketes, are the only existing 'homilies' of the oldest forms."[1] If, indeed, the Christian Fathers felt the need of this interlocutory method of instruction in the pulpit,[2] and yet ignored it in the teacher's chair, they must have been as contrary-minded in their processes of instruction as Herodotus says the Egyptians were in their religious and social customs.[3] But the free use of the question and answer form of statement in the commentaries and other religious writings of the Christian Fathers, even where those writings were not designed for elementary

---

[1] This statement of Paniel needs modifying, in view of the light recently thrown on the so-called " Second Epistle of Clement," which is shown to be an ancient homily by an unknown author—the oldest homily preserved to us. *This* homily, it is true, lacks the interlocutory form ; but there is a reason for this in the fact that, probably, as Lightfoot claims (*S. Clement of Rome*, Appendix, p. 306,) " it was not an *extempore* address, but was delivered from a manuscript," and was afterward made use of by being "read publicly to the Christian congregation at Corinth from time to time." In short, it is a record of the main points made by a teaching-preacher in one of his discourses, rather than an exhibit of his method of teaching.

[2] While these Lectures are passing through the press, I have a private letter from Professor Dr. M. B. Riddle, who is editing an edition of Chrysostom's works for the *Post-Nicene Fathers ;* and in this letter he says: " In editing Chrysostom I have been struck by the frequency with which he introduces objections or queries (*phēsin* [' He says '] is his word). While his homilies are continuous, there is a constant ideal interlocutory process. See *passim* his Homilies." The descriptions preserved to us of the freedom in conversation, and in the showing of approval or disapproval of the preacher, on the part of Constantinople audiences, in the days of Chrysostom, would indicate pretty clearly that the preacher was yet only the chief speaker—and not always that—at the regular services of the church. See, on this point, a scholarly article on " Constantinople in the Fourth Century," from the Quarterly Review, reprinted in *Littell's Living Age* for November 28, 1846, p. 431 f.

[3] *Hist.*, ii., 35.

religious instruction,[1] shows how familiar this method was
to them as an element in the ordinary teaching process.

The imperfect records which are left to us of the great
catechetical school at Alexandria would, however, seem
sufficient to prove that the teaching methods which had
before been found effective in the schools both of Jewish
religion and of Grecian philosophy, were made use of
at their best in that school of the Christian faith—and
presumably in similar schools elsewhere.   To begin
with, the influence of the thought and teachings of Philo
Judæus—mediator as he was between Moses and Plato—
on the founders of the great Christian school at Alexandria, is admitted on all sides.[2]   The commentaries of
Philo on the Pentateuch, as preserved in their Armenian
fragments, are arranged in the form of question and
answer much on the principle of the modern larger catechisms of the different branches of Protestant Christianity;
except that in Philo's work it is the pupil who asks the
question, and it is the teacher who answers it.[3]   These
interrogative commentaries of Philo are shown to have
been made a basis of the early Pentateuchal teaching of
the catechumens at Alexandria and beyond, as late as the

---

[1] See citations from Basil and Athanasius in Proudfit's article, as above; also,
articles "Apollinaris" and "Theodoretus" in Smith's *Dict. of Christian Biog.*
Basil's Greater and Lesser Monastic Rules, as well as his second book on
Baptism, are in the form of question and answer.   Apollinaris the Elder, aided
by his son of the same name, adapted the Gospels and the Epistles of the New
Testament "to the form of Socratic disputation."   Theodoret's commentaries
"upon the historical books of the Old Testament, from Genesis to 2 Chronicles,
are in the form of question and answer upon the more difficult passages."
"Fourteen books of questions and answers [on the Bible text] form the first
volume of Schulze's edition of Theodoret."

[2] See Bigg's *The Christian Platonists of Alexandria*, passim.

[3] *Opera*, VI., VII.   Comp. Vitringa, as cited at p. 20, *ante*.

days of Ambrose and Augustine;[1] and it is certainly fair
to presume that their substance and method were also
found available all the way between these times.

Clement, who was at the head of the Alexandrian
school before the close of the second century, tells in
his *Stromata* ("Miscellanies") of his indebtedness as
a teacher to the methods of his former instructors,—
presumably Tatian, Theodotus, and Pantænus.[2] And
these methods, as indicated by Clement, recognize the
fundamental idea of the learner's need of mental effort
as a means of receiving and retaining truth. Thus, for
example: "By teaching one learns;"[3] "Use keeps steel
brighter, but disuse produces rust on it;" "Wells, when
pumped out, yield purer water, and that of which no one
partakes turns to putrefaction." "In a word, exercise
produces a healthy condition both in souls and bodies."[4]
It is certainly fair to assume that the methods of teaching
which Clement recognized as the best, were not neglected
by him in his work as a teacher.

Origen, yet more distinctively than Clement, was a
representative teacher of the catechumens; as he was the
representative scholar of his age. Origen is, indeed,
characterized by Dr. Bigg, in his recent study of "the
Christian Platonists of Alexandria," as "the first great
preacher, the first great commentator, the first great dog-
matist" of the post-Apostolic Church.[5] The teaching

---

[1] See, *e. g.*, Harris's *Fragments of Philo Judæus*, p. 3 ; also Harris's *The
Teaching of the Apostles*, p. 63.

[2] See Clement's Works in *The Ante-Nicene Fathers*, II., 301 f.

[3] This is a repetition of Cicero's aphorism, *Docendo discimus,*—" By teaching
we learn." Impression is made in expression.

[4] *The Ante-Nicene Fathers*, II., 302 a.

[5] *The Christian Plat. of Alex.*, p. 115.

methods of Origen are, therefore, to be recognized as the best known methods of his day; and they, fortunately, are not obscure. Gregory Thaumaturgus, who was a pupil of Origen, sounded the praises of his teacher as a master in the Socratic method of instruction; "and for the way in which this teacher probed his [the pupil's] inmost soul with questions."[1] Neander, in treating the history and methods of the school at Alexandria, says: "The patience and skill which must be exercised by these Alexandrian teachers, in answering the multifarious questions which would be proposed to them, is intimated by Origen [in his notes on our Lord's manner of meeting captious questioners[2]] when he requires of the Christian teachers [or catechists] that they should follow Christ's example, and not show a fretful spirit, if they should be pushed with questions propounded not for the sake of learning, [from the teachers,] but for the purpose of putting them to the proof."[3]

Johann Mayer, the eminent Roman Catholic historian of catechetics, who argues against the idea that the interlocutory method was the prevailing one in the Early Church,[4]—even he recognizes the fact that in the treatment of *unevangelized* pupils the teaching process involved the freest use of question and answer. He shows by the testimony of Eusebius,[5] and by the statements of Origen in his controversy with Celsus,[6] that no attempt was made to win and train young heathen without full and thorough

[1] Art. "Gregorius Thaumaturgus," in Smith's *Dict. of Christian Biog.*

[2] *Matt.*, Tom. XIV., § 16.

[3] *Gen. Hist. of the Christian Religion and Church*, I., 528.

[4] *Gesch. d. Katechumenats u. d. Katechese*, pp. 6, 255, 269, 300.

[5] *Hist. Eccl.*, v., 10.   [6] *Contra Celsum*, iii., 52; vi., 10.

interlocutory instruction. In this line he says that the catechist "paid due regard to the individuality, to the age, to the sex, and to the rank of each person [thus dealt with], with the most generous considerateness,"—on the teacher's part. And thus it was, as he thinks, that "Origen devoted himself to the instruction of one person at a time, or of a few persons who were alike in spirit and in acquirements, or who were united in bonds of friendship." [1] But the proving of this proves more than this. If, indeed, the interlocutory teaching process was employed in the winning and training of the heathen because it was found to be the *best* method, it is hardly to be supposed that a *poorer* method was employed in the instruction of young Christians.

Origen, indeed, places the interlocutory method above the hortatory or didactic method, as a means of edifying the hearer. "We put the gospel before each one, as his character and disposition may fit him to receive it," he says; "inasmuch as we have learned to know 'how we ought to answer every man' [each one, individually].[2] And there are some who are capable of receiving nothing more than an exhortation to believe, and to those we address that [exhortation] alone; while we approach others, again, as far as possible, in the way of demonstration, by means of question and answer." [3] That is to say, in hopeful cases teaching was the method; in other cases, exhorting was all that could be attempted.

Augustine, again, would seem to put this matter of methods with catechumens beyond all reasonable doubt. In his book, "Catechising of the Uninstructed," prepared as a guide to a catechist at Carthage, he details the several

---

[1] *Gesch.*, p. 255.   [2] Col. 4 : 6.   [3] "Against Celsus," vi., 10.

steps in the process of wise catechising.   He insists that each pupil should be treated according to his individual needs; and that to this end the catechist should examine him by preliminary questioning as to his motives and as to his attainments, with a view to making the pupil's present error or lack the starting-point of his particular instruction.[1]   Similarly, all the way along in his teaching, the pupil, according to Augustine, must be watched and questioned, and carefully dealt with individually; so that he may be caused to *know* rather than merely be caused to *hear* the truth which is, for the time being, the substance of the catechetical instruction.   Every effort to secure both free questioning and frank answering by the pupil himself, is to be made by the catechist, step by step, in his course of catechetical teaching.[2]   It is the individual pupil who is to be taught; not the assembly which is to be harangued, in the instruction of catechumens.[3]   That is the point which Augustine emphasizes.

In a specimen discourse to catechumens on the Creed,[4] Augustine seems to illustrate his method of questioning by his frequent introduction of questions, to which he appends his own answers; as if this were in the line of his habit of teaching.   Thus: "What next? . . . 'was crucified, dead, and buried.'   Who?   What?   For whom? —Who?   God's only Son, our Lord.   What?   Crucified, dead, and buried.   For whom?   For [the] ungodly and sinners."   And so on in this discourse, which was to be the basis of instruction in the meaning of the articles of the Creed.   By all these glimpses of the current of events

---

[1] "Catechising of the Uninstructed," ch. 5; in *Nicene and Post-Nicene Fathers*, III., 288 *b*.   [2] *Ibid.*, chs. 8, 13.   [3] *Ibid.*, ch. 16.
[4] "On the Creed," ¿ 7, in *Nicene and Post-Nicene Fathers*, III., 371.

in the Early Church, it would seem clear that the *process* of religious teaching was much the same under both Jewish and Christian instructors, in whatever form the text of the teaching matter was presented.

In short, as Kraussold, a recent and very high German authority concerning the history of catechetics, sums up the case in the matter of the early Christian catechumenical schools: "The method of instruction was at first declaratory. That, at the same time, the interrogatory method was employed, is self-evident."[1] In other words, even if the teacher declared in advance what he intended to teach, when he came to attempt the teaching of that which he had declared, he used the ordinary and proper teaching method, which includes question and answer. That is "self-evident."

This much we know of the early Christian catechumenical and other catechetical schools, as illustrated by the great one in Alexandria, and by less prominent ones elsewhere; they included in their membership children and adults of both sexes;[2] among their teachers were laymen and women;[3] the scholars were taught individually;[4] the interlocutory method of teaching was used freely;[5] and the subject-matter of instruction began with the Old Testament story of creation, and went on to the most practical details of the Christian life.[6] And this is

---

[1] *Die Katechetik für Schule u. Kirche*, p. 18.

[2] See Bingham's *Antiquities*, Bk. ii., ch. 22, § 9; Bk. x., ch. 1, § 4.

[3] *Ibid.*, Bk. ii., ch. 22, § 9; Bk. iii., ch. 10, §§ 2, 3; Bk. viii., ch. 7, § 12; Bk. xiv., ch. 4, § 5.   [4] *Ibid.*, Bk. x., ch. 1, §§ 3, 6; ch. 2, § 5.

[5] *Ibid.*, Bk. x., ch. 2, § 7; Bk. xiv., ch. 4, § 26.

[6] *Ibid.*, Bk. x., ch. 1, §§ 6, 7.   Comp. De Pressensé's *Christian Life and Practice in the Early Church*, Bk. i., ch. 7.   See, also, articles on "Catechetics" and "Catechumens," in Herzog's *Real-Encyc.*; Smith and Cheetham's

in itself a description, or a delineation, of the Sunday-school of to-day, in its main and essential features.[1]

As the Christian Church gained in the scope of its power as an organization, and came to have control of extended communities, provinces, or nationalities, and as it reached out for the evangelizing of new countries, its formal recognition of the value of the church Bible-school corresponded yet more nearly with the ancient Jewish polity in the land of Palestine. When, for example, at the very beginning of the fourth century, St. Gregory, the Illuminator, entered upon his work of christianizing Armenia, he adopted a compulsory system of Bible-schools for the children in every city there; and by this means it was that Armenia was built up in the Christian faith.[2] And it would seem that at that period, as also earlier, there were public schools for the training of both heathen and Christian children in the knowledge of the Scriptures, in Mesopotamia, Cappadocia, Egypt, and else-where.[3] Bingham, indeed, calls attention to a specific

Dict. of Christian Antiq.; Encyc. Brit.; and McClintock and Strong's *Cyc. of Bib., Theol., and Eccl. Lit.;* and article on " Catechetical Instruction before the Reformation," in *Home, the School and the Church,* IV., 46 f.

[1] " In the Primitive Church, not only men and women, but children, were encouraged and trained up from their infancy to the *reading* of the Holy Scriptures; and the catechumens were . . . obliged to *learn* the Scriptures as a part of their discipline and instruction, . . . [moreover] children were trained up to the *use* of the Holy Scriptures. And of this we have undoubted evidence from many eminent instances of their practice [*e. g.*, Eusebius, Socrates, Sozomen, and Gregory of Nyssa, are here quoted in illustration of this custom]. . . . And it is observable, that as there were many catechetical schools in those times for explaining the Scriptures to the catechumens, so there were also schools appointed in many churches to instruct the youth in the knowledge of the Scriptures " (Bingham's *Antiq.,* Bk. xiii., ch. 4, § 9).

[2] *Ibid.,* Bk. xiii., ch. 4, § 9.

[3] *Ibid.;* also Bk. viii., ch. 7, § 12.

"canon attributed to the sixth General Council of Constantinople [A. D. 680], which promotes the setting up of charity schools [Robert Raikes' Sunday-schools] in all country churches;"[1] as practically they were already to be found in the cathedral churches generally.[2]

In all these Christian church-schools, as in the earlier Jewish church-schools, it was the Bible text itself which was the primary subject of study and of teaching. Very young children were taught to memorize the Scriptures, and at the same time to understand them.[3] Illustrations abound in ecclesiastical works of the fourth and fifth centuries, of persons who had become so familiar with the Scriptures as to be able to recite large portions of them —in some cases the entire Old and New Testaments— without the aid of a book.[4] Yet this memorizing of the Bible text was but incidental to the Bible-school *teaching;* it was not itself deemed the teaching.

Thus it is clear that the early Christian Church was not unfaithful to its trust, nor unmindful of the duty imposed upon it by the Great Commission. It organized Bible-schools far and near, as a means of instructing its converts, and of training its membership. And so it continued to do, so long as it wisely followed the injunctions of its Divine Founder. But as it grew in worldly prominence and lost in spiritual life, changes came in the methods of its training work. Its ritual services were expanded, and its teaching exercises were diminished. "Teaching gained in proportion as ritualism lost," says De Pressensé;[5] and conversely, teaching lost as ritualism

---

[1] *Antiq.*, Bk. viii., ch. 7, § 12.   [2] *Ibid.*, Bk. iii., ch. 10, § 4.

[3] *Ibid.*, Bk. x., ch. 1, §§ 6, 7 ; xiii., ch. 4, § 9.

[4] *Ibid.*, Bk. xiii., ch. 4, § 9.   [5] *The Apostolic Era*, Bk. ii., ch. 6, § 1.

gained. Or, as Proudfit represents it, when "the *ecclesi-astical* spirit overcame the *evangelical,* and the church grew . . . worldly and material in all her institutions and instrumentalities, . . . making more of a splendid ritual than of a pure faith, and magnifying church orthodoxy above vital piety, . . . catechetical instruction, of course, declined."[1]

In the recently issued valuable work of Mr. Henry C. Lea, on the history of the Inquisition, it is shown conclusively, by that impartial historian of the religious history of the Middle Ages, that the decline of the spiritual life of the Church was attributable to the neglect, by the Church, of its educational function.[2] It is also shown by Mr. Lea, as it has been shown by so many other historians before, that the gleams of a purer life, and the struggles toward a better state of things, meantime, were among and on the part of those who studied and taught the Bible, and who sought to secure Bible instruction for the people generally.

It stands out most clearly in the ecclesiastical history of the Middle Ages, that where the Christian life was purest, in those times of general decline, was where the Bible-school idea was adhered to most closely as a means of religious instruction and training.[3] Peculiarly was this

---

[1] See Proudfit's article, as before cited.

[2] *Hist. of the Inquisition*, Bk. i., chs. 1-6.

[3] The earlier form of "catechism," or manual for elementary religious instruction, consisted of the Creed, the Lord's Prayer, and the Ten Commandments, with or without explanation and comment. In this form it shows itself in the work of "Kero, monk of St. Gall (about 720); Notker, of St. Gall (d. 912); Otfried, monk of Weissenbourg (d. after 870), and others" (Schaff's *Creeds of Christendom*, I., 246). "One of the earliest—in fact, the first known catechism in the English language—was written by Wyclif. A copy of it, in the

the case with the Waldenses, the Albigenses, the Lollards or Wiclifites, the Bohemian Brethren or Hussites, and the Brethren of the Common Life.[1] Not the pure liturgy, nor yet the faithful pulpit, but the divinely appointed Bible-school—in its more primitive elements—was the distinctive means of their preservation from the wellnigh universal defection.[2]

British Museum, bears the date of 1372. . . . It was designed 'to teach simple men and women the right way to heaven.' The first three of the thirteen sections into which it is divided, contain catechisms on the Creed, the Lord's Prayer, and the Commandments." (See Dr. J. Hammond Trumbull's article on "Catechisms of Old and New England," in *The Sunday School Times* for September 8, 1883.) The "Primer," as "a manual of *primary* instruction in religious truth and practice," finds mention, at about the time of Wiclif, in Piers Plowman's Vision, and in Chaucer's The Prioresses Tale. Maskell (*Monumenta Ritualia Ecclesiæ Anglicanæ,* II., xlv) says of the Primer, that it "may have been well known in the early days even of the Anglo-Saxons; . . . for there never was a period, in the history of the English Church, when care was not taken to enforce upon all priests the duty of teaching their people the rudiments of faith, in the vulgar tongue, and to provide books fitted for that purpose." (See Dr. J. Hammond Trumbull's article on "The New England Primer and its Predecessors," in *The Sunday School Times* for April 29, 1882.)

[1] Schaff says (*Creeds of Christendom,* I., 569): "The Waldenses formed at first no separate church, but an *ecclesiola in ecclesia* ['a churchette within a church'], a pious lay community of Bible readers. They were well versed in Scripture, and maintained its supremacy over the traditions of men; they preached the gospel to the poor, allowing women also to preach"—or rather, perhaps, to *teach* in this "lay community of Bible readers;" as women taught in the catechumenical school at Alexandria, and as they teach in the Sunday-schools of to-day. The Waldensian Catechism presents important phases of Scripture truth. It "must have been written before 1500; while the Bohemian [Catechism] in the form in which it was presented to Luther, first appeared in print in 1521 or 1522. . . . Palacky brought to light (1869) a similar Catechism, which he derives from Hus before 1414" (Schaff, as above, I., 572).

[2] See Schaff's *Creeds of Christendom,* I., 246; art. "Catechisms," in Schaff-Herzog's *Encyc. of Relig. Knowl.;* art. "Catechumen" and art. "Education," in *Encyc. Brit.;* and art. "Catechetics" and art. "Catechisms," in McClintock and Strong's *Cyc. of Bib., Theol., and Eccles. Lit.*

An admirable illustration of this truth is furnished in the recorded testimony of Reinerius, an emissary from Rome to the Waldenses, in his report concerning the Bible-teaching prevalent among that people in the thirteenth century. "He who has been a disciple [in their fold] for seven days," he said, "looks out some one whom he may teach in his turn; so that there is a continual increase [of them]. If any would excuse himself [from learning] they say to him, 'Only learn one word every day, and at the end of the year you will have three hundred [words]; and so [you will] make progress.' . . . I have heard one of these poor peasants repeat the whole Book of Job by heart, without missing a single word; and there are others who have the whole of the New Testament by heart, and much of the Old; nor . . . will they listen to anything else, saying that all sermons which are not proved by Scripture are unworthy of belief."[1] The Waldenses, by the way, came originally from Lyons, where the cathedral catechetical school had long been of exceptional efficiency in securing religious instruction, however intermingled with error, to the young.[2]

From the beginning, in short, all the way down the centuries, the history of the Christian Church shows that just in proportion as the church Bible-school—the Sunday-school, as we now call it—has been accorded the place which our Lord assigned to it in the original plan of his Church, has substantial progress been made in the extending of the membership, and in the upbuilding—the "edifying"—of the body of Christian believers in the

---

[1] Cited in Henderson's *The Vaudois*, p. 102. See, also, Latrobe-Cranz's *Hist. of the Brethren*, p. 15 f.

[2] See art. "Waldenses," in Schaff-Herzog's *Encyc.*

knowledge of God's Word and in the practice of its precepts. And just in proportion as the Sunday-school agency, or its practical equivalent under some name or form, has been lacking, or has been ignored, has the Church failed of retaining and continuing the vital power of its membership.

Do not misunderstand me here. Every great reform, in the Church, or in nominally religious communities, since the days of John the Baptist and of Peter, has been brought about by *preaching*. Christians have been aroused from their sloth, and sinners have been startled in and from their sins, by the clarion voice of the herald-preacher. Preaching has been, and is, and is to be, the pre-eminent agency for the warning and calling of sinners, and for the exhorting and directing of saints. But the religious *training* of any people has been attained, and the results of any great reformation have been made permanent, only through a process of interlocutory, or catechetical, *teaching;* such as forms the distinguishing characteristics of the technical Sunday-school.

A few representative illustrations of this universal truth are as good as more. It was by preaching that the great Reformation of the sixteenth century was brought about; but no one of the chief reformers of that period was unwise enough to suppose that preaching was to retain and to build up in the pure faith of God's Word those who, through preaching, had been rescued from the embraces of error. Luther saw the need of a system of Bible-schools in the new Protestant world, as plainly as Simon ben Shetach saw that need in the ancient Jewish world. "Young children and scholars are the seed and the source of the Church!" rang out the warning voice of Luther. "For

the Church's sake, Christian schools must be established
and maintained," he added; "[for] God maintains the
Church through the schools."[1]   Luther even went so far
as to say that a clergyman was not fairly fitted to be a
preacher unless he had first been a teacher; that, in fact,
a bishop ought to give proof, before being a bishop, that
he had aptness to teach.   "I would that nobody should
be chosen as a minister if he were not before this a schoolmaster,"[2] was Luther's putting of this opinion.

Luther personally prepared two catechisms, a Larger,
and a Smaller, as helps to religious teaching; and his co-
workers and successors prepared others.   Calvin took a
similar view of the duty of the Church to instruct the
young and the ignorant by interlocutory teaching; and
he also prepared two catechetical lesson-helps, or lesson-
guides, first in French, and afterwards in Latin.   These
catechisms by Luther and Calvin were translated into
various languages, and were used widely among the
Protestants of Europe and of Great Britain.   Zwingle and
Beza in Switzerland, Knox in Scotland, Cranmer and
Ridley in England, and Usher in Ireland, and many other
representative leaders in the Reformation, were alive to
the importance of the revival of the primitive church-
school idea, as the hope of stability and growth for the
Church of Christ.   Just so far, in fact, as this divinely commanded method of religious training was newly adopted
and adhered to, were the best fruits of the Reformation
preserved and transmitted; and where there was chiefest
lack in this direction, the influence of the Reformers and
of their work gradually diminished, or faded away.[3]

[1] Cited in Schumann's *Lehrb. d. Paedag.*, p. 144.   [2] *Ibid.*
[3] See articles " Catechisms " and " Catechetics," in Schaff-Herzog's *Encyc.*,

Indeed, had it not been for the rising up at that time, in the Roman Catholic Church, of a new apostle of the church-school idea, and for the wonderful effectiveness of his work of restoring to that Church this primitive agency of religious teaching, it would seem that the power of the Church of Rome as such would have been permanently broken, or hopelessly hampered, by the labors of the reformers. Ignatius Loyola, the founder of the Society of Jesus, with Lainez, Aquaviva, Xavier, and others of his immediate associates, despairing of turning back the tide of battle against Rome and her institutions, as then waged under the pulpit leaders of the opposing host, conceived the plan of reaching out after the children of the combatants, and of rearing up in them a new generation of lovers and defenders of Rome.

The first great work of the Jesuits was the establishment of religious schools for the young, which were an advance in their methods on anything then known to the world. The very ideas which prevail in the management of our best modern Sunday-schools, church and mission, seem to have been carried out by the Jesuits in these schools of their forming.[1] And it was by this means that the Jesuits, in a single generation, according to the testimony of one of their chief historians, becoming " masters of the present by the men whom they had trained, and disposing of the future by the children who were yet in their hands, realized a dream which no one till the times

and in McClintock and Strong's *Cyc.* See, also, Porter's *The Educational Systems of the Puritans and Jesuits Compared*, pp. 26-35.

[1] See Steinmetz's *Hist. of the Jesuits*, I., 346-350; Karl von Raumer's *Gesch. d. Paedag.*, I., 288 f.; Ranke's *Hist. of the Popes*, I., 415-418; and Quick's *Essays on Educational Reformers*, pp. 2-20.

of Ignatius had dared to conceive."[1] The verdict of history on this point is summed up by President Porter, in his suggestion that Catholic and Protestant historians are agreed that it was by this religious school machinery that the Jesuits "arrested the Reformation in its onward and apparently triumphant advances," and that "the dividing line was fixed between the Protestant and Catholic sections of Europe, to remain till now almost precisely where it was drawn thirty years after Luther had broken with Rome."[2] It was practically by the Sunday-school agency that the Protestant Reformers hoped to make permanent the results of the Reformation. And it was by a more adroit and efficient use of the Sunday-school agency, in its improved forms, that the Church of Rome stayed the progress of the Reformation. *That* is the plain lesson of history.

Nor has the Church of Rome ever forgotten the lesson learned in that crisis hour of her history. The Council of Trent recognized the peril of the Church of Rome through the Protestant use of catechetical teaching, and it gave chief prominence to wisely planned efforts at meeting that peril. "The heretics have chiefly made use of catechisms to corrupt the minds of Christians,"[3] was the declaration of that Council. Therefore "the Holy Synod rightly decreed that both [the] pestilent preaching and the writings of the false prophets must be met by opposition;"[4] and felt it "necessary, even after so many written treatises

---

[1] Crétineau Joly's *Histoire Religieuse, Politique, et Littéraire de la Compagnie de Jesus,* I., 5 ; cited by Porter, in *Educ. Systems,* p. 23 f.

[2] Porter's *Educ. Systems,* p. 4.

[3] Preface to *The Catechism of the Council of Trent,* Question vi.

[4] *Ibid.,* Q. vii.

of Christian doctrine, to put forward a new catechism for
pastors, by the care of an Œcumenical Council, and the
authority of the Sovereign Pontiff."[1]   All pastors were
specifically charged by the Council of Trent with the duty
of instructing the young in the primary elements of the
Christian faith.[2]   And from that day to this the Church
of Rome has never, as before, neglected the divinely
appointed agency of Christ's Church for discipling and
training the young ; nor has it, since then, given a second
place to children in the ministrations of its priesthood.

It was in consequence of this lesson that St. Francis
Xavier (who is credited with the saying, " Give me the
children until they are seven years old, and any one may
take them afterwards ") gave the young and the ignorant
the first place in his evangelizing in India ; going through
the streets of Goa ringing a bell, and entreating parents
and householders to send their children and their slaves
to him to be instructed.[3]   It was in consequence of this
lesson that St. Carlo Borromeo devoted his energies so
largely to the gathering and teaching of children in Sunday-schools in his cathedral at Milan, and in his parish
churches near and far ; leaving at his death, in 1584,
seven hundred and forty-three of these Sunday-schools,
comprising more than three thousand teachers and forty
thousand scholars.[4]   It was in consequence of this lesson
that Cardinal Bellarmine, while Archbishop of Capua, a
little later than Borromeo's time, aroused himself to the
determination of securing elementary religious instruction

[1] Preface to *The Catechism of the Council of Trent*, Question viii.
[2] *Ibid.*, Q. xi.
[3] See *Méthode de Saint-Sulpice, dans la Direction des Catéchismes*, pp. 1-12.
[4] *Ibid.*

to every child in his arch-diocese, he setting an example to his under pastors by going personally into the parishes, and gathering about him the children and their friends for their familiar teaching; preparing meanwhile, as an aid in this work, simple catechisms,[1] one at least of which is an approved text-book in the Roman Catholic Sunday-schools of England and the United States to-day.[2]   It is in consequence of this lesson that the policy of the Roman Catholic Church, far more than that of the Protestant churches, has from that time to this been in the direction indicated by these labors of Loyola and Xavier and Bor-romeo and Bellarmine.

This policy it is that was illustrated by the recorded conversation of a Roman Catholic priest with one of our Protestant Episcopal bishops in the United States, some years ago, when the priest said to the bishop, in sub-stance: "What a poor, foolish people are you Protestants! You leave the children, until they are grown up, pos-sessed of the devil ; then you go at the work of reclaiming them with horse, foot, and dragoons.   We Catholics, on the other hand, know that the children are plastic as clay in our hands, and we quietly devote ourselves first to them.   When they are well instructed and trained, we have little fear as to their future."   And this policy of the Church of Rome, resulting as it did from this lesson in the history of that Church, has been recognized by many a wise Protestant scholar and thinker—all along these last three centuries—as worthy of more extensive

---

[1] See *Méthode de Saint-Sulpice, dans la Direction des Catéchismes*, pp. 1-12.

[2] " In 1870, the Œcumenical Council recommended the general use of the *Schema de Parvo*, a small catechism, which is little more than an abstract of Bellarmine's " (art. " Catechism," in *Encyc. Brit.*).

imitation by all lovers of God's truth, and all lovers of divinely indicated methods of working.[1]

Bishop Lancelot Andrewes, of the Church of England, for example, learned as he was in the Bible text and in ecclesiastical antiquities, writing on this subject within a century after the Reformation, pointed back to the teachings of Scripture and of Christian history in proof of the fact that interlocutory religious teaching was the hope, as it was the duty, of the Christian Church. It was by this means, he said, that Christianity made all its earlier conquests; "and when catechising was left off in the Church, it [the Church] soon became darkened and overspread with ignorance. The Papists, therefore, acknowledge that all the advantage which the Protestants have gotten of them [since the Reformation], hath come by this exercise [of catechetical instruction]; and it is to be feared that if ever they get ground of us, it will be by their more exact and frequent catechising than ours."[2] A century and a half later, these words of Bishop Andrewes seemed like fulfilled prophecy.

It is not that the various Protestant churches did not, at the time of the Reformation, realize the importance of the Sunday-school idea; nor yet that they did not form plans for the prosecution of certain phases of the Sunday-school work; but it is that various causes combined, as can be shown, to render the formed plans insufficient, or ineffective, for the purpose in view, and finally to bring

[1] A valuable treatise on the religious instruction of children by the Church, from the Roman Catholic stand-point, is the "*Méthode de Saint-Sulpice, dans la Direction des Catéchismes,* as above cited. It treats of the history, literature, and methods of the subject, quite fully. Incidentally it gives proof of the prevalence of the Sunday-school idea in the schools which it represents.

[2] *The Pattern of Catechistical Doctrine,* p. 8.

them into neglect. All the representative Reformed
churches were explicit, at the start, in recognition of the
divinely ordained mission of the church-school, or Sunday-school. The views of Luther, on this point, have
been already cited.[1] In the Heidelberg Catechism, where
the question is asked, "What doth God require in the
fourth commandment?" the answer comes, "First, that
the ministry of the gospel and the *schools* be maintained." In the Scotch Book of Discipline there stands
the acknowledgment that "one of the two ordinary and
perpetual functions that travel in the word is the office of
the doctor, who may be also called . . . *catechiser ;* that
is, teacher of the catechism and rudiments of religion."[2]
And this, in fact, was the Protestant position generally.

The General Assembly of the Church of Scotland, in
the first year of its existence, provided that while there
should be two public services on every Lord's Day, the
first service should include worship and sermonizing, and
the second should be given to worship and the catechising of the young and ignorant.[3] Again, a canon in
the Church of England, which dates back to 1603, and
which has never been repealed, requires that "every parson, vicar, or curate, upon every Sunday or holy day,
before evening prayer, shall, for half an hour and more,
examine and instruct the youth and ignorant persons of
his parish in the Ten Commandments, the Articles of the
Belief, and in the Lord's Prayer ; and shall diligently hear,
instruct, and teach them the Catechism set forth in the

[1] See p. 67 f., *ante.*

[2] See *Abridgment of the Acts of the General Assemblies of the Church of
Scotland*, p. 76 f.

[3] See Hetherington's *History of the Church of Scotland*, p. 55.

Book of Common Prayer." [1] The minister who fails of
attention to this duty is, on his first offense, by the provisions of this canon, to be reported to his bishop and to
receive a reprimand. A second offense is to subject him
to suspension; and on the third offense he is, if deemed
incorrigible, to be excommunicated. It would seem,
indeed, as if the Reformers realized that the hope of the
future pivoted on the continued and faithful ministry of the
Church to the young; and yet that the plans of the Reformers to secure the continuance of this ministry were practically a failure. And here is a mystery worth looking into.

A primary cause of the decline of the Sunday-school
work in Protestant churches generally, after the new
prominence given to it by the Reformers, seems to rest
in the widespread perversion of the very means designed
for its prosecution. It was in order to promote interlocutory teaching that catechisms, presenting truth in
the form of question and answer, were prepared in such
fullness and variety by Protestant church leaders.[2] But
the use of those catechisms widely degenerated into a
perfunctory service of asking rote questions with the purpose of securing memorized rote answers in reply, apart
from any necessary interchange of thought or of knowledge between teacher and pupil. And thus it came to
pass that catechism using stood in the way of catechetical
teaching; the stepping-stone becoming a stumbling-block.

So, again, the sermon, or the homily, was brought
by the Reformers to its earlier place as an adjunct of

---

[1] Canon lix., of 1603. See Gibson's *Codex Juris Ecclesiastici Anglicani*,
tit. xix, cap. 1, p. 453.

[2] See List of Catechisms in Mitchell's *Catechisms of the Second Reformation*,
pp. lxxxv-xci.

all principal services of worship, as a means of popular instruction in religious truth. But the sermonizing
being wholly separated from catechising, under the new
arrangement, lost its primitive place in a conference between teacher and taught, and degenerated widely into a
continuous discourse to passive, and often to inattentive
and unintelligent hearers. It is so much easier, on the
one hand, to preach than it is to teach ; and, on the other
hand, to hear than it is to learn ; it is so much easier to
tell what one knows or thinks, or what one thinks he
knows, than it is to find out another's spiritual lack and
needs and capabilities, and to endeavor to supply them
wisely,—that it is hardly to be wondered at, however
much it is to be regretted, that preaching (especially
under the pressure of the seeming needfulness of polem-
ical discourses[1]) gradually overshadowed teaching in the
work of the ministry in Protestant churches ; the children,
meanwhile, having practically only a form of religious
instruction without its power. And thus it was that
the teaching of the young wellnigh died out from the
churches of Protestantism through the misuse and abuse
of the agencies devised for its promotion.

All this was, however, an evil of administration rather
than of primary purpose and plan ; for it is evident from
the records of history that the Reformers had no thought
of overshadowing Bible-school teaching by pulpit preaching, nor yet of making the reciting and hearing of the

---

[1] In the Church of England, very soon after the enactment of the Canon of
1603, enjoining catechising, controversial preaching on dogmas usurped the
place of catechising ; and, in 1622, King James directed that catechising take
the place of afternoon sermons. Archbishop Laud again enforced catechising
instead of sermonizing on Sunday afternoons. (See Perry's *History of the
Church of England*, pp. 398, 415).

catechism a chief element in catechetical teaching. The catechism was, in every instance, prepared, not as the lesson itself, but as a lesson-analysis, a lesson-guide, a lesson-paper, duly authorized, for the time being, by a Church Lesson-Committee. It outlined the subject of study, but it was not designed to be the object of study. No prominent compiler of a catechism in the realm of religious truth, from the days of Philo Judaeus to the Westminster Divines, can, in fact, have supposed that his work would be followed in the blind and mechanical fashion which subsequently prevailed so widely for the making of catechism teaching a thing of dread to the child, and of unconcern to the teacher.[1]

Luther made himself clear on this point. In his Preface to his Smaller Catechism he enjoined it upon teachers to see to it that their scholars not only knew what was said in the catechism answers, but knew what was meant by them; "to take these forms [of statement] before them, and explain them word by word."[2] And as showing that these answers, even when thus explained and understood, were in no sense to be the limit of the pupil's teaching, Luther claimed that every child under catechetical instruction ought to know the truths of the entire gospel, the facts of the whole life and work of our Lord, by the time he was nine or ten years of age.[3] "Not only must they learn the word [of God] by heart," again he

[1] " May we not have just reason to fear," said Dr. Isaac Watts, (*Works*, III., 214,) in speaking of the use of the Westminster Catechism, " that the holy things of our religion have not only been made the aversion of children, but have been exposed to disreputation and contempt, by teaching them such a number of strange phrases which they could not understand?"

[2] See Köstlin's *Life of Luther*, p. 369 f.

[3] See Karl von Raumer's *Gesch. d. Paedag.*, I., 169 f.

said, . . . "but they must be asked, verse by verse, and must answer, what each [verse] means, and how they understand it."[1] Luther's Larger Catechism was not even arranged in the form of question and answer, but it was none the less a "catechism," in name and in fact, for being in the form of the lesson-guides of the Early Church catechumens.

Even before the Reformation there were formal injunctions in force in the Church of England, requiring all curates to *explain* to their hearers every sentence of the substance of the primers which those hearers were to memorize. Thus, in 1536–38, an injunction to the curates ran: "Ye shall, every Sunday and Holy-day throughout the year, openly and plainly recite to your parishioners, twice or thrice together, or oftener if need require, one particle or sentence of the Paternoster, or [of the] Creed, in English, to the intent [that] they may learn the same by heart: and so from day to day [ye are] to give them one little lesson or sentence of the same, till they have learned the whole Paternoster and Creed in English by rote. And as they be taught every sentence of the same by rote, *ye shall expound and declare the understanding of the same unto them.*"[2]

And when a "Catechism for Children" was given its place in the Prayer Book of Edward VI.,[3] that catechism

---

[1] Luther's *Deutsche Messe* (1526); cited in Gieseler's *Eccles. Hist.*, IV., 562.

[2] Quoted from Burnet's *History of the Reformation*, in Procter's *History of the Book of Common Prayer*, p. 390. Comp. Burnet's *Hist. of the Ref.*, I., 364, 507.

[3] "When the great hindrance to reformation was removed by the death of Henry, the instruction of the young and the ignorant was among the first particulars to which the advisers of Edward directed their efforts, in the Injunctions of 1547; and as soon as a Book of Service was prepared, a Catechism

was by no means understood as covering the substance of a Christian child's religious instruction. On the contrary, it merely covered the points at which the child was to be examined by the bishop, when brought to him for confirmation.[1] Various other catechisms were in use, more or less widely, in the Church of England, in the days of Edward and of Elizabeth;[2] and in order to secure uniformity in the religious teaching of the young, the Convocation of 1562 took steps for securing a catechism that should be the standard of religious instruction in all the schools.[3] This catechism was prepared by Dean Nowell, of St. Paul's, although it made free use of the material of earlier authors, including the work of Bishop Poynet.[4] Delayed in its issue by various causes, it was

was placed in it, that the exposition of these Christian elements might not depend on the care or ability of the curates" (Procter's *Hist. of Book of Com. Prayer*, p. 390).

[1] "The end and purpose of catechism [of catechising] is, in good and natural order, fitly applied to serve the good use of confirmation by the bishop, *at which time the bishop doth not teach but examine*" (Thomas Norton in his Preface to the English translation of Nowell's Catechism, in 1570. See Parker Society's edition of *Nowell's Catechism*, p. 109).

[2] See Procter's *Hist. of Book of Com. Prayer* (p. 392), with citation from Cardwell's *Documentary Annals*.

[3] "One considerable thing more passed the hands of this Convocation [1562]; . . . viz., the Catechism in Latin for the use of schools, and also for a brief summary of religion to be owned and professed in this reformed Church. And this is the same with that which is commonly known to this day by the name of Nowell's Catechism" (Strype's *Annals of the Reformation*, Vol. I., pt. i., p. 525 f.).

[4] "An intention was formed in the time of Edward and Elizabeth, to have another authorized Catechism [besides that in the Prayer Book] for the instruction of more advanced students, and especially those in public schools. . . . The original of this work is ascribed to Poynet, who was Bishop of Winchester during Gardiner's deprivation. It was published in Latin and in English in 1553, and is supposed to have had the approval both of Cranmer

finally issued in 1570. Originally written in Latin, it was
translated into English and Greek;[1] and several abridg-
ments or condensations of it were made. While entitled
Catechismus Puerorum ("Children's Catechism")[2] it was
specifically designed "to be a guide to the younger clergy
in the study of divinity, as containing the sum and substance of our reformed religion."[3] In other words it was,
like every other true catechism, an indication of the lines
along which the clergyman or schoolmaster should teach
the children and youth of his charge. In 1571 a canon
enjoined the exclusive use of Nowell's Catechism—in one
or another of its forms—in the work of religious instruc-

and also of the Convocation which sanctioned the Articles in 1552" (Procter's
Hist. of Book of Com. Prayer, p. 391 f.). Comp. Strype's *Memorials of Abp.
Cranmer*, p. 294. "Nowell informs the Bishops that he had not scrupled to
avail himself of the labors of others who had preceded him in this department
of theology, both as regarded arrangement and matter. . . . The Catechisms
of Poinet and Calvin are, perhaps, those with which Nowell's is most frequently and verbally coincident" (Corrie's Memoir of Nowell, in Parker Society's edition of *Nowell's Catechism*, p. vii). In drawing up his catechism,
Nowell "made much use of the Catechism set forth toward the latter end of
King Edward's reign" (Strype's *Annals of the Ref.*, Vol. I., pt. i., p. 525 f.).

   [1] See Strype's *Annals of the Ref.*, Vol. I., pt. i., p. 525 f.; Corrie's Memoir
of Nowell, in Parker Soc. ed. of *Nowell's Catechism*, p. vii ; Procter's *Hist.
of Book of Com. Prayer*, p. 393.

   [2] Corrie (Memoir, as above, pp. v, vi) shows that the *Catechismus Puerorum* approved by this lower house of Convocation March 3, 1562, was the
same as that published by Nowell in 1570.

   [3] " Besides this [Prayer Book Catechism], there was a Catechism set forth
by Edward VI., that is often mentioned in our accounts of the Reformation ;
which King Edward, by his letters patent, commanded to be taught in all
schools, and which was examined, reviewed and corrected, in the Convocation
of 1562, and published with these improvements in 1570, to be a guide to the
younger clergy in the study of divinity, as containing the sum and substance
of our reformed religion " (Gibson's *Codex Juris Ecclesiastici Anglicani*,
tit. xix., cap. 1).

tion by clergymen or schoolmasters;[1] and its use in this way was continued for years.[2] In incidental proof that catechising was understood to require more ability than is involved in merely hearing the catechism recited, an order of Convocation of 1588 is to the effect that "no unlearned unable person to catechise shall be admitted to any cure;" that is, no person so unlearned as to be unable to teach the truths outlined in the catechism, shall have a place of curate.[3]

The recently published discussions of the Westminster Assembly of Divines over the form of the Shorter Catechism issued by that body, show that the idea of having the answers in that lesson-help blindly memorized by children was not in the minds of its framers, save as an evil to be guarded against religiously. Some of the more prominent divines, including Palmer, who was called "the best catechist in England," and who presided over the Assembly's Committee on the Catechisms until his death,[4] desired to insert a series of minor, or subordinate, questions and answers with each principal question and answer, as a means of making the meaning of that main answer clear to the common mind.[5] The objection made

---

[1] See Cardwell's *Synodalia,* I., 128.

[2] "This Catechism [of Nowell's] was printed again [after 1570] in the year 1572; and in Greek and Latin in 1573; and so from time to time had many impressions; and it was used a long time in all schools even to our days; and pity it is, it is now so disused" (Strype's *Life of Abp. Parker,* p. 301).

[3] Cardwell's *Synodalia,* II., 572.

[4] See Biographical Sketch of the Rev. Herbert Palmer, in Mitchell's *Catechisms of the Second Reformation,* pp. li-liii; also p. x. See, also, Hetherington's *History of the Westminster Assembly,* p. 259.

[5] See Palmer's Endeavor, etc., in Mitchell's *Catechisms,* as above, pp. 93-118. See, also, Dr. Briggs's article "The Westminster Assembly," in *The Presbyterian Review,* for January, 1880, pp. 155-162; Mitchell's *The Westminster*

to this plan was not that the main answer was in itself sufficiently simple and clear, but that if the necessary helps to its simplifying were given in set form, this might lead to an undue dependence on them, and so to the neglect of the essential interlocutory process of teaching, which every teacher must choose for himself according to the requirements of his particular scholar. The fear was that the catechism lesson-outline might thus come to be deemed self-explanatory, and its answers memorized just as they stood; and so, as one of the divines expressed it, these misguided "people will come to learn things by rote, and can answer as a parrot, but not understand the thing."[1]

Assembly, pp. 407-441; and *Minutes of the Sessions of the Westminster Assembly*, pp. 91-94.

[1] See *Minutes of the Sessions of the Westminster Assembly*, pp. 91-94; also Mitchell's *The Westminster Assembly*, pp. 409-420. In advocating the introduction of minor explanatory questions as a help to the understanding of the answers to the main questions in the Catechism, Rutherford said: "[It is] said [that] the Apostles did not use such a way. I think they did use it." As to the proper method of catechising, he said: "It should be in the plainest and easiest way. It is a feeding of the lambs." And in enforcement of his claim that the Catechism could not explain itself, he added: "There is as much art in catechising as in anything in the world. It may be doubted whether every minister do understand the most dexterous way of doing it." What would Rutherford have said to the modern claim, that for a teacher or parent to hear a child repeat the main answers to the Westminster Catechism, is to teach the Catechism! Seaman, also, insisted that while "the greatest care should be taken for the answer" to every question in the Catechism, in order to have it present truth accurately, yet that answer was "to be formed not to the model of knowledge that the child hath, but to that [which] the child ought to have." In other words, each Catechism answer was designed to define a truth to which the child was to be led up by wise teaching, not to present a statement of truth which the child should repeat unintelligently. Mr. Delmy opposed any set form of simple explanatory questions, because the catechiser needed "to inquire into the measure of the knowledge of the party" catechised, and to frame his own questions accordingly.

The opinion of the Westminster Assembly on the point of a blind and unintelligent memorizing of the answers to its catechism by children, was expressed by Gillespie, when he said, in the discussion over its framing: "It never entered into the thoughts of any to tie to the words and syllables in that catechism."[1] As to the necessity of a free interlocutory method in the teaching of truth, his conclusion was that which is the conclusion of the best teachers of the ages; namely, that "the light of nature and natural reason leads men this way in the explanation of things."[2] It would seem, in short, that the very method of "learning" the Westminster Catechism, which has been more common than any other in the last two centuries, and which even has many advocates and admirers to-day, is a method which the Westminster Divines themselves stigmatized as "parrot" learning, and as contrary to "the light of nature and natural reason."[3]

---

[1] *Minutes of the Sessions of the Westminster Assembly*, p. 93.

[2] *Ibid.*

[3] If there is one fundamental principle in the teaching process, on which all modern masters in the theory and art of teaching are agreed, it is that the true order of learning involves a knowledge of the thought or thing as precedent, in the child's mind, to the memorizing of the words which express that thought, or which declare that thing.   Roger Ascham, earliest of great English teachers, protested against the method of blind memorizing, by which the learners' knowledge "was tied only to their tong and lips and neuer ascended vp to the braine and head, and therefore was sone spitte out of the mouth againe" (*The Scholemaster*, p. 88).   Comenius, whose pioneer teaching work was hardly less prominent on the continent of Europe than was Ascham's in England, was equally positive on this point.   "In teaching," he said, "let the inmost part, *i. e.*, the understanding of the subject, come first; then let the thing understood be used to exercise the memory" (cited in Quick's *Essays on Educational Reformers*, p. 57).   John Locke showed his wisdom in a like declaration: "I hear 'tis said," he wrote, "that children should be employed

The more eminent contemporaries and immediate successors of the Westminster Divines were at one with them in holding that true catechising is a very different matter from adhering to the mere letter of the catechism. Richard Baxter, in his "Reformed Pastor" and other works, pressed the importance and explained the methods of catechising; which he deemed the divinely approved plan of discipling those whom Christ's ministers can reach.[1] He insisted that catechising is a more difficult, as it is a more important, work than sermonizing; and he cited Archbishop Usher's opinion to the same effect.[2] Baxter's illustrations of catechising along the lines of the Westminster Catechism, and of simpler catechisms than this,[3] consist of the simplest inter-colloquial as well as inter-

in getting things by heart, to exercise and improve their memories. I could wish this were said with as much authority of reason as it is with forwardness of assurance, and that this practice were established upon good observation more than old custom." Of the use of the memory, he added : "Charging it with a train of other people's words, which he that learns cares not for, will, I guess, scarce find the profit answer half the time and pains employed in it" ("Thoughts Concerning Education," in Locke's *Works*, III., 80 f.). Pestalozzi, the father of modern education in Europe, was emphatic and unqualified in his assertion that "nothing should be learned by rote without being understood" (See Barnard's *Pestalozzi and Pestalozzianism*, p. 25). "Words which are the signs of things," he said, "must never be taught the child till he has grasped the idea of the thing signified" (Quick's *Essays*, p. 190). And so it has been held by all our later students of the theory and practice of teaching. As Dr. John S. Hart has expressed it : "This is the true mental order. Knowledge first, then memory. Get knowledge ; then keep it. Any other plan is like attempting to become rich by inflating your bags with wind instead of gold ; or, attempting to grow fat by bolting food in a form which you cannot digest" (*In the School-Room*, p. 58).

[1] "The Reformed Pastor," in *Practical Works*, XIV., 246-354.

[2] *Ibid.*, p. 318.

[3] Baxter prepared at least three elementary catechisms, after the publication of the Westminster Catechism (see his *Practical Works*, Vols. XVIII., XIX.).

locutory instruction in the truths of the catechism, as adapted to the needs of the particular pupil in hand.[1]

Dr. Isaac Watts was an enthusiast in the work of teaching children catechetically, and a radical in his hostility to the unintelligent memorizing of the Westminster Catechism by children. "The business and duty of the teacher [of children]," he said, "is not merely to teach them words, but [to teach them] things. Words written on the memory without ideas or sense in the mind, will never incline a child to his duty, nor save his soul. The young creature will neither be the wiser nor the better for being able to repeat accurate definitions and theorems in divinity without knowing what they mean."[2] In rebut-

---

[1] *Practical Works*, XIV., 316-322. " Why is not catechising more used by pastors and parents?" asks Baxter (*ibid.*, XV., 76). And then he adds by way of explanation : " I mean not the bare words unexplained without the sense, nor the sense in a mere rambling way without a form of words ; but the words explained." Of the difficulties of wise catechising he says : " I must say that I think it an easier matter by far to compose and preach a good sermon, than to deal rightly with an ignorant man [by the interlocutory method of teaching] for his instruction in the necessary principles of religion " (*ibid.*, XIV., 318). Giving illustrations of questioning as a test of the learner's knowledge, in the study of catechism truths, Baxter says : " So contrive your question that they may perceive what you mean, and that it is not a nice definition, but a necessary solution, that you expect. Look not after words, but things, and there [thereto] leave them [if you can do no better] to a bare yea or nay, or the mere election of one of the two descriptions which you yourself shall propound " (*ibid.*, XIV., 322). Comp., also, *ibid.*, II., 99 ; V., 530 f. ; XIX., 4, 12.

[2] *Works*, III., 208. Watts claimed that the Westminster Assembly did not design the Shorter Catechism for blind memorizing by young children, but prepared it as an outline of doctrine by which teachers should be guided in their work of instruction. " The Assembly's Larger Catechism," as he said, " was not composed for children, but for men ; to give them a large and full view of all the parts of our holy religion. The Shorter Catechism is but an abridgement of the Larger. . . . A multitude of the same Latinized and theological terms are used in it as in the Larger " (*ibid.*, III., 210). He remarked that more than twenty persons " who had a most high esteem for the

tal of the even then common suggestion that there is a possible gain to children in the unintelligent memorizing of statements of doctrine which it may be they will live to know the meaning of, Dr. Watts said, pithily: "Words are but as the husks of this divine food, whereby the souls of children must be nourished to everlasting life. Though the food is divine, it is possible the husk may be too hard for them to open.[1] Is it the best method for feeding and nourishing the bodies of young children, to bestow upon them [uncracked] nuts and almonds, in hope that they will taste the sweetness of them when their teeth are strong enough to break the shell? Will they not be far better nourished by children's bread, and by food which they can immediately taste and relish?"[2] This thought of Dr. Watts suggests the telling title of Dr. Bushnell's sermon on a kindred theme: "God's thoughts fit bread for children."

Even those simpler forms of catechism which Dr. Watts

Assembly's [Shorter] Catechism, and a great and just veneration for it," had already, before himself, prepared elementary catechisms designed to precede the use of the Assembly's. One of these writers he quoted, as saying: "When the venerable Assembly composed this form of instruction, it seems that few of themselves thought it designed or fitted for babes" (*ibid.*, III., 211). Watts argued, as modern educators would argue, that to cause a child to memorize the Catechism without understanding it, is to raise in that child's mind an added barrier to his subsequent understanding of the Catechism; hence "whatever catechisms are impressed on the memories of children in their most tender years, they [the children] should be taught the meaning of them, as far as possible, as fast as they learn them by heart" (*ibid.*, III., 215).

[1] "I have been informed," says Watts, (*ibid.*, III., 249,) "of one child who was asked what the chief end of man was, and he answered, 'His head;' another being asked the same question answered 'Death;' neither of them taking in the true idea or meaning of the words."

[2] *Ibid.*, III., 211 f.

himself prepared as lesson-helps for children were not designed by him for the children's blind memorizing. In using one of these, as in using the larger ones, "parents and teachers should use their utmost skill," he said, "in leading the child into the meaning of every question, when they ask it, and of every answer when the child repeats it, that the child may not hear and learn mere words and syllables instead of the great things of God and religion." And this seems to have been the purpose of all catechism makers of two and three centuries ago. The catechisms were intended as guides in Bible-study, not as substitutes for it, in the religious instruction of children.[1] It was by the perversion of this agency that the help became a hindrance, and that the hopes of the Reformers and their earliest successors for a permanent re-establishment of the primitive Bible-school agency were frustrated.

In America it was much the same as it was in Europe. The founders of New England had no thought of building up a Christian commonwealth without the Bible-school training agency. But as they looked upon the Church and the State as having a common oversight of this work, and upon the work itself as covering seven days in the week, their week-day schools were their Bible-schools, according to the ancient Jewish theory. Quite naturally,

[1] Principal Currie, while at the head of the Church of Scotland Training College, Edinburgh, expressed himself emphatically on this point. Writing of the manner and method of religious instruction for young children, he said (*Early and Infant School-Education,* p. 136): "An abstract style of teaching is unsuitable, however clear our proofs or simple our phraseology. The 'Catechism' is the exponent of this style of teaching, and *can never, therefore, be the vehicle of instruction by itself.* Its forms of expression are mere words to the child."

therefore, they gave the whole of the Lord's Day to worship and sermonizing, upon the presupposed basis of a week's catechetical teaching.

Nor did they suppose that the memorizing and reciting of catechism answers was catechetical teaching. John Cotton said, on this point: "The excellent and necessary use of catechising young men and novices . . . we willingly acknowledge; but little benefit have we seen reaped from set forms of questions and answers devised by one church, and imposed by necessity on another."[1] Cotton Mather, also, urged that the aim of catechetical teaching was an understanding of Bible truth. In an appeal to his brother ministers, in the dedication of his "Maschil; or, The Faithful Instructor," he emphasized the uselessness of attempting to train the young and ignorant by "well-composed sermons;" "whereas," he said, "if you will be at the pains (and can any pains be too much for the precious and immortal souls of your neighbors, O ye that have the care of souls?) to instruct them in the *interlocutory way* of teaching, which we call catechising, you have the experience of all ages to make you hope that vast would be the consequence, vast the advantage."[2]

But gradually, in New England, the week-day schools became thoroughly secularized. Catechetical teaching there, came first to be limited to a perfunctory teaching of the Westminster Catechism; and then to drop out altogether. And in this way it finally came about that where the Christian founders of New England had planned

---

[1] Cited by Dr. J. Hammond Trumbull in his article "Catechisms of Old and New England," in *The Sunday School Times* for September 8, 1883.

[2] Cited by Dr. J. Hammond Trumbull, in his second article, as above, in *The Sunday School Times* for September 15, 1883.

for even more of teaching than of sermonizing, the teaching was given up and only the sermonizing remained.
An untaught generation — untaught in any form of the
divinely appointed Bible-school — was a sure result; and
the religious decline of New England was inevitable.[1]
Here, as elsewhere, was illustrated that truth of ecclesiastical history which Bishop Jebb as an observant teacher
recorded, that all through the Christian centuries, "in
exact proportion as catechising [free and familiar interlocutory teaching, as he explained it[2]] has been practised
or neglected, in the same proportion have the public faith
and morals been seen to flourish or decline."[3]

Great preachers, also, as well as great teachers, all the
way along in the years of progress and of decline after
the Protestant Reformation, were as emphatic in their
affirmations of the importance of interlocutory teaching,
as God's agency of religious training, as they were of any
other primitive Bible truth rescued by the Reformation

[1] All the lessons of history would seem to show, that while interlocutory
Bible teaching has tended, even under the most unfavorable circumstances,
to preserve the religious vitality of the people practicing it, an adherence to
the unintelligent or parrot reciting of any set catechism has been followed by
a departure from the teachings of that catechism by the people practicing it.

[2] "Let not the common prejudice be entertained, that catechising is a slight
and trifling exercise, to be performed without pains and preparation on your
part. This would be so if it were the mere rote-work asking and answering
of the questions in our Church Catechism : but to open, to explain, and familiarly to illustrate these questions in such a manner as, at once, to reach the
understanding and touch the affections of little children, is a work which
demands no ordinary acquaintance, at once, with the whole scheme of Christian theology, with the philosophy of the human mind, and with the yet pro-
founder mysteries of the human heart. It has, therefore, been well and truly
said, by I recollect not what writer, that a boy may preach, but to catechise
requires a man " (Jebb's *Pastoral Instructions*, p. 198).

[3] *Ibid.*, p. 196.

from the oblivion of the Dark Ages.   It seems strange, indeed, as one reads their testimonies and appeals, that they did not have more permanent power over the thought and action of the churches in which these men were representative leaders.   Godly and earnest Bishop Hall said, toward the close of his well-filled life:[1] " There is no one thing of which I repent so much as not to have bestowed more hours in this public exercise of catechisme [of inter-locutory teaching]; in regard whereof I would quarrel with my very sermons; and wish that a great part of them had been exchanged for this preaching conference. Those other divine discourses enrich the braine and the tongue; this settles the heart; those others are but the descants to this plain song."[2]

Henry More, eminent as a divine, a philosopher, and a preacher, in the Church of England, in the days of Bishop Hall, and Archbishop Usher, and Richard Baxter, was equally explicit with these other men of God on this point.   " Concerning preaching," he said,[3] " that which is most remarkable is this, that whereas there are three chief kinds thereof, namely, catechising, expounding a chapter, and preaching, usually so called,—whereof the first [catechising] is the best, and the last [preaching, or ser-monizing] is the least considerable of them all,—this worst and last is the very idol of some men, and the others [are] rejected as things of little worth.   But assuredly they [the expounding of a chapter, and the catechising] are of most virtue for the effectual planting the gospel

---

[1] He died in 1656.   [2] Cited in Jebb's *Pastoral Instructions*, p. 367 f.

[3] In *The Great Mystery of Godliness* (1660), p. 37 f.; cited by Dr. J. Hammond Trumbull, in his article, as above, in *The Sunday School Times* for September 15, 1883.

in the minds of men; and of the two, as I said, catechising is the better because it enforceth the catechised
to take notice of what is taught him ; and what is taught
him is not so voluminous but that he can carry it away
and remember it forever."

George Herbert, model Christian pastor as he was, put
this truth sententiously when he said, in his " Country
Parson:" "At sermons and at prayers men may sleep
or wander, but when one is asked a question, he must
disclose what he is." [1] And sturdy John Owen was no
less positive in his convictions at this point than the most
zealous Churchman. " More knowledge," he said, " is
ordinarily diffused, especially among the young and ignorant, by one hour's catechetical exercise, than by many
hours' continual discourse." [2]

Churchman and Puritan, great preacher and great
teacher, in the days of new foundation-laying in Protestant Christendom, were at one in this opinion; as, indeed,
it would seem that every intelligent Bible student and
Christian thinker must always be : for in no sphere save
in that of religion—where alone interlocutory teaching is

[1] George Herbert's *Remains*, p. 165. That Herbert had no thought of con-
fining catechetical teaching to set questions and answers, is evident when he
says (p. 163): " Many say the Catechism by rote, as parrots, without piercing
into the sense of it ; " and, again, when he counsels the varying of the questions according to the capacity of the learner, in order to "draw out of
ignorant and silly souls, even the dark points of religion." " Catechising in
its true and original sense," said Bishop Law, a century later than Herbert,
" implies something more than the bare running over of an old form [even]
though that [form] consists of proper questions and answers, and contains
whatsoever is needful for faith and practice." Archdeacon Bather, who cites
this statement of Law, cites also, with approval, the yet earlier statement of
Dean Comber, that " sermons can never do good upon an uncatechised congregation" (see *Hints on the Art of Catechising*, pp. 6, 171).

[2] Cited by Dr. Steel in *The Christian Teacher in Sunday Schools*, p. 128.

divinely enjoined—was there ever attempted the folly of teaching primary truths, to the young and the ignorant, by unbroken discourse.   Perhaps the facts and the arguments in this entire case have never been put more concisely and tellingly than in the words of the loyal and royal old English preacher, Dr. Robert South.   "Nay," he said, " I take schoolmasters to have a more powerful influence upon the spirits of men than preachers themselves; . . . it being seldom found that the pulpit mends what the school has marred. . . . And for my own part I never thought a pulpit, a cushion, and an hourglass, such necessary means of salvation, but that much of the time and labor which is spent about them, might be much more profitably bestowed in catechising youth from the desk ; preaching being a kind of spiritual diet upon which people are always feeding, but never full ; and many poor souls, God knows too, too like Pharaoh's kine, much the leaner for their full feed.   And how, for God's sake, should it be otherwise?   For to preach to people without principles [without a basis of established convictions] is to build where there is no foundation, or rather where there is not so much as ground to build upon.   But people are not to be harangued, but catechised [instructed], into principles : and this is not the proper work of the pulpit, any more than threshing can pass for sowing.   Young minds are to be leisurely formed and fashioned with the first plain, simple, and substantial rudiments of religion. And to expect that this should be done by preaching, or force of lungs, is just as if a smith, or artist who works in metal, should think to frame and shape out his work only with his bellows." [1]

[1] South's *Sermons :* Sermon 49, " The Virtuous Education of Youth."

That the bellows has an important part in the work of bringing the gathered coals to a glow at the spiritual forge, so that they may heat the metal to a fitness for its hammering and shaping, no one will question. But the advantage of other agencies besides the bellows, in preference to a reliance upon that alone, in the proper work of the spiritual forge-tender, is well illustrated in a comparison of the labors of Whitefield and Wesley, in the English reformation of the eighteenth century, in which they toiled together. Whitefield had the greater bellows power; and the hardest iron softened in the coals which kindled and burned under the breath of his preaching.[1] Yet he made little use of any other agency than that; while Wesley took the pinchers and the hammer of the class-meeting agency, and saw to it that every individual member of the church organization put into operation by him was personally reached and trained through an interlocutory exercise, week by week, year in and year out. And now that which we know of Whitefield's work is chiefly in the recorded testimony of men who tell how the fires burned when he blew the bellows; while the gleam of new forges are seen all the world over, as a result of Wesley's conformity, in his methods of training, to the divinely appointed plan of church formation and church-life maintaining.

In spite, however, of the lessons of the Protestant Ref-

---

[1] This figure of the bellows, as applicable to the preacher, seems to have been in the mind of Whitefield himself, when he wrote to Governor Belcher, concerning a visit to Boston by his friend Gilbert Tennent, as following up his own beginning there: "This week Mr. Tennent proposes to set out for Boston, to blow up the divine flame recently kindled there." See *Home, the School and the Church*, V., 167.

ormation in its progress and in its checking; in spite of the concurrent testimony of great preachers and great teachers all along the centuries; in spite of the uniform indications of all ecclesiastical history; in spite of the specific injunctions of the great Head of the Church,— interlocutory Bible-teaching again declined in prominence in the Protestant churches of Europe, of Great Britain, and of America, during the seventeenth and eighteenth centuries, as it had declined in the universal Christian Church in the eight or ten centuries preceding the six-teenth. Here and there, as similarly through the Middle Ages, there were those who continued faithful to God's plan for the Church teaching of the young; and who were blessed and were a blessing accordingly. The Mora-vians, for example, lineal descendants of the Hussites, never wholly intermitted this method of working. They continued to give the first place to the Bible, and their first care to the children, in the work of religious instruc-tion. There were local churches, also, in every great body of Protestant Christians, which were distinguished for their recognition of the child-teaching duty of the Church, while that duty was ignored or neglected so widely in their communion at large. But these instances were exceptional. It seemed, indeed, as if, in the varying progress of the Christian centuries, the Sunday-school idea had less prominence in the seventeenth and eighteenth than in the third and fourth centuries. And this outlook gave little hope to the Church or to the world.

LECTURE III.

THE SUNDAY–SCHOOL: ITS MODERN REVIVAL
AND EXPANSION.

III.

THE SUNDAY SCHOOL: ITS MODERN REVIVAL AND EXPANSION.

Religious Declension in the Eighteenth Century.—Mid-century Revivals.—Zinzendorf's and Wesley's Work among Children. —The Sunday-school Beginnings of Robert Raikes.—Nature and Progress of this Movement.—Its Influence in England and Elsewhere.—Sunday-schools in America.—Illustrations of their Power.—As Seen by Foreigners.—As Imitated Abroad.—Improved Sunday-school Methods.—The International Lesson System.—Growth in Popular Bible Study.—The Sunday-school of To-day.

In whatever aspect it be viewed, the contrast between the religious life of the Protestant world in the sixteenth century and in the eighteenth, is a sad one. The decadence of moral and spiritual power in the Protestant nations of Europe and America, as a whole, despite its partial checks by religious revivals on both sides of the ocean, continued with generally accelerated force to the latter third of the eighteenth century; with its culmination in the volcanic outburst of the French Revolution, and the accompanying earthquake tremblings of the moral world.

On this point all historians are practically at one. In Germany the period in question is characterized, by the church historian Kurtz, as "the years of spiritual famine."[1]   Of the rationalistic cyclone which burst over his land at the close of that period, he says: "The storm came from abroad; but it was invested with the mighty power of the spirit of the age; and it found a dissolution and agitation going on within which brought sympathies and allies to it from all sides, and promoted the transition of the one extreme into the other."[2]   De Pressensé, writing of the corresponding religious decline in France, ascribes its origin, as does Kurtz, to countries beyond his own; but its effects he finds both at home and abroad.   "Nothing is so sad," he says, "as the religious history of the eighteenth century.   Piety languishes; science there is none, at least on the side of the defenders of Christianity.   In England and in Germany a parching wind blows over hearts and minds.   There is preached in the Protestant pulpits—in those which are standing—a religion without grandeur, without mysteries; which has neither the boldness of philosophy, nor that of faith."[3]

Looking at England from the stand-point of whatever historical writer we turn to, we find much the same state of things described there.   A historian of English literature says of the middle of the eighteenth century: "It was remarkable for the low tone of manners and sentiment; perhaps the lowest that ever prevailed in England."[4]   A historian of English jurisprudence says of the same period: "The upper classes were corrupt without refinement; the middle, gross without humor; and the lower, brutal with-

---

[1] *Text-Book of Church History*, II., 308.   [2] *Ibid.*, II., 277.

[3] *The Church and the French Revolution*, p. 15.

[4] Shaw's *Manual of English Lit.*, p. 315.

out honesty."[1] Bishop Ryle, with the evangelical sympathies of a Low Churchman, says: "The state of this country, in a religious and moral point of view, in the middle of last century, was so painfully unsatisfactory that it is difficult to convey any adequate idea of it. English people of the present day, who have never been led to inquire into the subject, can have no conception of the darkness that prevailed. From the year 1700 till about the era of the French Revolution, England seemed barren of all that is really good. How such a state of things can have arisen in a land of free Bibles and professing Protestantism is almost past comprehension. . . . There was darkness in high places, and darkness in low places; darkness in the court, the camp, the Parliament, and the bar; darkness in country, and darkness in town; darkness among rich, and darkness among poor;—a gross, thick, religious and moral darkness; a darkness that might be felt."[2]

A more recent history of the English Church in the eighteenth century, from the stand-point of a stauncher Churchman, while aiming to show that the state of things in that church was not so bad as is pictured by Bishop Ryle, bears added testimony to the general decline in religion and morals then existing in England. "That lax morality and religious indifference prevailed more or less among all classes during this period," it says, "we learn from the concurrent testimony of writers of every kind and creed. Turn where one will, the same melancholy

---

[1] Phillimore's *History of the Law of Evidence*, p. 546; cited in Forsyth's *Novels and Novelists of the Eighteenth Century*, p. 17.

[2] *The Christian Leaders of the Last Century*, p. 13 f.

picture is presented to us."[1]   Finally, such impartial and careful historians as Lord Mahon,[2] and Lecky,[3] and Green,[4] multiply detailed facts, and citations of contemporaneous opinion, in evidence of a measure of ignorance, of irreligion, and of immorality in the English community generally, in the latter half of the eighteenth century, which it is not easy now to realize.   As in the case of the French and German historians, the English writers on this period attribute the causes of the decline to influences beyond their own country; and they find occasion for gratulation in the thought that "if England was morally and spiritually in low estate at this period, she was, at any rate, in a better plight than her neighbors."[5]

America shows much the same decline in morals and religion during the eighteenth century as England and the continent of Europe, with a similar attempt on the part of historians to prove that its origin was in an influence which came from abroad.   Dr. Dorchester, in connection with his valuable compilation of facts in this line, says: "The corruption of manners, working downward through English society during the reigns of William III., Queen Anne, and the first two Georges, extended to American shores, changing the moral aspects of the people.   In the first third of the eighteenth century this deterioration was very plain.   The drinking habits, hitherto very mod-

---

[1] Abbey and Overton's *The English Church in the Eighteenth Century*, p. 302 f.   See, also, pp. 5, 25 f., 303-310.

[2] *History of England from 1713 to 1783*, VII., 330.

[3] *History of England in the Eighteenth Century*, Vol. II., ch. 9 ; Vol. VI., ch. 23.

[4] *History of the English People*, Bk. ix., chs. 1-4.

[5] *The English Church in the Eighteenth Century*, p. 311.   See, also, Lecky's *Hist. of Eng.*, II., 691.

erate, were increased, though [they were] not as bad as at the close of the century."[1]   Referring to the revivals under Edwards and Whitefield, in 1735–45, he says: "They were an incalculable blessing to the Colonial churches and communities, checking for a time the spread of immorality. But there speedily followed a long and troublous period (1750–1800) and its distracting events— the French and Indian wars; the conflicting agitations preceding the Revolutionary War; the war itself, with the usual depraving influences; . . . the general infusion of European skepticism and manners; and the spread of New England rum."[2] And he adds that "a detailed statement of American manners in the last quarter of the eighteenth century will exhibit a condition of immorality having no later parallel on our shores."

In his famous funeral sermon on Dr. Nathanael Emmons (which is said to have been read in advance to its subject by its author), the Rev. Thomas Williams expressed himself in similar terms of the moral aspects of the years following the Revolutionary War. "The scenes and events," he says, "which arose after the establishment of our national independence, in this country, in the Church of God on earth, and among the nations of the world, during his [Dr. Emmons's] ministry, were the most astonishing that have occurred in the records of uninspired history. In his day, the conspiracy of infidels and atheists against religion, government and humanity, against truth and peace, order and liberty, shook the foundations of kingdoms and nations; and attempted to destroy from the earth the Church and kingdom of God,

---

[1] *The Problem of Religious Progress*, p. 173.   [2] *Ibid.*, p. 177.

and the name and glory of the Lord Jesus Christ. In his day, the 'three unclean spirits, like frogs, were coming from the mouth of the dragon and from the mouth of the beast and from the mouth of the false prophet.'[1] . . . Through their influence impiety, infidelity and inhumanity, delusion, disorder and wickedness in every form, have arisen in New England, and in other parts of the world, above what was ever before known on earth. Error, folly and vanity, declension, lukewarmness and stupidity, have seized and destroyed many churches in this land; and have reached every church and town, every neighborhood and family."[2]

The first President Dwight, of Yale, in commenting on the sad state of things in this last-named period, says of its immediate causes: "Europe . . . consigned to these states a plentiful supply of the means of corruption. From France, Germany, and Great Britain, the dregs of infidelity were vomited upon us. From the '*Système de la Nature*' and the 'Philosophical Dictionary,' down to the 'Political Justice' of Godwin, and the 'Age of Reason,' the whole mass of pollution was emptied in upon us as a deluge."[3] A little later Dr. Lyman Beecher, looking back upon this time, said with like emphatic earnestness: "When that mighty convulsion took place, which a second time burst open the bottomless pit, and spread darkness and dismay over Europe, every gale brought to our shores contagion and death. Thousands at once breathed the tainted air, and felt the fever kindle

---

[1] Rev. 16: 13.

[2] *Discourse on the Official Character of Nathanael Emmons*, p. 67 f.

[3] Dwight's *Travels*, IV., 380.

in the brain. A paroxysm of moral madness and terrific innovation ensued."[1]

As to the *fact* of the existing decline in public morals and in religious life on both sides of the ocean in the latter half of the eighteenth century, there would seem to be no room for question; but as to its primary *cause*, the reasons generally given by historians are fairly open to challenge. Even though it be shown that influences of evil are at work in the world, is that in itself sufficient to account for the failure of the Church of Christ to maintain its purity and its power? Is the Church, indeed, dependent for the savor of its saltness on the measure of good which it absorbs from the community about it? Or is it its very mission to be at its best when the world is at its worst? Rightly furnished, the Church of Christ is proof against all outside evil. When the Church fails to withstand evil, and when its spiritual life declines, the cause of trouble is to be sought within the Church, and not beyond it. Then is the time to look for the neglect, or for the misuse, by the Church, of God's appointed means and methods in the line of its legitimate working.

If the families of Christian missionaries in a heathen land were, one after another, lapsing into heathenism, would it be deemed sufficient to ascertain the precise form of error into which they lapsed, and to locate the geographical direction from which it reached their neighborhood? Would not the necessity be recognized of learning what essential guards about those Christian families had been lacking amid their heathen surroundings? Why then should it be concluded satisfactory to account

---

[1] *Sermons Delivered on Various Occasions*, p. 110.

for the low state of the Protestant churches of Europe and America in the eighteenth century, by an enumeration of their temptations, and an identifying of their tempters, without giving chief prominence to their so general neglect of the church-school, or the Sunday-school, as God's appointed agency for winning and training the young?

God has chosen to give power to his Church in and through the means and measures of his pointing out. To the school idea he has assigned a foremost place in the right workings of the Church of Christ. Whenever that idea is lost sight of, or is obscured, the Church is a loser in its holding power and in its power of progress. It is only when that idea is kept in due prominence that the Church has a possibility of filling its place and of doing its proper work. That that idea was obscured in the Protestant world, during the latter part of the seventeenth and the first half of the eighteenth century, is a fact which admits of no dispute. Even in England, where the state of things was better than in some other countries, the religious teaching of the young was sadly neglected. Abbey and Overton, the English Church historians already cited, say at this point: " In the latter part of the seventeenth and through the earlier years of the eighteenth century, we find earnest Churchmen, of all opinions, sorely lamenting the comparative disuse of the old [and still enjoined] custom of catechising [of the interlocutory teaching of the young] on Sunday afternoons. Five successive archbishops of Canterbury— Sheldon, Sancroft, Tillotson, Tenison, and Wake—however widely their opinions might differ on some points relating to the edification of the Church, were cordially agreed in this."[1] And as to another prominent religious training agency at the same period, these writers say: "If we ask what was the state of the Universities, which ought to be the centres of light, diffusing itself throughout the whole nation, the training-grounds of those who are to be the trainers of their fellow-men, we have the evidence of such different kinds of men as Swift, Defoe, Gray, Gibbon, Johnson, John Wesley, Lord Eldon, and Lord Chesterfield, all agreeing on this point, that both [of] the great Universities were neglectful and inefficient in the performance of their proper work."[2]

"For more than sixty years after the death of [Queen] Anne [1714]," says Lecky, "the history of education in England is almost a blank."[3] Referring to the latter half of the eighteenth century, Lord Mahon says: "Throughout England the education of the laboring classes was most grievously neglected; the supineness of the clergy of that age being manifest on this point as on every other."[4] And by this neglect of God's appointed training agency, as a means of holding those who were already within the fold of the Church, and of hopefully reaching those who were without, the decline of life and power in the Church, as the controlling force in the community, was assured—and was brought about. Only God knows what would have been the result to the Church and to the world, if the church Bible-school agency had not been revived and made newly prominent under circumstances which led to its extension and to its expansion in a measure beyond all precedent.

---

[1] *The English Church in the Eighteenth Century*, p. 469.
[2] *Ibid.*, p. 303.   [3] *Hist. of Eng.*, VI., 276.   [4] *Hist. of Eng.*, VII., 332.

To begin with, there were remarkable revivals of religion near the middle of the eighteenth century, in connection with the work of Zinzendorf in Germany, of Wesley and Whitefield in Great Britain, and of Edwards and Whitefield in the United States. But these revivals, and the work of these great men, could, in the very nature of things, have permanent power only as the methods and agencies put into fresh operation by them corresponded to God's appointment, and were, in his providence, suited to the work to which they were applied. As in the case of Luther and Calvin and Knox, and again of Loyola and Xavier, Zinzendorf and Wesley realized that no revival could be permanent in its results, nor could any reformation be an abiding one, except by means of reaching and systematically training the young; and it was in the light of this fundamental truth that they prosecuted their evangelizing and upbuilding work most successfully.

Zinzendorf and his co-workers preached directly to the children, gathered large numbers of them into the church-fold,[1] and at the same time arranged for the personal training of the converts individually, by clustering them in small classes under special teachers.[2] Wesley followed

---

[1] In 1727 there was a remarkable revival among the Moravian children at Bertholdsdorf and Herrnhut, which had its beginning in a discourse to the girls by Count Zinzendorf. (See Cranz's *Hist. of the Brethren*, p. 119 f.). For evidence of Zinzendorf's interest in the religious training of children, by the church, see, also, Spangenberg's *Life of Zinzendorf*, p. 85 f.

[2] In an address delivered July 2, 1747, Count Zinzendorf mentioned that just twenty years before then, [that is, July 2, 1727,] on the day commemorative of the visit of Mary to Elisabeth, the idea came to him of organizing the people of his charge into "bands or societies," or small classes; and he added: "These were established throughout the whole community the following week, and have been productive of such blessed effects, that I believe [that] without such an institution the church would never have become what it now

Zinzendorf in both particulars.[1] He laid great stress on the work among children, and on the class instruction of converts. "Unless . . . we can take care of the *rising generation*, the present revival of religion," he said, "will be *res unius aetatis;* it will last only the age of a man."[2]

is. The societies, called bands, consist of a few individuals met together in the name of Jesus, amongst whom Jesus is, who converse together in a particularly child-like manner on the state of their hearts, and conceal nothing from each other, but have wholly committed themselves to each other in the Lord. . . . In each of them a brother or a sister, according to the sex [of the band or class], was commissioned to take particular charge of the rest. When they met they either read something of an edifying nature, sang, and prayed, or else conversed together." It was about this time that Zinzendorf also revived the primitive "love-feast" among his people. (Spangenberg's *Life of Zinzendorf*, pp. 86-89.)

[1] One of Zinzendorf's helpers was Peter Boehler, born at Frankfort-on-the-Main, in 1712. He was made a bishop at Herrnhut in 1748. While at London, as a Moravian worker, early in 1738, he became acquainted with John Wesley, and seems to have put his stamp upon him permanently. Tyerman records that Wesley "was induced [by Boehler] to become a member of the first Moravian society in Fetter Lane [London]." The rules of that society, framed "in obedience to the command of God by St. James, and by the advice of Peter Boehler," provided that the members "should be divided into bands, of not fewer than five nor more than ten; and that some one in each band should be desired to interrogate the rest, and should be called the leader. Each band was to meet twice a week." The details of the plan of exercises, and of the scope of management of these bands, would seem to indicate, beyond a question, the origin of the idea of the subsequent system of Methodist class meetings (see Tyerman's *Life and Times of John Wesley*, I., 195 f.; also Wesley's Journal for May, 1738, *Works*, I.). In the summer following his first connection with the Moravian society in London, Wesley visited Zinzendorf at Herrnhut. In his journal at that time he describes the methods of Moravian church organization and discipline, similar to those which Boehler had disclosed to him. This system impressed Wesley to such an extent that he wrote out its details in full in his journal; and the future showed the value which he attached to it. (See Wesley's Journal for August, 1738, and for February and March, 1742 [*Works*, I.]; also Tyerman's *Life of Wesley*, I., 377-381, 446, 463.)

[2] Tyerman's *Life of Wesley*, III., 23. See, also, Wesley's Sermons: Sermon 94, on Family Religion (*Works*, VII., 73).

And in that statement Wesley touched the truth of truths concerning God's method of giving permanent power to the work of his Church. To his preachers, Wesley followed this affirmation with the injunction: "Spend an hour a week with the children, in every large town, whether you like it or not. Talk with them every time you see any at home. Pray in earnest for them."[1] Lecky, in his careful review of the methods and influence of the Wesleyan movement, says: "The Methodists appear to have preached especially to children;" and he cites the words of Wesley when describing, "among other cases, a remarkable revival among children at Stockton-upon-Tees, in 1784: 'Is not this a new thing upon the earth? God begins his work in children. . . . Thus the flame spreads to those of riper years.'"[2] Moreover, from the beginning of his more active labors, Wesley insisted that all who were brought under his instruction should be gathered in "bands," or "classes," for their personal training.[3] So far the Wesleyan movement included important elements of the Sunday-school agency; and in the same measure that movement had a possibility of continuance and permanency.

But there was still a lack, and the effect of it was obvious. The *methods* of the Wesleyans, like those of the Moravians, were limited to those bodies of Christians, even while the *influence* of their work extended far beyond them. Their evangelizing efforts among children were

---

[1] Tyerman's *Life of Wesley*, III., 23.

[2] *Hist. of Eng.*, II., 665. For accounts of Wesley's work among children, see his Journal, for Aug. 19, 1776; Dec. 2, 1778; April 5, April 27, June 7, 1782; May 18, June 8, 1784, etc. (*Works*, IV.).

[3] Tyerman's *Life of Wesley*, I., 379.

but occasional, as visiting preachers had opportunities in that direction. And the training of converts in their bands, or classes, was mainly in the sphere of Christian experience. There was still needed a revival of the primitive church-school agency, to be made use of alike by every branch of the Church of Christ, for the persistent and systematic teaching of children and of the child-like, in the " all things" of the Holy Scriptures. Unless that agency should reappear, the Church of Christ must continue crippled for its divinely directed work, and the best results of the latest revival, like those of former days, must be confined to the lifetime of its chief promoters. It was the timely meeting of that lack which proved a new beginning of good to the Protestant Christian world.

It was in the city of Gloucester, England, in July, 1780,[1] that Robert Raikes, the editor and proprietor of

[1] It is a singular fact, that, for more than three-quarters of a century, the beginning of Raikes's work was understood to be 1781, instead of 1780. The Jubilee, or half-century celebration, of the Raikes movement, was in 1831. The more careful histories of the Sunday-school, such as Pray's and Watson's, were positive in fixing its start in 1781; and cyclopedias and modern church histories, generally, accepted this as the correct date. Yet the Centenary of Sunday-schools was observed in 1880; the inscription on the pedestal of Raikes's statue, erected at that time in London, gives 1780 as the date of his first Sunday-school; and, practically, no question now exists that this is correct. Raikes's letter concerning his work, published in the Gentleman's Magazine for June, 1784, says that it was "about three years" before that writing that he began his first Sunday-school. Here, perhaps, is the origin of the idea that the beginning was in 1781. But that letter of Raikes is dated "November 25th," hence must have been written as early as 1783. Moreover, the date of the beginning of the Gloucester Sunday-schools is given as 1780 on the monument of the Rev. Thomas Stock, a co-worker with Raikes in their starting (Pray's *Hist. of Sunday-schools*, p. 137); and a Bible presented, at the beginning of this work, to Mr. King, in whose house the first Sunday-school was started by Raikes, bore in it the date of "July, 1780." (See Gregory's *Robert Raikes*, p. 72.)

The Gloucester Journal, who had already interested himself in philanthropic efforts at prison reform, gathered the
poorer children of a manufacturing quarter of that city
into the rooms of a private house of the neighborhood,[1] for
their Sunday instruction in reading and in the elementary
truths of religion. "The children were to come soon
after ten in the morning, and stay till twelve; they were
then to go home and stay till one; and after reading a
lesson they were to be conducted to church. After
church they were to be employed in repeating the catechism till half-past five, and then to be dismissed, with an
injunction to go home without making a noise; and by
no means to play in the street."[2] Four women were
employed as teachers in the school, at the rate of a shilling a day.[3] And this was the beginning of the modern

[1] "It was at the house of a Mr. King, in St. Catherine Street, that the first
Gloucester Sunday-school was started, in the month of July, 1780. Mr. King
was at the time steward to Mr. Pitt, who represented Gloucester in Parliament
for some years" (Gregory's *Robert Raikes*, p. 72).

[2] A letter from Robert Raikes, dated June 5, 1784, in the Appendix to
Turner's *Sunday Schools Recommended*, p. 41.

[3] Describing his conversation with a woman of the neighborhood, where he
started his first Sunday-school, Raikes says: "I then inquired if there were
any decent, well-disposed women in the neighborhood who kept schools for
teaching to read. I presently was directed to four: to these I applied, and
made an agreement with them to receive as many children as I should send
them upon the Sundays, whom they were to instruct in reading and in the
Church Catechism. For this I engaged to pay them each a shilling for their
day's employment. The women seemed pleased with the proposal. I then
waited on the clergyman before mentioned [the Rev. Thomas Stock], and
imparted to him my plan; he was so much satisfied with the idea, that he
engaged to lend his assistance by going round to the schools on a Sunday afternoon, to examine the progress that was made, and to enforce order and deco-
rum among such a set of little heathen" (Raikes's Letter in *Gentleman's
Magazine* for June, 1784). Gregory (*Robert Raikes*, p. 72) says that, "prior
to the establishment of the school, Mr. Raikes and the Rev. T. Stock went to

Sunday-school movement. This was the revival, under new auspices, of the divinely appointed church Bible-school. This was the starting-point of a new period of life and hope to the Church of Christ, and, through the Church, to the world.

There seems to have been absolutely nothing new in the Sunday-school plans of Robert Raikes. Schools of a similar character, and apparently with all the essential features of his school, were organized in Upper Egypt, and in Armenia, and elsewhere in the East, more than fourteen centuries before his day.[1] All the way along the intervening centuries there had been repeated revivals of this agency of evangelism and of religious instruction, with more or less of success. The seventeenth and eighteenth centuries had not been without attempts in this direction, in England, Ireland, Scotland, Wales, and the United States.[2] But in the providence of God the times

---

Mrs. King's house, and engaged the services of Mrs. King as the first teacher, at a salary of 1 *s.* 6 *d.* per Sunday, of which sum Mr. Raikes contributed a shilling and Mr. Stock sixpence." It is possible, therefore, that Mr. Stock added a sixpence to Mr. Raikes's shilling in the case of one teacher. Indeed, Mr. Raikes wrote on another occasion : "The stipend to the teachers here is a shilling each Sunday, but we find them firing, and bestow gratuities as rewards of diligence, which may make it worth sixpence more" (Raikes's Letter to Mrs. Harris, in Pray's *Hist. of Sunday-schools*, p. 145).

[1] See p. 62 f., *ante.*

[2] It has already been shown (p. 74, *ante*) that a form of Sunday-schools was inaugurated by the General Assembly of the Church of Scotland, in 1560, and that as early as 1603 a similar system was in operation in the Church of England. Yet a certain curious interest attaches to the record of sporadic instances of Sunday-school work, in fields where that work was not systematically and generally prosecuted, after its post-Reformation decline, and before its revival by Robert Raikes. Therefore it is that the following instances of such work may properly be mentioned just here ; although it is by no means probable that they stand alone in the history of such undertakings in the

were now ripe for a revival of the church-school idea in this form, and for its progressive prevalence beyond its extremest limits of a former day.

Mr. Raikes had a peculiar advantage, in his position as the editor of a weekly periodical, with its opportunity of enabling him to make widely known the good results of his new enterprise. Yet it was not until his experiment had had a successful trial of more than three years that he made an announcement of it in his periodical.[1] His earliest sketch of his work, thus given to the public, in November, 1783, (without, however, the mention of his own name in connection with it,) seems to have attracted the attention of Colonel Richard Townley, of Lancashire, and to have incited him to a desire to introduce similar

---

period and countries covered by them. Sunday-schools are known, or are claimed, to have been conducted in Bath, England, (by the Rev. Joseph Alleine,) in 1665-68; in Roxbury, Massachusetts, in 1674; in Norwich, Connecticut, in 1676; in Plymouth, Massachusetts, in 1680; in Newton, Long Island, (by the Rev. Morgan Jones,) in 1683; in England, (by Bishop Frampton,) in 1693; in Berks and Montgomery counties, Pennsylvania, (by the Schwenkfelders,) in 1734; in Ephrata, Pennsylvania, (by Ludwig Höcker,) in 1740; in Bethlehem, Connecticut, (by the Rev. Dr. Joseph Bellamy,) in 1740; in Philadelphia, Pennsylvania, (by Mrs. Greening,) in 1744; in Norham, Scotland, (by the Rev. Mr. Morrison,) in 1757; in Brechin, Scotland, (by the Rev. David Blair,) in 1760; in Catterick, England, (by the Rev. Theophilus Lindsey,) in 1763; in Columbia, Connecticut, (by the Rev. Eleazer Wheelock,) in 1763; in Bedale, England, (by Miss Harrison,) in 1765; in High Wycombe, England, (by Miss Hannah Ball,) in 1769; in Doagh, County Antrim, Ireland, (by William Galt,) in 1770; in Bright, County Down Ireland, (by the Rev. Dr. Kennedy,) in 1774; in Little Lever, near Bolton, England, (by James Heys,) in 1775; in Mansfield, England, (by the Rev. David Simpson,) in 1778; also, about the same time, in Asbury, England, (by the Rev. Thomas Stock); and in Dursley, England, (by William King).

[1] In a letter written by Mr. Raikes, in 1787, to Mrs. Harris, of Chelsea, it is said: " My eldest boy was born the very day I made public to the world the scheme of Sunday-schools, in my paper of November 3d, 1783." See Pray's *Hist. of Sunday-schools*, p. 147.

schools into the large manufacturing counties of York and Lancaster. The latter, therefore, applied to the mayor of Gloucester, and through the mayor to Mr. Raikes, for added information on the subject. A letter from Mr. Raikes, dated November 25, in response to this inquiry, was published "in the Leeds and Manchester papers of December, 1783, and January, 1784;"[1] and in June, 1784, it was given in full in the pages of the influential Gentleman's Magazine, of London. Another descriptive letter by Mr. Raikes, concerning his Sunday-schools, was published, a little later, in the Arminian Magazine, edited by John Wesley. Yet again he spoke through the pages of the European Magazine.[2] These accounts of the origin and progress of Mr. Raikes's work were reproduced in various forms in the metropolitan and provincial press of Great Britain, and did much to call public attention to the new undertaking in its importance and its possibilities. It is said, indeed, that "by this means the knowledge and nature of Sunday-schools were 'diffused with the rapidity of lightning throughout the world.'"[3]

While this Sunday-school movement began within the pale of the Church of England, it was at first purely an individual, rather than an ecclesiastical, movement; as indeed wellnigh all great movements of progress or of reform have been, from the days of John the Baptist to those of Luther, and of Loyola, and of Knox, and of

---

[1] These facts are given in the Appendix to Turner's *Sunday Schools Recommended.*

[2] See Gregory's *Robert Raikes*, pp. 59, 85. Gregory says that this letter was dated June 5, 1785; but Turner, in his *Sunday Schools Recommended* (p. 40), as already noted (at p. 110, *ante*), gives its date as June 5, 1784.

[3] Pray's *Hist. of Sunday-schools*, p. 152.

8

Wesley.   With the approval of some church dignitaries, and against the opposition of others,[1] it extended itself into the field of all religious denominations throughout the United Kingdom, and afterwards over the ocean.   Bishop Porteus, then of the see of Chester, and later of London, was its early and earnest advocate.   The bishops of Norwich, Salisbury, and Llandaff, and the Dean of Canterbury, followed him in commending it.   The earls of Ducie and of Salisbury gave it approval.   John Newton, William Cowper, Thomas Scott, and Mrs. Trimmer, were hearty in its support.   William Fox and Jonas Hanway secured the organization of a general Sunday-school society, with its centre at London.   Ladies of fashion undertook the work of Sunday-school teaching.[2]   Then the Queen herself gave fresh impetus to the new movement by adding to it

[1] Speaking of the early days of the Sunday-school movement, Sir Charles Reed said, at the Raikes Centenary, in London, in June, 1880: "When Sunday-schools were first instituted in this country they were fiercely attacked. It is not to be supposed that they had an easy progress.   They were attacked by prelates in the pulpit.   The Bishop of Rochester notably denounced it [the Sunday-school movement], and urged the clergy not to support it; and the Archbishop of Canterbury was the first man in that day to call the bishops together to consider whether something could not be done to stop this great enterprise." (See *The Sunday School Chronicle*, for July 1, 1880, p. 354.) Later, the Presbyterians of Scotland, and the Congregationalists of New England, were represented among the opponents of the Sunday-school as it battled its way into deserved favor.

[2] For detailed proofs of the facts here referred to, see, among other works, Lloyd's *Sketch of the Life of Robert Raikes, and of the History of Sunday Schools;* Pray's *History of Sunday-schools* (a book which has proved a thesaurus of facts and suggestions for subsequent writers on both sides of the ocean); Watson's *The First Fifty Years of the Sunday-school;* Watson's *The Sunday-school Union : Its History and Work;* Gregory's *Robert Raikes;* Paxton Hood's *The Day, the Book and the Teacher;* Power's *Rise and Progress of Sunday-schools;* and the Centenary numbers of *The Sunday School Chronicle*, July, 1880.

the stamp of royal favor. Sending for Robert Raikes, she learned from his own lips the story of his work and its progress; and, as he reports it, "Her Majesty most graciously said that she envied those who had the power of doing good by thus personally promoting the welfare of society, in giving instruction and morality to the general mass of the common people; a pleasure from which, by her situation, she was debarred."[1] And so Sunday-school teaching came to be not only reputable but fashionable among the better classes of the English people; and this in itself was a means of good to those better classes, apart even from any good which came from it to those whom they taught. Thus it was that there was a beginning of better days to the English-speaking Christian world through the re-introduction into church activities of the divinely appointed Bible-school agency.

It has been so common to ascribe all the quickening of interest in religious and philanthropic enterprises, which characterizes the closing years of the last century and the opening years of this, to the evangelical revival and the Methodist movement growing out of it, that it may be well to consider how little real progress had been made in the more than fifty years of revived Christian life in England which preceded the new beginning of the Sunday-school, in comparison with the progress made in the twenty years, or even in the ten, which immediately followed that. It was just after Raikes had started his first Sunday-school, that John Wesley published his "Estimate of the Manners of the Present Time," in which he said of England generally: "A total ignorance of God is almost

---

[1] Raikes's letter to the Rev. Bowen Thickens, cited in Gregory's *Robert Raikes*, p. 95.

universal among us. The exceptions are exceeding few, whether among the learned or unlearned. High and low, cobblers, tinkers, hackney coachmen, men and maid servants, soldiers, sailors, tradesmen of all ranks, lawyers, physicians, gentlemen, lords, are as ignorant of the Creator of the world as Mahometans or pagans."[1] A little later he testified again: "There is not, on the face of the earth, another nation (at least, that we ever heard of) so perfectly dissipated and ungodly [as England]; not only so totally 'without God in the world,' but so openly setting him at defiance. There never was an age, that we read of in history, since Julius Cæsar, since Noah, since Adam, wherein dissipation and ungodliness did so generally prevail, both among high and low, rich and poor."[2] With all fair qualifyings of these extreme statements of Mr. Wesley, it is evident that there was much to be done in the way of bringing the community to a good measure of religious life and of common morality, at the time when the Sunday-school element became a factor in reformatory agencies, after more than fifty years of the evangelical revival of the eighteenth century.[3]

Lord Mahon presents a very dark picture of English social life at the time of which Mr. Wesley here speaks, and *he* points to the Sunday-school beginning as marking a new era of national reform.[4] Green, speaking of the days which followed the close of the American Revolution, just after the beginning of Raikes's work, says: "It was then [not before, but *then*] that the moral, the philanthropic, the religious ideas which have moulded English

---

[1] *Works*, XI., 152.   [2] *Ibid.*, VI., 424.
[3] See Wesley's Sermons: Sermon 94, § 3 (*Works*, VII., 77).
[4] *Hist. of Eng.*, VII., 333 f.

society into its present shape, first broke the spiritual torpor of the eighteenth century."[1] And again Green says specifically: "The Sunday-schools established by Mr. Raikes of Gloucester . . . were the beginning of popular education"—[in England].[2] Lecky, also, refers to "the establishment of Sunday-schools" as "an important step" in the line of "a revived interest in [popular] education."[3] As showing the national and social prominence which was quickly gained by the Sunday-school system as a factor in the forces of Christian civilization, it is a noteworthy fact that Adam Smith, with his clear perception of the needs and the hope of society as such, declared of this

---

[1] *Hist. of the English People*, IV., 272.   [2] *Ibid.*, IV., 273 f.

[3] *Hist. of Eng.*, VI., 277. At a centenary celebration under the auspices of the Church of England Sunday School Institute, in London, in July, 1880, the Rev. J. F. Kitto, in his formal address from the Institute, to the Archbishop of Canterbury, said on this point: "It is very difficult for us in this day accurately to estimate the effect which has been produced upon our nation by the attention which was so forcibly directed at that time [in 1780] to the necessity of the education of the young. We believe that it is scarcely too much to say that the system of national elementary education which has been called into existence during the last hundred years owes its origin in great measure to the persevering efforts of those who were instrumental in the foundation of Sunday-schools. . . . One hundred years ago it was a rare thing for the child of a laboring man to be able even to read, but to-day we can point to the gratifying fact that, amongst all the 20,000 scholars who are assembled here to-day, by Your Grace's invitation, there is probably not one who is in a similar condition of ignorance. Nor is this the only or the chief result of the formation of Sunday-schools. The seed of Christian faith and Christian enterprise which was sown by Robert Raikes and his associates has now borne fruit in almost every parish in our land, and its influence has spread far beyond the confines of our own country, or the limits of our own Church; so that wherever our Christianity extends, the importance of the Sunday-school is recognized as the nursery and training-school of the church; and the zeal and activity of thousands of voluntary teachers have been enlisted in its behalf" (*Thirty-seventh Annual Report of the Church of England Sunday School Institute*, 1880-81, p. 47 f.).

agency that " no plan has promised to effect a change of manners, with equal ease and simplicity, since the days of the apostles "[1]—when, in fact, its prototype was in its pristine prominence. And the pessimistic Malthus was moved, about the same time, to utter a warning against the nation's leaving the entire education of the common people to the Sunday-schools.[2]

John Wesley recognized the potency of the new Sunday-school agency, and he immediately incorporated it into the policy of his great undertaking. To this fact the Methodist Church organization owes a large measure of its success, if indeed it is not indebted to it for its continuance as well as for its steady growth. " I verily think," wrote Wesley, "these Sunday-schools are one of the noblest specimens of charity which have been set on foot in England since the time of William the Conqueror."[3] Again he wrote to his brother Charles: "I am glad you have set up Sunday-schools. . . . It is one of the noblest institutions which has been seen in Europe for some centuries, and will increase more and more, provided the teachers and inspectors do their duty."[4] And well he might think thus. About the time of the opening of Raikes's first Sunday-school, more than fifty years from the beginning of the great revival, the aggregate membership of the Methodist communion, all the world over, was a little more than fifty thousand.[5] Within four years from the public announcement by Raikes of the beginning of his work in Gloucester, the Sunday-schools of the

---

[1] Cited in a letter of Robert Raikes to William Fox, in Lloyd's *Sketch of Robert Raikes*, p. 55.   [2] See Lecky's *Hist. of Eng.*, VI., 278.
[3] Tyerman's *Life of Wesley*, III., 522.   [4] *Ibid.*, III., 604.
[5] *Ibid.*, III., 620.

United Kingdom had a membership of about a quarter of a million;[1] and from that time onward the progress of the Methodists, as of wellnigh every other body of Protestant Christians, was accelerated beyond all precedent.

At first the Sunday-school had paid teachers, and its instruction was mainly limited to lessons in reading, and in the Church of England Catechism. Afterward it secured voluntary teachers,[2] and its lessons included the memorizing of Bible verses. Gradually its plans and methods were expanded, until they comprised the systematic study of the Bible in limited lessons, week by week, with a classification of scholars in accordance with their ages and attainments. And with this progress in the character of the school itself, there was a corresponding progress in its influence in the direction of securing new agencies for the extension of Christian knowledge.

That the Sunday-school was not only the beginning of the English system of public school education, but that step by step that system was prompted and promoted by the success of Sunday-school teaching, is evident by the records of history.[3] Penny postage in Great Britain, with all that it has done for the diffusion of intelligence in that realm, is shown to have been specifically urged and advocated with a view to its bearing on the newly extended

---

[1] See Raikes's letter to Mrs. Harris, in Pray's *Hist. of Sunday-schools*, p. 147.

[2] It has been generally understood that the beginning of voluntary teaching was in Bolton, England, in 1785; but at the Raikes Centenary in London, in 1880, Sir Charles Reed claimed this honor for Oldham, England. He said: "In Oldham the first voluntary teacher was found who declined to receive money, and undertook the charge of classes in schools for nothing" (*The Sunday School Chronicle*, for July 1, 1880, p. 354).

[3] See Watson's *The First Fifty Years of the Sunday-school*, pp. 25-40; 107-112; 118-125.

correspondence between teachers and scholars in the
Sunday-schools, and between those who had been taught
to read in the Sunday-school.[1]   The British and Foreign
Bible Society—first of the societies of that character,
which in the aggregate have now sent out into the world
more than one hundred and fifty millions of Bibles and
Testaments, in at least two hundred and eighty languages
and dialects—was immediately the result of an effort to
provide Bibles and Testaments for those who had learned
in the Sunday-school to use them, and to wish for them.[2]
The Religious Tract Society, of London, was likewise
started in order to furnish good reading to those who,
through the Sunday-school, had become interested in
good reading.[3]   It need hardly be added that the new
popular interest in the religious training of the young
and the ignorant in our home communities, and the new
appreciation of the vital truths of Christianity through
personal Bible-study, were a cause of that larger interest
in the world's religious needs which led to the new foreign
missionary movement for the evangelizing of the world,
which, in fact, began with the organization of the London
Missionary Society in 1795, and of the Church Missionary
Society in 1799—less than twenty years after the beginning of Raikes's Sunday-school work.[4]

In short, it is evident that the great religious decline
of the eighteenth century was consequent on a lack of
the divinely designated church-school agency for the
winning and training of the young; and that the great

[1] See *The [London] Sunday-school Union : Its History and Work*, p. 128.
[2] See Watson's *The First Fifty Years of the Sunday-school*, pp. 64-68.
[3] See *The Jubilee Memorial of the Religious Tract Society*, p. 11 f.
[4] See Lecky's *Hist. of Eng.*, VI., 275.

religious advance of the nineteenth century is consequent upon a revival and expansion of that agency, with its legitimate influence and outcome. To the reintroduction of that feature into the Protestant Church polity we owe, under God, the chief measure of whatever, in our religious life and methods of work, make and mark this century— as superior to the centuries which it follows.

A recent tribute to the vastness of the work wrought through the Sunday-school in Great Britain, rendered by so competent and impartial an observer as Mr. John Bright, is worthy of notice just here. In a public address, only a few months ago, Mr. Bright said: "In my mind, the Sunday-schools have been the foundation of much of what is good amongst the millions of our people. I my-self am of opinion that—I will not say no attempt has been made, but—no attempt has been at all successful to show the enormous gain which our people have received from the institution of Sunday-schools, and from the zeal and continuity by which they have been supported. . . . I believe that there is no field of labor, no field of Chris-tian benevolence, which has yielded a greater harvest to our national interests and national character than the great institution of Sunday-schools."[1] And in this estimate of this evangelizing and educating agency, Mr. John Bright but echoes back, as the verdict of history, the careful measure of its power which was given by Mr. Adam Smith, a century ago, as an utterance of prophecy.

And now, instead of pursuing the historical course of religious progress in Great Britain and Ireland, where the Sunday-school in its revived form first had prominence,

[1] See *The Church Sunday School Magazine,* for July, 1887, p. 572 f.

it will, perhaps, be better to look at the influence of the
modern Sunday-school movement here in America, as
illustrative of the share which that movement has contributed to the religious progress of this century both
here and abroad.   The conditions of American life tend,
in fact, to bring into clearer exhibit the relative power of
the Sunday-school as the agency of agencies in the promotion of this progress.

America has been practically saved to Christianity and
the religion of the Bible by the Sunday-school.   No
country has ever been held permanently to that religion
in its perennial vitality, without the aid of the Sunday-
school or its substantial equivalent.   And no country
was ever more difficult of such holding, or was more
obviously dependent on this means of its holding, than
America.   At the time when the Sunday-school was introduced as a practical power in the American community,
unbelief and error were sweeping away the barriers of
sound religious conviction in the older portions of our
country; while an incoming flood of godless immigration
was threatening to ingulf hopelessly all vestiges of Christianity as a vitalizing force in the newer communities
of our extending border population.   The new agency
practically stayed the progress of error and unbelief, and
rescued the children alike of those who had lapsed from
the faith, and those who had never had faith.[1]

It is difficult to realize at this distance of time the change

---

[1] For the credit of introducing the modern Sunday-school into the United
States, there are many claimants.   It would seem that in several places, on
this side of the ocean, a Sunday-school which was started within a few years
after Raikes's beginning in Gloucester, was continued for a time, and then
given up, without leaving an immediate successor.   Thus a Sunday-school was
organized, under the direction of Bishop Asbury, at the house of Mr. Thomas

which the Sunday-school quickly wrought in America, in the prevailing sentiment of parents, teachers, and pastors, concerning the religious needs and the religious capabilities of children, as objects of church effort and of church care; and the advance which was speedily made in popular Bible knowledge in the community generally. A help to the understanding of the case, so far, may be found in the expressions of joy over this change on the part of those who were personal observers of it.

In 1814, the Rev. Dr. Lyman Beecher preached and

Crenshaw, in Hanover County, Virginia, in 1786; yet but little is known of it save its beginning. A minute in favor of organizing Sunday-schools was adopted by the Methodist Conference in Charleston, South Carolina, in February, 1790; yet no record is found of Sunday-schools organized in consequence of this minute. In December, 1790, a meeting was called in Philadelphia to consider the importance of this work; and early in January, 1791, the First-Day or Sunday School Society was formed, for the purpose of securing religious instruction to poor children on Sunday. This society has continued in operation to the present day; yet its schools, like those of Robert Raikes, had paid teachers during the earlier years of its operation. In 1791 a Sunday-school was started in Boston; in 1793 one was started in New York City, by Katy Ferguson, a colored woman; in 1794 one was started in Paterson, New Jersey; in 1797 Samuel Slater secured the organization of one in Pawtucket, Rhode Island; in 1800 one was started in Pittsburgh, Pennsylvania. In 1803 a Sunday-school was gathered by Mr. and Mrs. Divie Bethune, in New York City; and subsequently other schools were begun by them. Mrs. Bethune was a daughter of Mrs. Isabella Graham. Mr. Bethune had seen something of Raikes's work in England, and the New York school was started in imitation of that. In the same year with this beginning in New York, a Sunday-school was begun in Portsmouth, New Hampshire; the year following, one was started in Baltimore, Maryland. In 1809 a systematic Sunday-school movement was organized in Pittsburgh, Pennsylvania. The Rev. Robert May, from London, gave a new start to Sunday-schools, in Philadelphia, in 1811, which proved a beginning of permanent progress. A local union for Sunday-school work was organized in New York in 1816; another in Boston the same year; and another in Philadelphia in 1817. These societies became the nucleus of The American Sunday School Union, a national society, organized in 1824.

published his soon famous sermon on the Waste Places of New England,[1] in which he drew a gloomy picture of the religious destitution in the field of his moral outlook; while at the same time he outlined the possibilities of good to the community through yet unattempted endeavors at systematic religious instruction by the Church in the homes of church-members and beyond. Fourteen years after this (in 1828) Dr. Beecher republished that sermon; and he added to it this note, concerning his ideal plans of reform in the direction of the church instruction of children: "Since this was written, the system of Sabbath-schools has more than realized all that at the time [of the sermon writing] had been asked or thought."[2] A year later than this testimony by Dr. Beecher, President Francis Wayland, in a sermon before the American Sunday School Union, expressed his wonder over the progress in the understanding of children, as well as in their instruction, within the period of a single decade. "Who would have supposed," he said, "that the memory, the judgment, the understanding, and the conscience, of so young a child [as was then under infant-school instruction] were already so perfectly formed and so susceptible of improvement?" "And if I be not much mistaken," he added, "the instruction now given to infants, in these invaluable nurseries [the infant-schools], is more philosophical, and does more toward establishing correct intel-

[1] Although the sermon had immediate reference to Connecticut, Dr. Beecher said that his remarks concerning that state were, "with slight modification, applicable to New England generally;" and it will hardly be questioned that, in that day, the average moral standard in New England was at least up to that of the country elsewhere.

[2] *Sermons Delivered on Various Occasions*, p. 128.

lectual and moral habits, than was attainable, when I was
a boy, by children of twelve or fourteen years of age, in
grammar schools of no contemptible estimation." [1]

In similar thought, the Rev. Dr. E. N. Kirk, who
was born in 1802, thanked God, in his maturer life, that
the dark days of his childhood were "passed, passed forever," those days "when *indoctrination* and *restraint* were
the highest aims of parents, preachers, and teachers, and
[when] amusement [was] the chief aim of authors, who
wrote for children!" [2] while the Church of Christ seemed
to have no faith in the possibility of an intelligent Christian life by a child as a child. As showing that these
men did not misrepresent the ignorance of the child-
nature which prevailed among Christians of the age
before Sunday-schools, it may be mentioned that good
Dr. Doddridge, who was foremost in his time as a worker
in behalf of children, coolly said in a published sermon,
with reference to a child of, say, five years old: "Without
a miracle, it cannot be expected that much of the Christian scheme should be understood by these little creatures,
in the first dawning of reason, though a few evangelical
phrases may be taught [to them], and sometimes, by a
happy kind of accident, may be rightly applied." [3] And
here in America, as late as the years 1828-30, one of the
subjects of serious discussion in our religious magazines
was, "Can Children Reason?" In support of the affirma-
tive of this question, there were proffered the answers

---

[1] Sermon on *Encouragements to Religious Effort* (1830), p. 12.

[2] *Address to the Convention of Sunday-school Teachers*, Pittsfield, June 24,
1863, p. 6.

[3] Sermon on Submission to Divine Providence in the Death of Children
[1736]. (*Sermons and Religious Tracts*, I., 89.)

to questions given by children of nine, ten, and twelve years old, which went to show "that children are capable of thinking and reasoning for themselves."[1]

The Rev. Albert Barnes, in 1850, looked back upon the dearth of religious reading for children in the days of his boyhood (he was born at the close of last century) in contrast with the extensive literature for childhood provided by and for the Sunday-school in its first half-century of progress. All that he could have obtained for his boyhood's reading, had he had limitless means at his command, "would," he said, "have required little more than Franklin paid for his whistle;" but now he found available such treasures in that line as had no parallel in all history in the rapidity of their invaluable accumulating.[2] And even before this review of the half-century's progress by Mr. Barnes, the Rev. Dr. Isaac Ferris, afterwards Chancellor of the University of the City of New York, declared, in 1834, that the candidates for the theological seminary coming from the instructions of the Sunday-school at that time, had "knowledge, on several branches, in advance of the instruction of the seminary itself;" because of the new helps available in the Sunday-school to the understanding of Jewish antiquities, of the geography and the manners and customs of Bible lands, of ecclesiastical history, and of Scripture analysis.[3]

With a better understanding of the religious capabili-

---

[1] See *American Sunday School Magazine*, and *The Sunday School Visitant*, for 1828-29.

[2] Sermon on *Christianity as Applied to the Mind of a Child in the Sunday-school* (1850), pp. 38-42.

[3] *An Appeal to Ministers of the Gospel in Behalf of Sunday-schools* (1834), p. 28 f.

ties of childhood, there came, throughout the country, an increase of wise care for the children, in the home, in the school, and from the pulpit. Children were gathered into the church-fold in numbers unprecedented. Bible knowledge was increased among children, and by means of children. Revivals of religion had new frequency and new power; and the ordinary ministrations of the pulpit reached intelligent hearers, where before there had been only hearers who were not sufficiently instructed to comprehend the forms of truth declared to them. Thus a careful observer of the progress of events, writing in one of the prominent English religious magazines, ascribed the peculiar power of the great revivals in America from 1828 to 1832 to the superior methods of Bible study in American Sunday-schools. The progress of infidelity was checked, the sweep of error was stayed. Instead of losing ground steadily, in its relative hold upon the increasing population, evangelical religion began to make gain. So it was in the older portions of our country. So it was in the newer communities, where the pioneer Sunday-school kept pace with the extremest advance of immigration, reaching and teaching the children of parents who of themselves would never have sought the place of religious worship or teaching.

Just a few illustrative instances of the work which has been going on in all parts of our country for the past three-quarters of a century, may aid in bringing to mind the current of events during that period. In the congregation of the old First Church in Norwich Town, Connecticut, some seventy years since, a young girl came out from her family—the first of its members to do so —and confessed her child-like trust in her Saviour.

Learning something of the Sunday-school work of Divie Bethune, in New York City,[1] she gathered a little Sunday-school in the galleries of her home church. The church authorities deemed this a desecration of God's day and of God's house, and forbade her the use of the galleries. She withdrew with her little charge to a neighboring school-house. Public sentiment, including the expressed opinion of her own pastor, secured her exclusion from that building also.[2] She tried again on the church steps; and she maintained a footing there until the gallery was again opened to her, and her Sunday-school had gained its right to live. The father and the mother of that little girl followed her into the church-fold. Every other member of her family came there also. She became the wife of the Rev. Dr. Myron Winslow, as a missionary worker in Ceylon. Three of her sisters also became missionaries. One of her brothers died just as he entered the ministry. Another brother went West as a home missionary, and gathered a church and Sunday-school there. A daughter of hers labored as a missionary's wife in India, and died leaving several sons, two of whom afterward entered the ministry. On the occasion of the fiftieth anniversary of the organization of the Sunday-school she had started, I heard the pastor of her church pay a glowing tribute to her memory, as he read aloud the names of twenty-six ministers and missionaries who

---

[1] See p. 123, *ante.*

[2] Nearly thirty years ago I was told, on the testimony of an eye-witness, that when the old pastor of the church passed the school-house where this young teacher had her Sunday-school for a season, he shook his ivory-headed cane toward the building, and said in honest indignation, "You imps of Satan, doing the Devil's work!"

had already gone out from that Sunday-school as a centre of Bible-study and of Christian influence. And that incident is a fair illustration of the work wrought by the Sunday-school, in the family, in the church-fold, and in the community at large, in the field of our older churches, since the Sunday-school obtained its new foothold in America.

Some years ago I attended the one hundred and fiftieth anniversary of the First Church in Pomfret, Connecticut. Pomfret is one of the many country parishes of New England which have lost much of their ancient prominence, as local centres, by the drawing away of population and business into the valleys, along the mill-streams and the railway lines. The pastor of the Pomfret church, in his historical discourse, showed that during the last half-century of the period commemorated, the average congregation had dwindled from about ten or twelve hundred, to, say, a hundred and fifty or two hundred persons. This would have been a discouraging feature in the church history, but for the Sunday-school addition to the power of that waning congregation. Prior to the settlement of the pastor who organized the Sunday-school of that church, it would seem that there had never been any children received into full church-membership there. But he turned his attention to the little ones, and it was said at his funeral that "the children of the Sabbath-school loved him as they did their own eyes." And now, with the Sunday-school in continued operation from his day to the present, there had been more additions to the membership of the church in the last fifty years than in the first one hundred; and this with a congregation of only one-fifth or one-sixth of its former

size.[1]   As a listener to that historical discourse said
dryly: "It would seem that while fewer people went to
church in Pomfret, more went to heaven, after the Sunday-
school was started there."   Nor is that Pomfret record a
better one than we should have a right to look for in a
church with, as over against a church without, a Sunday-
school in such a town as Pomfret.

Within my own day, and within my own range of
personal observation, a young layman went into one of
the back streets of the city of Philadelphia, and gathered
a Sunday-school of less than thirty scholars.   He has
continued in charge of that Sunday-school to the present
time.   Its membership is now more than two thousand.
A church which was organized on the basis of that
Sunday-school has a membership of upwards of seventeen hundred, while another flourishing church has been
established as one of its offshoots.   And similar instances
of church organization on the basis of Sunday-school
beginnings could be pointed out in every large city
of America.

In our newer communities a very large proportion of
all the churches organized within the past half-century
have had their beginning in a Sunday-school—without
the influence of which a church could neither have been
formed nor have been continued in such a neighborhood.
And the magnitude of this pioneer Sunday-school work,
with its results of church gathering, is one of the marvels
of the century.   Take a specimen incident from its history
for an example.   Some thirty years ago a little girl was a
scholar in a pioneer Sunday-school, in a new community

---

[1] *The 150th Anniversary of the Organization of the First Church of Christ
in Pomfret, Conn.*, (1866,) pp. 31-33, 55, 61, 62.

in Illinois. She induced her father to come with her to that Sunday-school. He, although a man of strong native qualities, was wholly uneducated—even to the limited extent of a public-school training. He was lame, and he had a serious impediment in his speech. There, in the Sunday-school, he submitted himself in child-like trust to the Saviour. Then, full of love for that Saviour, and of gratitude for the Sunday-school agency which had brought to him a knowledge of the Saviour, he, Stephen Paxson, went out and essayed the gathering of other Sunday-schools in needy neighborhoods beyond. He became a missionary of the American Sunday-school Union, and in that service he gathered more than twelve hundred Sunday-schools with an aggregate membership of sixty thousand scholars and teachers. Scores of churches were established on the basis of those Sunday-schools; and when he entered into rest one of his sons was continuing and widely extending his work, which now goes on with increasing volume as the years pass by.[1]

In this way it is that the Sunday-school has become the prime church agency for pioneer evangelizing, for Bible teaching, and for the religious instruction and care of children, in every denomination of Protestant Christians in America, as also among Roman Catholics and Jews, and even among such an anomalous religious body as the Mormons. From an aggregate membership of a few hundreds at the beginning of this century, it has come to include, within the evangelical Protestant bodies alone, from eight to ten millions, or nearly one-fifth of the entire population of the United States. Meanwhile

---

[1] See *A Fruitful Life* (a memoir of Stephen Paxson).

its influence is manifest, in the fact that while, from 1800
to 1880, the aggregate population of this country has
nearly ten-folded, the number of communicants in the
evangelical Protestant churches has nearly thirty-folded.[1]

Observers from other lands are, perhaps, readier than
ourselves to recognize the peculiar value of the Sunday-
school in a country like our own, without a state church,
without the possibility of systematic religious instruction
in the public schools, and with so large a proportion of
irreligious families coming to us from across the ocean,
to swell our population year by year. For example, on
the occasion of our Centennial Exposition in 1876, the
French Government had here a Commission, studying
the principles and methods of primary instruction in the
United States. Two years later a voluminous report on
the subject was published by the French Government, as
prepared by Monsieur F. Buisson, the president of that
Commission; and it was evident that no department of
primary instruction in this country had impressed that
careful observer as more important and noteworthy than
that of the Sunday-school. "The Sunday-school," he
said, "is not an accessory agency in the normal economy
of American education; it does not add a superfluity; it
is an absolute necessity for the complete instruction of
the child. Its aim is to fill by itself the complex mission
which elsewhere is in large measure assigned to the
family, the school, and the church." "All things," again
he said, "unite to assign to this institution a grand part
in the American life. Most diverse circumstances co-
operate to give it an amplitude, a solidity, and a popu-

[1] Dorchester's *Problem of Religious Progress*, p. 545.

larity, which are quite unique. For denominational leaders, for those whom above all the interests of their church preoccupy, the Sunday-school is pre-eminently the instrument of propagandism." [1] And this is a fairer view of the case than that which is held by many who have had even better opportunities than M. Buisson of studying the Sunday-school in its workings and in its influence here in America. Professor Émile de Laveleye, of the University of Liège, Belgium, in his work on popular education, published a few years before M. Buisson's report, spoke with no less warmth of the Sunday-school system of the United States, in its power and in its importance. "The Sunday-school," he said, "is one of the strongest foundations of the republican institutions of the United States." [2]

Nearly as many teachers and scholars are in the Protestant Sunday-schools of the United States to-day, as are in all the rest of the Protestant world besides, although the Sunday-school has its recognized place and power in every quarter of the globe. [3] The circumstances under

---

[1] *Rapport sur l'Instruction Primaire à l'Exposition Universelle de Philadelphie, en 1876,* pp. 464-476.

[2] *L'Instruction du Peuple,* p. 358.

[3] The estimated statistics of the Sunday-school, in 1887, as gathered by Mr. E. Payson Porter, of Philadelphia, show, in round numbers, for the United States, one million teachers, and eight million scholars; and, for the rest of the world, one million teachers, and eight and a half million scholars. If these teachers received the *per diem* allowance for these services which was deemed a fair one, both in England and America, in the early days of the Sunday-school, the outlay for their work would be, in the United States alone, about $250,000 a week, or $13,000,000 a year, and more than twice that sum for the world as a whole. In the light of this fact, there is added force in the statement of Lord Hatherly, at the Raikes Centenary, that the Sunday-school is an evangelizing instrumentality by which there are secured

which it was developed in this country, gave to the Sunday-school here a distinctive character, as an agency both of evangelizing and of church-training, which makes it, in a peculiar sense, a pattern for imitation elsewhere. Hence it is that the American Sunday-school as an institution has found a foot-hold in most of the countries of Europe, and is gaining in membership and in confidence there, with the best results to the Church of Christ and to the community at large.

It is now about twenty-five years since Mr. Albert Woodruff, a Christian layman of Brooklyn, New York, while a traveler in Germany, was moved to undertake the starting of a Sunday-school on the American plan, with voluntary teaching by laymen and women, in the German capital. He saw that with all that was done for the religious instruction of German children, through the family, through the parochial school, as a part of the system of public education, and through perfunctory catechetical teaching in the churches, there was still a sad lack of popular Bible-study as Bible-study, and of voluntary Bible teaching by Christian laymen and women; and that the consequence of this lack showed itself there, as it shows itself under like circumstances everywhere, in the growth of skepticism and error and unbelief throughout the community—even in the higher institutions of learning. From that humble beginning the foreign Sunday-school work of America has come to be no mean factor in the evangelizing activities and in the edifying labors

"visiting agents, and good agents, and well-instructed agents, with a minimum of expense and a maximum of benefits." Who would think of complaining of the trifling expense to the churches of the Sunday-school of to-day, in view of the priceless value of its unpaid workers?

of the world at large. The London Sunday-school Union has, from the first, co-operated heartily with American workers in this new movement.[1] And now, in Germany alone, there are some three thousand Sunday-schools, comprising, say, thirty thousand teachers and three hundred thousand scholars. "The work is now spread all over Germany," writes one of its more prominent promoters; "and all clergymen who are not rationalists have Sunday-schools. Even the latter have opened children's divine services, without classes; [mainly] because they cannot find teachers [in sufficient number] who, out of love for Jesus, would devote themselves to this work."

Not only in Germany, but in wellnigh every country of continental Europe, the modern Sunday-school has been making steady progress within the past quarter of a century, from the impulse and under the watchful oversight of Christian workers, banded together, in the United States and in England, for the purpose of promoting the extension and improvement of this means of evangelization and of religious training. Meanwhile, in every foreign field where American or English missionaries are at work, the Sunday-school is growing in prominence as an agency of church extension and of church upbuilding. And thus, in a truer sense than ever before, the disciples of our Lord are laboring, all the world over, in

---

[1] At the Raikes Centenary, in London, in June, 1880, Mr. A. Benham, chairman of the Continental Committee of the London Sunday School Union, said on this point: "'Honor to whom honor' is an apostolic injunction, and right cheerfully do we accord to our highly esteemed friend and fellow-worker, Mr. Albert Woodruff, of Brooklyn, the honor of having been the pioneer of this great work. By him was laid the foundation on which has been erected the superstructure; and for what has been done up to the present time we thank God, who has, in his providence, vouchsafed so rich a blessing on the

accordance with the requirements of his pre-ascension injunction: "Go, make scholars of all nations."

Nor has the progress of the Sunday-school here in America been less marked and important in the measure and character of its instruction than in the growing magnitude of its numbers. From an unintelligent and unrestricted memorizing of Bible verses as the highest attainment of its earliest Bible-study, it passed, as did the Sunday-school in Great Britain, to the special study of limited lessons from the Bible text, week by week; and finally to the systematic study of the entire Bible as the Bible, in a series of carefully selected lessons for a continuous seven years' course, which is common to Sunday-schools generally, under the designation of the International Lesson Course. And now, under the influence of this course of instruction, the best and freshest work of the best and strongest Bible scholars on both sides of the Atlantic is made available as a help to the ordinary study of the average teacher in his preparation for the weekly teaching of his scholars.

The International lessons were formally inaugurated at the beginning of 1873, under a recommendation from a purely voluntary and an undenominational assemblage of Sunday-school workers, in a national convention for the United States; that recommendation being subsequently approved by Sunday-school workers in Canada and in England.[1]   At the start, not a single denomination

---

labors already expended on this work" (*The Sunday School Chronicle,* for July 3, 1880, p. 368).   The American workers in this movement are associated under the designation of The Foreign Sunday School Association, with its headquarters at the home of Mr. Woodruff, 130 State Street, Brooklyn, New York.

[1] The best available sketch of the movement which resulted in the Inter-

was, as a denomination, in favor of the International lesson plan. Wellnigh every great religious publishing house was opposed to it; nor could any one of those houses adopt it without rendering useless valuable plates and copyrights of series of lesson-helps. On all sides there was more or less of reluctance to accept the new system in all its essential features, and from some quarters the opposition to it was outspoken and prolonged. Hence that system secured an established position only through its tested merits, and in response to a popular conviction and demand which could not be overborne, nor successfully resisted.

One of the chief points in discussion at the time of the adoption of this lesson system, and which is still a point in its criticism, concerns the wiser method of selecting passages from the Bible, in order to its thorough and systematic study. Four plans had, severally, their earnest and conscientious advocates. First, a system of Bible doctrines, as indicated by a common creed of evangelical Christians, or as outlined in the principal catechisms of the churches, was preferred by many as a basis of sound Bible teaching. Second, personal duties, God-ward and man-ward, were thought by not a few to be the most important basis of practical Bible teaching. Third, the life of our Lord Jesus Christ in prophecy and in history, especially as its main features are indicated in the seasons of the Church year, was deemed by a multitude the fitting basis of reverent Bible teaching. Fourth, the Bible itself as a book, as the Book of books, with its exhibit of doctrines, and of duties, and of the life of Christ, was

national lesson plan is Gilbert's *The Lesson System ; the Story of its Origin and Inauguration.*

more generally looked upon as pre-eminently the basis of systematic Bible teaching; and this latter plan it was that was adopted as the plan of the International lesson system.

Steadily this system of Bible-study has won its way in the world. Almost without exception the great denominational publishing houses have made its lessons the basis of their course of instruction. While the Episcopalians have adopted it less generally than any other portion of the Protestant community, it is used in many of their Sunday-schools; and by a large proportion of the Sunday-schools of other Protestant Christians in the United States and abroad, including the foreign missionary stations of the world. While it is not easy to ascertain the number of persons who are using these lessons regularly, it can safely be said that at least from five to seven millions are now engaged, week by week, in the study of the same passage from God's Word, in accordance with the plan of the International lesson course. And so it has come to pass that at the very time when the Bible as a single whole is most severely assailed by its opponents from without the Christian fold, and most seriously questioned by its critics from within that fold, a larger number of persons than were ever before engaged in its careful study are becoming intelligently acquainted with its contents as the inspired record of a revelation from God.

A vast body of biblical literature has been created to meet the demands of the new army of Bible students. So long as there was no one phase of biblical truth which centred the interest of the community generally at any given period, there was no justification in publishing, in periodical or in book form, special helps to the elucidation of any one phase above another of such truth. But when that centring of popular interest was secured through the International lesson course, an immense constituency was already assured to any publication in the line of the studies of that course. Authors and publishers alike were prompt to recognize this new state of things, and they were aroused and stimulated to its meeting. Fresh aids to Bible-study were multiplied, and the demand for them increased even faster than their supplies. Commentaries, cyclopedias, works of biblical research, were called for to an extent before undreamed of. Important works by European specialists which would not have been thought of for popular demand in America, were now issued on this side of the water in rival editions; and the library of the average country clergyman, or of the more intelligent lay teacher, can now be supplied with volumes which otherwise could have found a place only in the better furnished of our city libraries.

The foremost scholars of the foremost universities of the world have been summoned to bear a part in the elucidation or the illustration or the application of the current lesson themes. Thus, for a single example, the honored President of Yale University is now, and for some time has been, guiding critically the New Testament studies of more than a hundred thousand Sunday-school teachers, week by week, in the line of these International lessons. For several years before him, the venerable ex-President Woolsey led similarly in this line of guidance; while the universities of Oxford and of Leipsic and of Neufchâtel from over the ocean, have contributed of their scholarship to swell the current of Bible learning for the regular supply of teachers in our American Sunday-schools.

Popular magazines and secular newspapers now feel the necessity of recognizing the field and scope of the International lessons in the catalogue of their ordinary or of their special attractions. The very atmosphere of the Christian community is surcharged with the spirit of these lessons, through their united study and teaching. Biblical theology as biblical theology has a new and a firmer hold upon the minds and hearts of teachers and of taught. And the lines of division between schools of dogmatists, and between denominations of believers, grow dimmer in the brighter glow of the great truths of the Bible which Bible students rejoice in together, as they sit side by side under the teachings of their common Redeemer.[1]

Many a young layman, in one of our better conducted American Sunday-schools, trained under the influence of this system of International lesson study, is to-day more familiar with the Bible as the Bible, than was the average young minister of a generation or so ago. One of the more prominent pastors in the United States, himself not yet past middle life, said to me, not long ago, as he spoke of a young man, still under eighteen years of age, who had received his chief learning in Bible knowledge under the influence of the International lessons, and who was now to enter college: "He knows more of the Bible, when he enters college, than I knew of it when I left the theological seminary; for he has had advantages in Bible-study such as we knew nothing of in Sunday-school, in college, or in the seminary, in my days there." Yet that pastor was the son of a New England clergyman, a gradu-

[1] It is a noteworthy fact that the increased desire for Christian union, and the increase of apparent readiness for its attainment, has corresponded in its growth and progress with the spread of this system of common Bible-study.

ate of one of the choicest Christian colleges of New England, and an alumnus of one of the more prominent theological seminaries outside of New England. Moreover, it was because he had kept himself abreast of the modern Sunday-school movement, with its mighty sway of systematic Bible-study, and knew its practical power, that he spoke as he did of those facts with which many another pastor might be familiar, but is not.

It is even now recognized as a serious question, whether a young man who is in preparation for the ministry can afford to be outside of the direct influence of this Bible-studying movement during his undergraduate years in college and in seminary; and whether the provisions in these schools of preparation are yet such as to send from them into the ministry men furnished with Bible knowledge, and with a knowledge of methods of Bible teaching, in that measure which will bring them abreast, at the start, of the Bible students whom they are likely to find, in the communities to which they go, as the product of the agencies and influences now operative outside of the preparatory schools. And it is in the line of the solving of this question that plans for Bible-study in the college curriculum are being discussed with earnestness among instructors in this University, and beyond it,[1] and that the Faculty of Yale Divinity School has shown its readi-

[1] There was never a time when the systematic study of the English Bible had as large prominence as to-day, among the better class of students in American colleges generally Such a gathering as the "College Students' Summer School and Encampment for Bible Study," under the direction of Mr. Moody, at Northfield, Massachusetts, (where from three hundred to six hundred of the brighter students of the foremost American colleges pass several weeks in this occupation, year by year,) would have been an impossibility twenty years ago, or earlier.

ness, by inviting this course of lectures, to make available to its students whatever facts or suggestions may be brought to bear upon it out of the experiences or the study of any one who has given it special attention.

And this is the record and the aspect of the modern Sunday-school movement. In the latter third of the eighteenth century, Bible-study and Bible teaching were a minor factor in the activities of the Christian Church, and the tide of vital godliness was at a very low ebb on the shores of all Christendom. In the latter third of the nineteenth century, Bible-study and Bible teaching have a prominence never before known in the world's history, and vital godliness is shown and felt with unprecedented potency in the life and progress of mankind. This change is due to God's blessing on the revival and expansion of the church Bible-school as his chosen agency for Christian evangelizing and Christian training.

LECTURE IV.

THE SUNDAY-SCHOOL: ITS INFLUENCE
ON THE FAMILY.

IV.

THE SUNDAY-SCHOOL: ITS INFLUENCE ON THE FAMILY.

Supposed Rivalry of Sunday-school and Family Influence.—The Family, God's Primal Training Agency.—The Church-school Divinely Ordained as a Complement of the Family.—The Christian Church a Larger Family.—Family Religion Prior to the Modern Sunday-school and Afterwards, in England.—In Ireland.—In Scotland.—In Wales.—In the United States.—God's Agencies Never Conflict.—Family Religion Pivots on Sunday-school Efficiency.—Cause of the Popular Error at this Point.—Mythical Boundary of the Good Old Time.—Claims of the Sunday-school under the Great Commission.

In considering the nature and the history of the Sunday-school as an agency of the Church of Christ for the discipling and training of the young, it would not be right to ignore an objection to it, or a fear concerning it, which, from its new beginning in its present form, has had prominence in the minds of its warmest well-wishers, as well as of many of its severest critics; and that objection or fear is, that a natural tendency of the Sunday-school is in the direction of releasing parents from a sense of their responsibility for the religious instruction and care of their children; and that, as a consequence of this tendency, the work and influence of the Sunday-school are liable to bear adversely on the family—as God's primal training agency for the human race. I say it would not be right to ignore this; for if, indeed, this objection be valid, or this fear be well founded, the Sunday-school neither can have, nor ought to have, the intelligent approval of the lovers of God's order in the plans of God's ordering.

When God created man, God ordained the family for the good of man and for the glory of God. The first human pair were set as the founders and the illustrators of the family for all time to come. "And God created man in his own image, in the image of God created he him; male and female created he them. And God blessed them: and God said unto them, Be fruitful and multiply, and replenish the earth, and subdue it; and have dominion."[1] "He which made them," says our Lord, "from the beginning made them male and female, and said, . . . The twain shall become one flesh. So that they are no more twain, but one flesh."[2] "And wherefore one?" asks and answers the prophet Malachi. "He sought a godly seed."[3] The family was designed of God for the uprearing of children in and for the service of God.

> "Lo, children are an heritage of the Lord:
> And the fruit of the womb is his reward.
> As arrows in the hand of a mighty man,
> So are the children of youth.
> Happy is the man that hath his quiver full of them."[4]

The divine injunction to parents was and is: "These words which I command thee, . . . shall be upon thine heart: and thou shalt teach them diligently unto thy children, and shalt talk of them when thou sittest in thine house."[5] "Command your children to observe to do all

---

[1] Gen. 1: 27, 28.   [2] Matt. 19: 4-6.   [3] Mal. 2: 15.
[4] Psa. 127: 3-5.   [5] Deut. 6: 6, 7.

the words of this law. For it is no vain thing for you; because it is your life."[1]

The institution thus ordained of God for a specific work must not be hindered in its mission, nor can it safely be rivaled or slighted. Any agency subsequently introduced for the religious instruction and care of the young, which claims a divine authorization, must be able to prove its efficiency in the line of unqualified co-operation with the family, or yield its claim to divine authorization. "For God is not a God of confusion, but of peace."[2] His plans never conflict. "All things" which he ordains *work together for good*"[3] in his cause. If the Sunday-school is in conflict, or even in rivalry, with the family in its sphere, then the Sunday-school is not worthy of confidence or of approval. So far there ought not to be any question among Christian thinkers or Christian workers. Now, what are the facts in the case?

That the objection, or the fear, referred to, has been and still is of wide-spread prominence, is as unmistakably true as is the fact that proof of the well founding of that fear should be destructive of the good name of the Sunday-school. Nearly seventy years ago Dr. Thomas Chalmers, in mention of "the more familiar objections which have been alleged against Sabbath-schools," said: "There is none which floats so currently, or is received with greater welcome and indulgence, than that they bear with adverse and malignant influence on family religion—that they detach our young from the natural guardianship of their own family, and come in place of

[1] Deut. 32 : 46, 47.   [2] 1 Cor. 14 : 33.   [3] Rom. 8 : 28.

that far better and more beautiful system which at one time obtained over the Lowlands of Scotland."[1]

As in Scotland, so in America, the Sunday-school was challenged as endangering the responsibility of the family for the religious training of the young. President Heman Humphrey, of Amherst College, for example, in a sermon before the American Sunday School Union, in 1831, cautioned parents "against devolving the whole business of religious education upon others," especially upon Sunday-school teachers. "I greatly fear," he said, "that even many Christian parents are in fault here; and I do know that some devoted teachers have almost doubted, on this account, whether their labors were of much use."[2] Two years later the Rev. Dr.—afterwards Bishop—Henshaw, in a similar advocacy of the Sunday-school cause, said: "This species of charitable effort has been objected to as interfering with the domestic relation, and relaxing the sacred tie by which parents and children are bound together." And quite naturally he added: "If this objection were valid and well sustained, it would be impossible upon Christian principles to vindicate, much more to advocate, earnestly, the system in question."[3]

While urging afresh the claims of the Sunday-school work in America, in 1845, the Rev. Dr. Archibald Alexander said: "I have recently heard it strongly objected to the whole system of Sunday-schools, that their tendency is to prevent family instruction, by furnishing parents with an apology for neglecting the instruction of their own

---

[1] *Select Works*, X., 207.

[2] Sermon on *The Way to Bless and Save our Country*, p. 18.

[3] Sermon on *The Usefulness of Sunday-schools*, p. 9.

children. It is alleged that formerly it was the custom of pious parents to spend their Sabbath evening in cate-chising and instructing their children and domestics; but now this has become very rare; and the delinquency is ascribed to the Sabbath-school system, which takes the work out of the hands of the parents, and gives it to irre-sponsible and often incompetent hands."[1]

In 1850, the Rev. Albert Barnes dwelt with warmth on the possible peril to the family from the Sunday-school. "From the nature of the case," he said, "there is danger that the true design of the Sunday-school will be mis-understood, abused, and perverted; that it will send back an influence into the family which will wholly defeat one of the great ends of the domestic organization. This danger arises from the impression which is likely to be left on the minds of parents, that they can thus transfer their obligations to train their children in the doctrines and duties of religion to others."[2]

As lately as 1881, Bishop Talbot, of Indiana, said:[3] "A Sunday-school of the modern pattern may not inaptly be defined to be an institution to save unfaithful parents and sponsors trouble. . . . In its present religious aspect, it usurps the functions both of the family and of the church." Of the former days, in contrast with these, he said: "In the mother Church [of England], when Sun-day-schools were begun, there was no room for them, and no need of them as religious organizations. Every parent, himself religious, took care to instruct his chil-

---

[1] *Suggestions in Vindication of Sunday-schools* (enlarged edition), p. 40.

[2] Sermon on *Christianity as Applied to the Mind of a Child*, p. 29.

[3] In his Convention Address.

dren in religion. Every pastor claimed them as a part of his flock whom he was to feed according to Christ's command. They were catechised by him 'openly in the church,' and trained in all Church doctrine and practice, as well as in Bible truth. Now all this is changed."

And so, all the way down to the present time, prominent representatives of the different branches of the Church of Christ in America have been sounding the note of warning against allowing the Sunday-school to usurp the duties and responsibilities of the family, or have been giving expression to the fear that the family has suffered, or is suffering, or is likely to suffer, from a tendency of the Sunday-school in this direction. On the face of it, it would seem that there must be some basis in fact or in sound reason for all this assumption on the part of intelligent and thinking men; yet I do not hesitate to affirm, and to undertake to prove, that the teachings of Scripture, the lessons of history, and the logical consideration of the principles involved, unite to show its utter baselessness; to show, indeed, on the contrary, that the Sunday-school neither has had, does have, nor can have, any other influence on the family, than that of quickening, promoting, and improving the measure and the methods of home religious instruction. And to the proof of this proposition I now invite attention.

The Bible record shows, that God in his wisdom ordained and established the church-school, for which the Sunday-school now stands, to meet and supply an existing lack in the family; and to be—while not a substitute for, nor yet a mere supplement to—a complement of the family in the religious instruction and training of

children. All history gives evidence that just in proportion as the church-school, of earlier or of later times,
has flourished or has declined, family religion has waxed
or has waned. And an examination of the principles
which are operative in the case would indicate that this
could not be otherwise.

The family was the first agency ordained of God for
the religious training of the race; and it stood alone as
an agency for that work until the Flood. But the family,
by itself, so far failed of filling its place, and of accom-
plishing its mission, that God chooses to say that it
repented him that he had made man;[1] and he swept the
race from being, save a single household, which he spared
to bridge over the chasm of destruction. And when God
began anew, with a peculiar people, he gave to his Church
a measure of responsibility in the sphere of the family,
while he lessened in no degree the responsibility of the
family as previously imposed on it. And from that time
onward one of the chiefest duties of parents has been
to secure to their children the teachings of the church-
school, as well as of the home.

Abraham was a teacher before he was a parent;[2] as
witness his three hundred and eighteen "instructed"[3]
retainers; and he was a better parent for being a teacher.
Of the days of Moses, it is declared in Deuteronomy,[4]
that the Lord's command for all Israel, at certain stated
periods, was: "Assemble the people, the men and the
women and the little ones, and thy stranger that is within
thy gates, that they may hear, and that they may learn,

[1] Gen. 6: 5-7.   [2] Comp. Gen. 14 : 14; 15 : 1-6; 18 : 19.
[3] See note on this point, at p. 6 f., *ante.*   [4] Deut. 31 : 9-13.

and fear the Lord your God, and observe to do all the words of this law; and that their children, which have not known, may hear, and learn to fear the Lord your God, as long as ye live in the land whither ye go over Jordan to possess it." And so it was that the church-school, in its germinal form, was brought into the world, to make the family what it should be.

Gradually the Jewish system of religious training was developed, with its progress from the service of the Tabernacle and of the Temple to the social services of the synagogue and the accompanying exercises of Bible-study and teaching, until it attained its crowning glory of being God's agency for the earthly training of the Holy Child Jesus. The importance of the church-school as an essential complement of the family in those days, in the land of Palestine, is shown in the teachings of the Rabbis on that subject. They tell it to the credit of King Hezekiah, that he carried his two sons on his shoulders to the synagogue school.[1] They praise the memory of Rabba bar Hunna because he would not break his fast in the morning till he had taken his son to such a school.[2] The Talmud teaches that a father's duty to lead his son to school in the morning precedes every other duty;[3] and it even suggests that a woman is entitled to a richer share than man in the Divine promises, because she sees to it that her children go to the place of Bible-study.[4] Thus it was, for example, that young Timothy with a Jewish mother[5] was sure not only to have home instruction in the Holy Scriptures before he

[1] See p. 6, *ante.*   [2] Qiddushin, 30 *a.*   [3] *Ibid.*
        [4] Berakhoth, 17 *a.*   [5] 2 Tim. 1 : 5.

England. Hannah More's correspondence with William Wilberforce and Mrs. Kennicott and others, describing the various communities in which she and her friends organized Sunday-schools, is in itself sufficient to prove this fact.[1] Of a parish of two thousand persons, within three miles of the cathedral city of Wells, she says: "We went to every house in the place, and found every house a scene of the greatest ignorance and vice. We saw but one Bible in all the parish, and that was used to prop a flower-pot."[2] Two other villages visited by her were found even more "ignorant and depraved" than this one.[3] Of yet another village, where she began a Sunday-school with more than a hundred scholars, she says, "There were not any boys or girls of any age whom I asked, that could tell me who made them."[4] And so it was wherever she pursued her investigations. It is evident, indeed, that it was not among the lower classes, any more than among the upper, of English society, that home religious instruction was in such prominence a century ago as to be imperilled by the introduction of the Sunday-school.

Moreover, that family religion has been extended and given power in English homes, in corresponding measure with the progress of the Sunday-school in England, is a fact capable of explicit proof. The average English home of to-day has in it a religious atmosphere wholly unknown to the average English home of a century ago. Of the prevalence of family worship, for example, in England, in these later times, an intelligent American

---

[1] *Memoirs of Hannah More*, Vol. I., ch. 6.   [2] *Ibid.*, I., 389.
[3] *Ibid.*, I., 388.   [4] *Ibid.*, I., 393 f.

observer has said: "Scarcely a family, at least none who lays claim to any degree of respectability, fails to have family [religious] service, at least [one] part of the day. . . . The servants come in, bringing with them their Bibles and the benches on which they sit. Men [even those] who do not 'profess religion,' as it is understood among us, seldom sit at meat without [saying] 'grace,' as it is here called. . . . At her breakfast-table, where the Queen appears as the woman, and lays aside the queen, she frequently says grace." Such a stronghold has this custom of family worship now acquired in England, that, as I happen to know, an eminent author, who has written against the dogma of a personal God, has retained the habit of leading his household in daily family prayers, according to the practice in which *he* was trained—after the new beginning of Sunday-schools in England. Of the immediate cause of this improvement in English household religious life, with all the gain that accompanies it, so intelligent and impartial a historian as Lord Mahon says, unqualifiedly, after describing the dark days of a century ago: "Among the *principal* means which, under Providence, tended to a better state in the coming age, may be ranked the system of Sunday-schools."[1]

There is one peculiar feature of the Sunday-school work in England which brings into yet clearer prominence the value of Sunday-school teaching as a promoter of family religious teaching, and which ought not to be omitted in this review. In England, the children of the upper classes in society are not, as a rule, in attendance at the Sunday-school as scholars. *They* are mainly

[1] *Hist. of Eng.*, **VII.**, 333.

dependent for their religious instruction on the home, and on the private school, and on whatever of formal catechetical exercises apart from the Sunday-school is secured to them in their parishes. Now how does the home religious instruction which at this enlightened day they receive, compare with that which is given in families from which the children are sent regularly to Sunday-school? The answer to this question ought to throw light on the tendency of the Sunday-school in its influence on the family, as a means of religious instruction. And in order to give force to the answer, all testimony on the subject ought to come from clergymen and other workers in the Church of England who are in sympathy with the classes referred to, and who are in a measure responsible for their right training.

Within the past three or four years a "symposium" on the subject of "the religious instruction of the children of the upper classes" in England extended through an entire year, in successive numbers of The Church Sunday School Magazine, the organ of the Church of England Sunday School Institute.[1] This symposium was participated in by clergymen and laymen of prominence in the Church of England, and by women whose position or whose services gave special weight to their opinions or testimony on the subject considered. From all that was shown in the course of that discussion, and in articles which followed it in the same magazine, it is evident that the children of the upper classes, in England, who are dependent on home religious instruction, are lamentably lacking in those elements of religious knowledge which

[1] See *The Church Sunday School Magazine*, from November, 1884, to October, 1885.

the Sunday-school supplies so fully; that the contrast between those who are taught in the Sunday-school and those who have only home instruction is so great as to cause alarm for the consequences of the home-neglected and the Sunday-school neglecting children of England's upper classes; and that the most hopeful agency for supplying the existing lack is some fresh adaptation of the Sunday-school idea.

The Very Rev. the Dean of Winchester has recently called attention to the fact that, according to trustworthy statistics, wellnigh all the children of teachable age in England are in the Sunday-school, "with the important exception of the well-to-do classes;" and of the condition of those children who are not yet reached by the Sunday-school he says, illustratively: "I was talking with that remarkable woman, Miss Beale, the other day. She has under her eye about seven hundred girls of the gentle-folk kind at Cheltenham. She asked me whether I was aware of the incredible ignorance in religious matters of the children of the wealthier classes, and said she was daily more and more horrified at the discoveries she made. And I feel convinced that if we all had her means of discovering the darkness of the land, we should also feel as much scared as she did. We are waking up to our shortcomings in this field of work."[1] And another clergyman, who says he agrees with English clergymen generally in finding "a far greater and clearer knowledge of the Scriptures" among children who come for confirmation from the Sunday-school, or from the National School, than among those whose religious instruction

---

[1] See *The Church Sunday School Magazine* for March, 1886, pp. 259-264.

has been only at home and in private schools, is sure that "the Sunday-school is the one efficient agency" for supplying the lack of home religious teaching in the upper classes of England.[1]

In short, the record of history shows that, in England, family religion was at a very low ebb when the modern Sunday-school was introduced there; that, in proportion as the Sunday-school in England has made progress, family religion has there been extended and improved— in the immediate sphere of the Sunday-school and beyond it; and that to-day family religion in England is at its best where Sunday-school instruction is most highly prized, and is at its poorest where the Sunday-school is ignored or is depreciated, and where, in fact, the family is looked upon as the only legitimate agency for the religious instruction of children. And as it has been in England, so it has been, in the same measure, or in larger, all the world over, wherever the influence of the Sunday-school on the family is capable of an intelligent tracking for a series of years.

Turn now to a glance at Scotland, in the light of a century ago and of to-day. Scotland has been called "the land of family religion;" but that designation was originally acquired in the days when the Protestant Reformers had re-instituted the church-school as a means of promoting religion in the home;[2] and it has gained new force in these later days, under the impulse which the Sunday-school has given to family religion in Scotland, as elsewhere. It is not true that home religious instruction was, in any sense, a prominent feature in the Scottish life

[1] See *The Church Sunday School Magazine* for January, 1885, pp. 165-167.
[2] See Lecky's *Hist. of Eng.*, II., 47 f.

of a century ago. "An intelligent traveler who visited Scotland in 1787," and who is cited by Lecky as a competent witness of the state of things there, has this to say of the people whom he observed: "The common people of Scotland are more than a century behind the English in improvement; and the manners of the Lowlanders in particular cannot fail to disgust a stranger. All the stories that are propagated of the filth and habitual dirtiness of this people are surpassed by the reality; and the squalid, unwholesome appearance of their garb and countenances is exceeded by the wretchedness that prevails within their houses."[1] This, be it remembered, was just before the modern Sunday-school obtained a foot-hold in Scotland, with an opportunity of showing the tendency of its influence on family religion. "It is certain," adds Lecky, "that during a great part of the eighteenth century hard drinking and other convivial excesses were carried among the upper classes in Scotland to an extent considerably greater than in England, and not less than in Ireland;"[2] nor does Lecky limit his exhibit of prevalent Scottish immoralities in that day to hard drinking.[3]

But to limit the investigation to that of the mere form of family religion, as such, at that time in Scotland, does not improve this picture. Dean Ramsay, writing thirty years ago of the generation before his own, in Scotland, says: "Take, as an example, the practice of family prayer. Many excellent and pious households of the former generation would not venture on the observance [of it],

---

[1] Skrine's Travels in the North of England and part of Scotland, pp. 71, 72; cited in Lecky's *Hist. of Eng.*, II., 84 f.

[2] *Hist. of Eng.*, II., 96.   [3] *Ibid.*, II., 97, 98.

I am afraid because they were afraid of the sneer. There was a foolish application of the term 'Methodists,' 'saints,' 'over-righteous,' and so on, where the practice was observed. It was to take up a rather decided position in the neighborhood; and I can testify that less than fifty years ago a family would have been marked and talked of, for a usage of which now throughout the country the *exception* is rather the unusual circumstance." [1] Not much crowding out of religion from the family, by the Sunday-school, in the half-century's progress *there!*

To this testimony it is sufficient to add the specific and conclusive exhibit of the whole case for Scotland, made by Dr. Thomas Chalmers; whose competency and fairness as a witness few would venture to question. "Is it possible," he asks, in his "Polity of Nations," "for any man at all acquainted with the chronology of Sabbath-schools, to affirm that they are the instruments of having overthrown the family religion of Scotland? . . . The truth is that, for many years previous to the extension of this system, a woful degeneracy was going on in the religious habit and character of our country; that [at this period] . . . the religious spirit, once so characteristic of our nation, has long been rapidly subsiding, . . . and now the state of the alternative is not whether the rising generation shall be trained to Christianity in schools, or trained to it under the roof of their fathers; but whether they shall be trained to it in schools, or not trained to it at all. . . . So far from [the local system of Sabbath-schools] superseding the household system of education, its direct consequence is to establish that [household]

---

[1] *Reminiscences of Scottish Life and Character,* p. 12.

11

system in places where it was before unknown; or to
restore it in places where, through the decay of Christianity for one or more generations, it had for some time
been suspended. . . . Nor can we conceive any degree
of piety or Christian wisdom, on the part of parents, that
should lead them to regard a well-conducted Sabbath-
school in any other light than as a blessing and an
acquisition to *their* children."[1]

Ireland was even less favored than England or Scotland
in the matter of family religion a century ago;[2] hence it
had more to gain and less to imperil, in that line, than
either of those countries, through the introduction of the
Sunday-school.   In fact, of some parts of Ireland at the
opening of this century, it is said by one historical writer,
that "even the Protestant children were 'no better than
heathens;'" while of the latter part of last century another historian affirms, that "the great mass of the Irish
Catholics were either absolutely illiterate, or were left to
the slight, uncertain, and often perverting, teaching of the
hedge schoolmaster."[3] After a quarter of a century's
progress of Sunday-school work in Ireland, the Parlia-
mentary Report of the Irish Education Inquiry said of
the influence of Sunday-schools in that land: "The influence on moral character, which has already been produced
in those parts of Ireland where institutions of this kind
have been formed, is attested by undoubted authority.
A marked improvement in principle and conduct, an
increased respect to moral obligation, a more general

[1] *Works*, X., 208-212. See, also, Lecky's *Hist. of Eng.*, II., 96-98.
[2] See Young's *Tour in Ireland in 1776-1779;* also Sir George Nicholls's *History of the Irish Poor Law*, p. 14.
[3] Lecky's *Hist. of Eng.*, VI., 451.

observance of relative duties, and a greater deference to the laws, are invariably represented as among the fruits of the education there received; and we entertain no doubt that it is one of the most powerful instruments for raising the character and advancing the general welfare of the people."[1]

Nearly forty years later the Rev. Dr. Urwick, of Dublin, in citing this report, said further of the influence of Sunday-schools in Ireland that, in addition to promoting popular Bible-study, and general education, and the evangelizing of the young, and the spirituality of the churches, they had done much to extend and to improve family religion in the community. "The mere fact," he said, "that children attend the Sunday-school, brings the subject of religion, week after week, before the minds of the parents, and is a standing admonition that the fear of God should be the law of the household. What the children learn at the school they naturally speak of at home, and, in many cases, [they] become in their turn teachers of the true, and witnesses for the right, in the family circle. To this must be added friendly visits from the Christian persons who instruct the children on Sundays. . . . Their example, counsels, and kind intercourse, operate powerfully to purify and bless, rendering the dwelling, however humble, like the house of God and the gate of heaven."[2]

But it is in Wales that the influence of the Sunday-school, in improving the community and in bringing religion into the family, is marked and obvious above all

[1] Cited by W. F. Lloyd, in his *Life of Robert Raikes*, pp. 74-81.
[2] See *Report of the Proceedings of the General Sunday School Convention*, London, Sept. 1-5, 1862, p. 25 f.

that is shown so clearly in England, Scotland, and Ireland. As Scotland has been called "the land of family religion," Wales has been called "the land of Sunday-schools." It is probably true that in Wales a larger proportion of the entire population is to be found in the Sunday-school than in any other community of like extent throughout the globe. And it is probably also true that in no other part of the world is there a community of like extent so thoroughly evangelized as Wales, or one where family religion is so nearly universal. Yet Wales had no marked superiority in its religious standing over other parts of Great Britain, at the opening of this century, or at the close of the last.

The Rev. Thomas Charles, of Bala, who was chiefly instrumental in introducing the Sunday-school into Wales at that period, found that, in a considerable stretch of country, not one person in twenty could read the Bible; while in entire neighborhoods only a single person had received any instruction in reading. The only bright spots were where circulating Bible-schools, on the week-day, had been set up by the Rev. Griffith Jones, some fifty years before.[1] In the Sunday-schools as founded by Mr. Charles, and as continued to the present day, in Wales, not only children, but adults, join in Bible-study; so that entire communities are direct sharers in the benefits of such study. In speaking of the need and value of his work after a quarter of a century's trial of its results, Mr. Charles said: "Where the [Sunday-] schools are neglected, . . . there is no progress made in any way whatever in regard to divine things: where the schools

[1] See Lecky's *Hist. of Eng.*, II., 656 f.

are low, the cause of religion will almost always be found to be so too."

Some forty years or more subsequent to this testimony of Mr. Charles, a report of one of the Assistant Commissioners of the Royal Education Commission affirmed : "The Welsh Sunday-school can well afford to allow itself to be tested by the results it has achieved. In little more than half a century, it has been the main agency in effecting that change in the moral and social population of the country, to which a parallel can scarcely be found in history. . . . There can be no mistake here as to the cause; we have to deal with no complications in the social condition of the population of the Principality; it is traceable, as it were, step by step, to the Sunday-school as the main social agency. In disseminating among a whole population religious knowledge, the Sunday-school [in Wales] has fulfilled its mission."[1] And this is the way in which the Sunday-school has shown its tendency, as bearing upon family religion, in that corner of the globe where the Sunday-school sway has been chiefest, and where family religion stands highest.

America was not so different from Great Britain and Ireland, in the lack of home religious instruction just before the introduction of the Sunday-school; nor has it proved so different in the new impulse given to family religion by the Sunday-school. The Sunday-school was not a considerable factor in American social life until a quarter of a century later than its re-introduction into Great Britain; hence it is necessary to count family

[1] These facts are from Mr. Hugh Owen's paper on " The History and Influence of Sunday-schools in Wales," in *Report of the General Sunday School Convention*, 1862, pp. 35-47.

religion in America as practically unaffected by the Sunday-school down to 1815 to 1820. And what was the state of things in this country for a quarter of a century prior to then?

Take, for example, our American colleges, founded as they were for the express purpose of providing the means of a thorough Christian education. It is obvious that their students would fairly represent the better class of Christian families in the community; and that the religious attitude of those students would go far to indicate the nature and effectiveness of the home religious instruction then prevalent in that class of families. Now the fact is capable of explicit proof, that, at the close of the last century and at the beginning of this, a college student who reverently accepted the Bible as a divinely inspired book was an exception in our colleges generally. In 1795 there were only eleven church-members out of a hundred and ten students in Yale College; while many of the students had adopted the names of prominent English and French infidels, and were open in the advocacy of infidel opinions.[1]　Four years later, with a larger number of students, the number of church-members was reduced to five; and at one communion service only one student communicant was present.[2]　Nor was Yale College, at this time, a marked exception among the colleges of New England in the low religious standard of its students generally. It is said, indeed, of Bowdoin College, in 1807, that "only one student [among the undergraduates] was willing to avow himself a Christian."[3]

[1] See Dwight's *Theology*, pp. 20-26.
[2] Professor Chauncey A. Goodrich, in *American Quarterly Register*, X., 294.
[3] See Dorchester's *Problem of Religious Progress*, p. 99.

Outside of New England the colleges made little, if any, better show. Bishop Meade, of Virginia, writing of the condition of affairs in his own state, in 1811, and earlier, says: "Infidelity, indeed, was then rife in the state, and the College of William and Mary was regarded as the hot-bed of French politics and religion. I can truly say that then, and for some years after, in every educated young man of Virginia whom I met I expected to find a skeptic, if not an avowed unbeliever."[1] President Ashbel Green, of Princeton College, says of his fellow-students in his undergraduate days there (1778-82): "I was at that time the only professor of religion among them, and a number of them were grossly profane."[2] Again he says: "There were . . . not more than five or six who scrupled to use profane language in common conversation."[3] As late as 1814, only twelve out of one hundred and five students were church-members.[4] Chancellor Kent, who graduated from Yale in 1781, and who was, for years, an instructor in Columbia College, said, in the latter part of his life : " In my younger days there were very few professional men that were not infidels; or at least they were so far inclined to infidelity that they could not be called believers in the truth of the Bible."[5] And this, be it remembered, is a suggestion of the choicer aspects of American family life before the days of Sunday-schools.[6]

---

[1] *Old Churches, Ministers, and Families of Virginia*, I., 29.

[2] Jones's *Life of Ashbel Green*, p. 133.

[3] Cited in Dorchester's *Christianity in the United States*, p. 287.

[4] Jones's *Life of Ashbel Green*, p. 620, note.

[5] Cited in Dorchester's *Problem of Religious Progress*, p. 98.

[6] It is a very common thing to ascribe the change in the condition of our American colleges to revivals of religion, and even to point to the precise

Added gleams of the state of things in the households and schools of that period are given to us in various memorial sermons and local histories. Thus the Rev. Dr. Abel McEwen, of New London, Connecticut—the man who won the valedictory in the contest with John C. Calhoun, at the time of his graduation from Yale—says of the community in which he was settled in 1806: "Little of family religion could be found. Households, at their meals, sat down to eat and rose up to play. Few children or domestics heard the head of their house ask a blessing or give thanks at their table. So far as careful inquiry can be relied on for the knowledge of facts, in but two families in this whole congregation [of the First Church] was daily family prayer maintained; though prayer, Saturday evenings, was, every week, offered by one other householder at the head of his family.[1] Probably in two other houses, perhaps in three, belonging to two other religious denominations [in this community], family prayer was, by laymen, daily offered."[2]   Is there need of

date of the revival in this or that college which ushered in the better day there. But it will be remembered that similar revivals had taken place in former times, without securing that permanent continuance of religious interest in our colleges which has been co-existent with Sunday-school progress. The great awaking in the days of Edwards and Whitefield was quite as potent, for the time being, in our colleges, as any or all of the revivals at the beginning of this century; but the decline which followed the former did not follow the latter. The family without the Sunday-schools bore no comparison, so far, with the family and the Sunday-school, as a religious training agency.

[1] Saturday night, it will be remembered, was by many looked upon as the beginning of the Sabbath; hence a service of family worship at that time would be in a sense a Sabbath service. Thus it is that Burns sings of The Cotter's Saturday Night, in Scotland, in those days when, according to Chalmers, family religion was there generally suspended.

[2] *Half Century Sermon*, p. 15 f.

testimony to show that household religion has stood better in that community since Sunday-school influences were felt in its family life?

The Rev. Dr. Heman Humphrey had a similar story to tell of the state of family religion in Fairfield, Connecticut, at the time of his settlement there, a few years later than Dr. McEwen's settlement at New London. Speaking not only of Connecticut but of all New England, in 1812, the Rev. Dr. Lyman Beecher said: "From various causes the ancient discipline of the family has been extensively neglected. Children have neither been governed nor instructed in religion as they were in the days of our fathers. . . . Thousands of families . . . have either not reared the family altar, or have put out the sacred fire, and laid aside together the rod and the Bible as superfluous auxiliaries in the education of children."[1] And two years later Dr. Beecher said, concerning this decline of religious instruction in the family, and the exclusion of "the Bible and catechetical instruction" from the common school: "The result was a brood of infidels, and heretics, and profligates; a generation prepared to be carried about, as they have been, by every wind of doctrine."[2] In 1819, the Rev. Abel Flint, of Hartford, Connecticut, affirmed: "It is also a melancholy fact that few children receive suitable religious instruction from their parents or others at home." The Rev. William Cogswell, of Dedham, Massachusetts, writing in 1826, said: "We regret to be compelled to acknowledge that family worship is comparatively but little observed. . . . The neglect of this duty to so great an extent is a lam-

---

[1] *Sermons Delivered on Various Occasions*, p. 83.　　[2] *Ibid.*, p. 111.

entable and an alarming consideration.   It is a reproach
upon our age." [1]

A writer in The Christian Spectator, in 1819, treating
of this subject, said : "The neglect of parents in regard to
the religious culture of their children has, during the last
century, greatly increased; and forms one of the most
decisive and alarming proofs of the gradual deterioration
of our population.   The scrupulous attention of our
ancestors to this duty was a conspicuous trait in their
character, and contributed greatly to the production and
maintenance of that strictness and purity of morals which
have so much distinguished the inhabitants of New
England. . . . The gradually increasing neglect of the
religious instruction of children, originating obviously
from the decline of parental faithfulness and piety, while
it is a most melancholy proof of the gradual retrograda-
tion of our population in morals and religion, suggests
and justifies, unless it is speedily arrested, alarming
apprehensions for future generations. . . . No incon-
siderable portion of the children and youth of this state
[Connecticut] in which more than anywhere else the
means of religious instruction abound, are lamentably
ignorant of Christianity.   In some other parts of the
country the evil is undoubtedly greater." [2]

Referring to the closing years of the eighteenth century, a historian of the Presbyterian Church in the United
States says : "The cause of religion, in many parts of the
land, seemed to be on the decline, and the prospect grew
darker and more discouraging with each succeeding year."
He cites an official utterance of the General Assembly in

[1] *The Assistant to Family Religion*, p. 27.
[2] *The Christian Spectator*, May, 1819.

proof of the fact, that not only was there, in the community at large, "a general dereliction of religious principles and practice amongst our fellow-citizens; a great departure from the faith and simple purity of manners for which our fathers were remarkable; a visible and prevailing impiety and contempt for the laws and institutions of religion; and an abounding infidelity which in many instances tends to atheism itself;" but even within the bounds of the church itself "'a dissolution of religious society' seemed to be threatened, by 'the supineness and inattention of many ministers and professors of Christianity.'" And he adds that "the profanation of the Sabbath, *the neglect of family religion and instruction,* ingratitude to God for his benefits, 'profligacy and corruption of public morals, profaneness, pride, luxury, injustice, intemperance, lewdness, and every species of debauchery and loose indulgence,' were sins which greatly abounded."[1]

Of that portion of Kentucky which was first occupied by Presbyterian families, it is said that in 1793 a religious decline had already shown itself. "The seeds of French infidelity had been sown broadcast over it. . . . Lawlessness largely prevailed. Family education and religion fell into neglect."[2] A visitor to Western New York in 1798 wrote, that "religion has not got west of the Genesee River."[3] Several years later than this, "the practice of family worship" is declared by Bishop Meade to have been "indeed a novelty in that day in Virginia."[4] And the Rev. Dr. Archibald Alexander, in repudiating the

[1] Gillett's *History of the Presbyterian Church,* I., 297 f.   [2] *Ibid.,* I., 420 f.
[3] Cited in Dorchester's *Problem of Religious Progress,* p. 185.
[4] *Old Churches, Ministers, and Families of Virginia,* I., 34.

suggestion that it was the Sunday-school which had brought family religious training into neglect, says emphatically: "The fact is that this neglect had taken place very extensively in this country many years before this institution was thought of."[1]   And this seems to be the concurrent testimony of all who speak by the record of authenticated facts.

If, indeed, it be true that the tendency of the Sunday-school is to diminish the measure and power of family religion in its field, it ought to have made short work of the little there was remaining for it to destroy at the time it first came into prominence in the United States.   But while family religion is not yet what it should be in this country, it was never so good, nor was there ever so much of it, as since the influence of the Sunday-school has been brought to bear in its favor.

A few years ago the present President of Harvard University made public the result of an inquiry on his part concerning the habit of family prayers in the homes from which came the students of his charge.   Out of seven hundred and forty-one families represented by his undergraduates, two hundred and eleven, or about two-sevenths of all, were reported as accustomed to have family prayers.[2]   Even though it might well be wished that a more satisfactory showing than this could be made in such a university, there is reason for believing that it is a far better one than could have been made by Harvard, or by Yale, or by Princeton, eighty or a hundred years ago.   And who will claim that Harvard has gained

[1] *Suggestions in Vindication of Sunday-schools*, (enlarged edition,) p. 40.
[2] *Annual Reports of the President and Treasurer of Harvard College*, 1880-81, p. 18 £.

more than other Christian colleges of the United States in this particular, since the Sunday-school became a power in the land?

In truth, the Sunday-school has proved a means, all our country over, of bringing family religion into families which before were without it, and of raising the standard and improving the character of family religion where it already had a place. On this point I venture to bear my personal testimony, instead of citing the opinion of others who have borne testimony in the same direction. For now thirty years I have given this subject close attention, with a wide and varied field of observation. I have personally visited tens of thousands of families, in city and village and country, in a range of twenty-nine states, extending from Maine to California, and from Minnesota to Florida. I have become acquainted, by sight and by inquiry, with the religious habits of families as families where the Sunday-school was prominent, where the Sunday-school was a minor factor in the community, and where there was no Sunday-school; and I have also watched the course of things year by year from without. Invariably have I found that the measure and standard of family religion corresponded with the measure and standard of Sunday-school activities in each and every community.[1] Moreover, if the Sunday-school came into

[1] It might almost be said that the Sunday-school disclosed to Christian parents generally the religious possibilities of childhood, and so prepared the way for the fitting religious training of children at home and in the sanctuary. Even where the memorizing of the Westminster Catechism was insisted on in the home, before the days of the Sunday-school, the very children who had a part in it were likely to be ignorant of the way of salvation, and to be counted by their parents incapable of an understanding of that way. Where, indeed, a child was taught set forms of prayer, the idea of a child's framing for itself

a community where there was no family religion, family religion was revived there; while if the Sunday-school declined in a community where family religion had prevailed, family religion was sure to decline correspondingly.

I go farther than this, as bearing on the question of the tendency of the Sunday-school to lessen or to increase a sense of parental responsibility for the home religious

a prayer of faith was hardly conceivable to the average Christian parent. A New England clergyman's wife told me, years ago, that when, as a child, she and one or two of her playmates were interested in the subject of personal religion, they dared not be detected by their parents in social prayer, lest their action should be deemed irreverent, and they were necessitated to seek Christ clandestinely. Similar statements have been made to me by many of those who remembered the ante-Sunday-school age; and I have personally found vestiges of this feeling in primitive New England neighborhoods, where parents actually objected to the attendance of their children at a Sunday-school while "too young to be Christians." Even in the sanctuary, the children, as a rule, had no place in the family pew prior to the Sunday-school day; but they were huddled together in the galleries under the watch and rod of the tithing-man. In the first *Annual Report of the Connecticut Sunday School Union*, (1826,) a change in this particular is reported from the church in Farmington, over which the father of President Porter, of Yale, was pastor. "One of the most serious impediments to the successful prosecution of our object," says the report (p. 12), "has always, hitherto, been the long-established and inveterately fixed custom of seating parents and heads of families separately from their children and households; and these, instead of being located in situations favorable for the restraining influence of their teachers, were, in accordance with long established usage, improperly indulged with the liberty of choosing their own seats, and changing them from Sabbath to Sabbath, in different parts of the galleries of the church; thus, through a faulty construction of some parts of the house, they easily could, and often did, cluster in companies and engage in frivolity, while screened from the view of the congregation at large. . . . The efforts of the tithing-men, and the most careful endeavors of Sabbath-school teachers, were insufficient to remedy the evil." At last, however, the endeavors of the Sunday-school had secured a place for the children of Christian parents in the family pew, in the church at Farmington, as in many another church elsewhere. And so it is that the Sunday-school has been the means of extending the scope and improving the character of family religious instruction and influence.

instruction of the children. One of my assistants, while I was in charge of Sunday-school missionary work in New England, at my request, made specific inquiry on this point, in more than three thousand homes, visited consecutively in back districts and border neighborhoods where were no Sunday-schools. Very many of the homes thus canvassed were the homes of confessing Christians; all of them were the homes of parents who knew that unless *they* instructed their children in religious matters, those children would remain uninstructed. In not above six of those more than three thousand families did the parents claim to give any systematic or specific religious instruction to their children. All the others frankly admitted that their children were without such instruction. Never in my canvassing—personally or by proxy—of homes represented in the Sunday-school, have I found reason for supposing that the proportion of homes where religious instruction was an important feature of the home life was not more than one hundred times larger than *that*. Even where in the immediate field of a Sunday-school I have found an exception of a Christian parent who deliberately kept his children away from Sunday-school in order to their better teaching at home, I have never yet found the household worship and the home religious instruction of the children to compare favorably with such worship and instruction in the better class of homes represented in the membership of the Sunday-schools.[1]

In short, I believe that whatever we have, in America,

[1] Both in measure and in methods, family worship and household religious instruction, in the homes of those who have been reached by the modern Sunday-school, are far in advance of anything that was known in the best

of satisfactory home religious instruction, is largely due to the Sunday-school; and that our still existing lack, in this direction, in the home, is to be reached and supplied through a wise use and a wise improving of the Sunday-school, as the divinely appointed complement of the family for the religious teaching of the young. And as in America in modern times, so everywhere and always, the brightest days of family religion have been coincident with, and have been consequent upon, the efficiency of church-school work in the community. It stands to reason, as well as accords with revelation, that this should be so.

Is it true that the tendency of outside medical counsel for the sick, in any family circle, is to diminish the measure or the quality of the home nursing there? Is it true that attendance at meetings for social prayer, or at gatherings for public worship, is liable in itself to lessen the attendant's interest in his family prayers, or in his private devotions? Is it true that the influence of a village singing-school is to prevent the parents and children who patronize it from singing together in their own homes? Is it true that free public libraries are likely to make home reading a less prominent feature in the families of those who visit them? Would any one claim that schools and colleges have a natural tendency to lessen the responsibility of parents for the education of the children who are sent to those institutions of learn-

cared for homes of our godliest ancestors. Children are now given an intelligent part in the exercises of family worship, and are won to an interest in the theme of the Bible lesson for the week or for the day, which would not have been deemed a possibility to persons of their age in the days before the Sunday-school. On this point I speak out of my personal knowledge in a wide and varied field of observation.

ing; or that the absence of such quickening agencies of education would increase the readiness of parents to teach their own children faithfully in their homes? How unreasonable, indeed, the suggestion that because children are sent to the place of Bible-study, and come back from it full of interest in its teachings, and full of questions raised by its exercises, the parents of those children are less likely to have a part in their children's religious instruction, than if there were no outside promptings to such a work for the little ones![1]

There is certainly a gain to young children in the sympathy and the stimulus of numbers as a means of impression and of instruction; and no child can be brought to the same standard of religious intelligence and feeling without this aid as with it. It is equally certain that, in securing this aid to his child, a wise parent ought to look well to the classmates and to the teacher who are to be the means of its securing. If, indeed, the parent is one who will *not* be at the pains to watch at a point like this,

---

[1] While preparing this lecture for delivery, I had a conversation on its subject with a mother of exceptional intelligence and devotedness, who had hitherto conscientiously kept her little daughter away from the Sunday-school, in order that that child's religious instruction might be secured exclusively in the home circle. To my surprise I learned that the child was now a pupil in the Sunday-school, her mother attending there with her. "But how is this?" I asked. "I thought you felt that the *home*, and not the *Sunday-school*, was the place for a child's religious teaching." "That's what I do think," she replied. "But I found that unless I had a set time for the home teaching, and a special subject of study, I was liable to let the day pass by without giving all the attention to it it deserved. So now I go to the Sunday-school with my child, in order to secure her right teaching there." Few mothers whom I have ever known would be less likely than that mother to fail of fidelity to her child in the matter of home religious instruction; and the difficulty *she* found in the attempt to get on without the Sunday-school would be far more of a difficulty to Christian mothers generally.

12

that parent is clearly most unlikely to be faithful and
wise in the home religious teaching of his child; and *his*
child will probably gain more, in this line, in the average
Sunday-school as it stands, than in his home as it is constituted. If, on the. other hand, the parent is one who
will give attention to a matter like this, he ought to
realize that his child can never be as well taught and
trained in the home alone, as in the home with the co-
work of the divinely appointed church-school,—the
family's complemental training agency for the young;
for there is absolutely nothing in the Word of God, in the
lessons of history, or in the teachings of sound reason,
to justify a parent in shutting up a child to the family
alone in all the course of its religious education.

But it will naturally be asked, How could an impression that the influence of the Sunday-school does, or that
it may, bear adversely on family religion, or on the
parental sense of responsibility for the religious instruction of children, come to prevail so widely for a long
series of years, unless it had something in fact, in reason,
or in Scripture, for its justifying, or for its prompting?
And this very natural question can very easily be answered.
It is a principle in human nature to glorify the past un-
reasonably and unreasoningly; and then to seek plausible
reasons for the supposed degeneracy of the present, in its
contrast with the ideal standard of the days of old.[1] And

---

[1] The Hebrews in the wilderness looked back upon the good old days of
their hard bondage in Egypt, and their cry was: " We remember the fish
which we did eat in Egypt for nought [without cost]; the cucumbers, and
the melons, and the leeks, and the onions, and the garlick : but now our soul
is dried away; there is nothing at all" (Num. 11: 5, 6). Meanwhile the
Egyptians themselves were looking back to the better days before the Pharaohs; when the hero-kings were preceded by the demi-gods, and the demi-

this principle it is that has prompted so many, first to believe that there was a good old time when parents generally were faithful and efficient in the religious train-ing of their children, and then to consider a possible cause of the present obvious lack of the imagined former perfectness. This baseless belief that it is the Sunday-school which has brought about the state of things where not every parent is faithful, nor every child is properly cared for at home—as "once it was," is no anomaly in human belief. It is one of that endless series of blunders which Qoheleth rebukes, for this age as for all ages: "Say not thou, What is the cause that the former days were better than these? for thou dost not inquire wisely concerning this."[1] There is no gain in searching for the cause of a state of things that exists only in fancy.

It is, indeed, an instructive pursuit to follow back the train of regrets over this decline of family religion, in our own country for an example, as bearing on the matter of the influence of the Sunday-school in this direction. Just when was that good old day of godly homes and of faithful parental instruction, throughout the community, of which so much is said approvingly? Was it, say, fifty years ago? That was the very time when such men as Humphrey and Henshaw and Alexander, as already cited, were insisting that it was not the Sunday-school which had brought about the supposed unfavorable contrast with

---

gods by the gods themselves (Brugsch's *Egypt under the Pharaohs*, I., 33). The classic Greeks were sure that their present Iron Age had followed the Heroic, which again had followed the Brazen, and that the Silver, and that the Golden (Hesiod's *Opera et Dies*, lines 109-201). It is always the long ago that was the choicer time. Pope might have sung: "Man never *is*, but always *has been* blest."

[1] Eccles. 7 : 10.

the family religion of a former day.   What if we go back twenty-five years more?   Then it was that, as McEwen and Flint and Meade and Cogswell and Gillett tell us, there was a day of peculiar neglect of home religious teaching.   If we push the inquiry to a century ago, we strike the time of which Lyman Beecher speaks, as the day when the bottomless pit was reopened, and which all historians agree as marking perhaps the lowest level of family religious life in our history.

To go back to the middle of last century carries us to the beginning of that decline which, according to the elder Dwight, and to Dorchester, followed the revival under Edwards and Whitefield, and culminated only at the close of the century.   Yet a quarter of a century earlier we reach the ante-revival day, which Jonathan Edwards speaks of as "a far more degenerate time (at least among the young people)" than perhaps "ever before."[1]   Hear what the Rev. Thomas Prince, of Boston, has to say on this subject, in 1730.   As he saw it, the "wonderful work of the grace of God begun in England and brought over hither [say from 1620 to 1630] was carried on while the greater part of the first generation lived, for about thirty years; and then the second generation rising up and growing thick on the stage, a little after 1660 there began to appear a decay; and this increased to 1670, when it grew very visible and threatening, and was generally complained of and bewailed bitterly by the pious among them; and yet much more in 1680, when but few of the first generation remained."[2]   It would never do to claim that the good old days of New England were the days of

---

[1] In Prince's *The Christian History*, for 1743, p. 112.   [2] *Ibid.*, p. 93 f.

Thomas Prince, a century and a half ago. We must get back of that time.

In 1706, Dr. Cotton Mather in a sermon on "The Good Old Way," which he bewailed with vain regrets, declared: "There is a general and a horrible decay of Christianity among the professors of it. . . . Ah! sinful nation. Ah! children that are corrupters. . . . The complaints of the corruptions in the lives of Christians [in New England], little short of universal, are everywhere, every day, wounding our ears."[1] In 1700, "the Reverend and Renowned Mr. Samuel Willard, pastor of the South Church in Boston, and vice-president of Harvard College," in a sermon on "The Perils of the Times Displayed," specified particularly, as one of the existing perils, "the grievous neglect of family worship."[2] Yet a little earlier, (1683,) the Rev. Samuel Torrey, of Weymouth, in an election sermon before the General Court of Massachusetts, moaned out: "How is religion dying in families, through the neglect of the religious service and worship of God, and of the religious education of children and youth in families! Truly, here and hereby religion first received its death wound"[3]—in New England. We shall need to push on by that point, in our search for the Paradise days of New England.

Dr. Increase Mather, father of Cotton, writing a preface to this sermon of Mr. Torrey's, said pithily: "The complaint is that New England is not to be found in New England."[4] And in his own treatise, published five years before this, under the title, "Pray for the Rising Generation," his testimony was: "The body of the rising

---

[1] In Prince's *Christian History*, p. 104.
[2] *Ibid.*, p. 101.   [3] *Ibid.*, p. 98 f.   [4] *Ibid.*, p. 99 f.

generation is a poor, perishing, unconverted, and (except the Lord pour down his Spirit) an undone generation."[1] Among the specific characteristics of those who were coming out from the New England home influences of that day, he instanced "many that are profane, drunkards, swearers, lascivious, scoffers at the powers of godliness, despisers of those that are good, disobedient."[2]   In the election sermon for 1670, the Rev. Samuel Danforth, of Roxbury, was sure that the good days were long before his own.   "Who is there left among you," he asked, "that saw these [New England] churches in their first glory?   And how do you see them now?   Are they not in your eyes in comparison thereof as nothing?"[3]

And this carries us back, step by step, to the generation immediately following that of the first settlers of New England, in our search for the time when—if ever before these Sunday-school days—children were properly instructed in religion by their parents in the home circle, and gave evidence of that parental faithfulness in their behalf, as they went out into the world.   In the light of the facts of history, is it quite worthy of a thoughtful and an intelligent Christian of to-day to take up this funereal wail over the departed glory of family religion, which has come echoing down through the centuries, and to add to it the already antiquated suggestion, that the mythical corpse was murdered by a supposed Sunday-school rival?

There is a lesson to be learned just here, as at many another point, from the customs and traditions of the Jews.   The Jews have their tradition of a long-ago day when all parents were competent and faithful in the

---

[1] In Prince's *Christian History*, p. 97 f.   [2] *Ibid.*   [3] *Ibid.*, pp. 94-97.

religious training of their children in the family; but the Talmud teaches that that day was considerably more than two thousand years ago; and that after it had passed away, if indeed Joshua ben Gamla had not revived God's agency of the synagogue-school, making attendance at it obligatory on all children, "the law would have been forgotten in Israel."[1] And since the revival of the syna- gogue-school, a Jewish parent is deemed faithful to his children, only while he secures to them the influences and instructions of that school in addition to all that he can do for them in his home at its very best.[2] And in this fact a Christian parent may find a suggestion of his duty as a Christian parent. The ideal of family religious in- struction includes wise and faithful parental teaching, in preparation for and in co-operation with the best available instruction in the divinely appointed church-school agency. And the measure and the quality of such religious instruc- tion in the family was never so great and so good as at the present day; and this because of the unvarying tendency of the widely extended Sunday-school agency to promote and to improve religious instruction in the family.

And here I rest the exhibit of the Sunday-school, in its origin, in its development, in its influence, in its disclosed power, and in its undisclosed possibilities. I have said nothing so far of its defects or of its lack, or of the faults and the follies in its popular management; not because I deem these slight or few, but because I would give em- phasis to its sacredness, and to the grandeur of its mission in spite of them. The deficiencies and the abuses of the

---

[1] Baba Bathra, 21 *a.*   [2] See p. 152 f., *ante.*

Sunday-school are mainly the result of its undervaluing, and its consequent neglect, by the Church of Christ and by the more prominent representatives of that Church—in the family, in the pulpit, in the college, and in the theological seminary. Seeing, therefore, as I have seen, this chosen child and this designated heir of our Lord Jesus Christ left to itself as a homeless waif, subject even to the scorn and the sneer of disciple and of rabbi, I am less ready to point at the obvious signs of its vagrant life and of its vicious surroundings, than to take it by the hand and bring it again into the very centre of the circle where our Lord himself is teaching, in order that his voice may be heard afresh, saying of this object of his love: "See that ye despise not one of these little ones; for I say unto you, that in heaven their angels do always behold the face of my Father which is in heaven;" and in order that there may be a new force to his words concerning the primary mission of his disciples: "Go ye therefore, and make scholars of all the nations, baptizing them into the name of the Father and of the Son and of the Holy Ghost: teaching them to observe all things whatsoever I commanded you: and lo, I am with you alway, even unto the end of the world."

When the Sunday-school is viewed in this light, it will be practicable and profitable to discuss fairly the methods of its improvement and of its wise conduct. And so, I trust, we are now qualified to enter upon that discussion.

LECTURE V.

THE SUNDAY-SCHOOL: ITS MEMBERSHIP
AND ITS MANAGEMENT.

V.

THE SUNDAY-SCHOOL: ITS MEMBERSHIP AND ITS MANAGEMENT.

The Missionary Feature of Modern Sunday-school Beginnings.—Church and Mission and Pioneer Sunday-schools of To-day.—What Is and what Ought to Be.—Children and the Child-like Belong in the Sunday-school.—Power of Numbers in Promoting Sympathy.—Taking in Truth by Absorption.—Evangelizing through the Sunday-school.—Two Specimen Schools in Connecticut.—How Sunday-schools are Managed.—How they Ought to Be.—Church Control.—Church Direction.—Church Support.—The Ideal Future.

Who are in the Sunday-school of to-day, and how the Sunday-school of to-day is managed, are simple questions of fact. Who ought to be in the Sunday-school as the church Bible-school, and how the Sunday-school as the church Bible-school ought to be managed, are questions of principle, involving the whole theory of church organization, and of legitimate church activities. Both these lines of questioning have their practical value in a discussion like this, and both demand recognition.

In its modern revival, under the lead of Robert Raikes, the Sunday-school was designed chiefly for the reaching and the teaching of otherwise neglected children, those whom its new apostle characterized as "little ragamuffins." In England, the missionary and evangelistic

idea is still peculiarly associated with the Sunday-school;
even though the distinction between "ragged schools"
and church Sunday-schools is now clearly recognized
there. It is not generally understood, in England, that
a Sunday-school attached to a church is one of the
regular services of the church, which all the children of
the church ought to attend as a matter of course; nor is
the Sunday-school in England commonly looked upon
as the place of Bible-study and teaching for all the members of the congregation, as it has been in Wales from
the beginning of its revival there.

In America, the modern Sunday-school began on the
English plan; but it was speedily adapted to the new
conditions existing here; and it now presents several
distinct phases of Christian effort with corresponding
differences in its membership. There are still mission
Sunday-schools in our American cities, composed chiefly
or wholly of children of the poorer and of the more vicious
classes in their neighborhood. But as there are no permanent and well-defined class distinctions in the American
population, these mission-schools are rather outside re-
cruiting-stations than camp training-posts for the Christian
host. Scholars who are rightly influenced by these
mission-schools pass out from them into schools of a
higher grade elsewhere. Meanwhile Sunday-schools in
the local churches include, as a rule, the children of the
church-members and of the other members of the congregation, together with more or fewer children from
outside families; also young people and adults in varying
numbers in different communities.

As distinct, however, from the local church-school on
the one hand, and from the city mission-school on the

other hand, there is the pioneer Sunday-school, in its incipient form or in its development, which has largely shaped the characteristics of the representative American Sunday-school. On the borders of our advancing and extending population, beyond the limits of existing church organizations, a Sunday-school is gathered as the first and for the time as the only religious assembly of the neighborhood. Into that Sunday-school the children are brought together. Through the children, the parents, as far as may be, are led to attend it. With the growth of numbers and interest, other services of worship and of preaching are added to the service of Bible-study. By and by a church organization is effected as an outgrowth of the Sunday-school. In such a case the Sunday-school is likely to retain its prominence as a gathering-place for young and old alike. It had the first place in the affections and confidence of the community about it; and that place it will not lose without a reason. It may be that such a pioneer Sunday-school is in the fore-front of civilization in our newer states or territories;[1] or again in a quarter of a city which is filling up with the city's growth; or in a newly started factory village; or in a border district of a country township of our older states on the Atlantic coast.[2] In any case the membership of

---

[1] Missionary workers sent out by the American Sunday School Union have gone with the advancing wave of population, since the formation of the society in 1824. They have organized neighborhood Sunday-schools at the average rate of three a day for now sixty-four years; aggregating nearly eighty thousand schools, with a membership of nearly four millions. And this is an undenominational work, in addition to all that has meanwhile been done by the denominations severally.

[2] As a rule, every new attempt to pre-empt a field for a church organization in a city or a village, nowadays, begins with the gathering of a Sunday-

such a Sunday-school is not likely to be limited to children from unevangelized homes; nor, indeed, to *children*
from any homes.

The responsible oversight and management of the Sunday-school in America are as varied in their source and
in their form as are the nature and the composition of its
membership. The earlier Sunday-schools here, patterned
on the Robert Raikes idea, were organized by individuals
or by an association of individuals, and were independent
of church control. Even where, in process of time, the
Sunday-schools in our older communities were practically
adopted by local churches, the original independency of
organization and management was in many a case continued; so that to-day it is not an unusual thing to find
a church Sunday-school wholly distinct in its organization
and control from the church of which it claims to be a
part. It has its own "constitution and by-laws," it
chooses its own officers, appoints its own teachers, directs
its own work, collects and disburses its own funds, with
an independency that could not be exceeded if it were
itself a General Council of the churches of undivided
Christendom.

In many cases, it is true,—and it is well that it is true,—
this independent organization of the Sunday-school has

---

school. It matters not what is the denomination, the method is the same.
The lessons of experience in the field of church extension during the past
sixty years have shown the value of reaching the parents through the young,
instead of hoping to reach the young only through the parents. Said the
Rev. Dr. Daniel Curry on this point: "Not only is there force in the familiar illustration of the Alpine shepherd's taking up the lambs in his arms
when he would induce the mother sheep to follow him, as that illustration
is generally understood, but it has an added force when we realize how much
easier it is to carry two little lambs under one's arms, than to lug one old
sheep up hill."

been formally abandoned, and the control of the school surrendered to the local church with which, before, it was linked. In the case of entire denominations,—such as the Protestant Episcopal, the Methodist Episcopal, and the Presbyterian,—the control of the Sunday-school has been unequivocally asserted by the general church authority. Yet, even in these denominations, where in a particular case a Sunday-school organization has preceded the organization of a church in its immediate field, the early feeling of independency quite naturally continues to have more or less sway with the Sunday-school membership after church control over the Sunday-school has been assumed.

And thus it is that there are anomalies in the organization of Sunday-schools, and practical difficulties in their direction and control. So far as to the existing membership and management of the Sunday-school of to-day. Now as to the true ideal in both these spheres.

The membership of the Sunday-school ought to include the children and the child-like from the families of church-members and of non-church-members,—all who need Bible-study and are capable of it. Under the old Jewish system of synagogue-school training,[1] every child of a Jewish parent was to be a scholar in a synagogue-school from the time he was six years old. Even in the choicest Jewish home, the parents had no right to limit a child's advantages to his home religious training, after he had come to that age. Entering the synagogue Bible-school thus early, the Jewish scholar never came to an age for graduation from that school. He was to continue in it

---

* See Lecture I., *passim.*

during his earthly life-course, and at death he was supposed to pass on into the heavenly Bible-school beyond. There were three departments in the synagogue Bible-school, making three grades of its membership. The primary department comprised scholars from six to ten years of age. The intermediate department included those from ten years old to fifteen. The senior department was made up of all who were over fifteen years old. And this threefold classification, with due allowances for different degrees of maturity at a specified age, is a natural and reasonable one for Bible-schools, or Sunday-schools, always and everywhere.

Nearly sixty years ago, while the Sunday-school in its new form was but a minor agency of religious instruction in America, so wise and conservative a teacher of teachers as the Rev. Dr. Archibald Alexander, of Princeton, said of the scope and limits of Sunday-school membership: "It appears to me . . . that the system of Sunday-school instruction might be greatly enlarged, both as it relates to the pupils received under . . . tuition, and as it relates to the subjects of instruction. In regard to the former, my plan would be so large as to include all persons who need instruction, from the infant of two years up to the man of a hundred years of age. . . . My idea is, that the whole church should form one great Sabbath-school, and that all the people should be disciples or teachers; or sometimes the one and sometimes the other, according to circumstances."[1] And this mode of instruction Dr. Alexander held to be "as much authorized [in the Bible] as public preaching, and in its place as necessary."

---

[1] *Suggestions in Vindication of Sunday-schools*, (1829,) p. 24 f.

Similarly, some twenty years since, the Rev. Dr. Thomas Smyth, of Charleston, long a minister of note and of influence in the Presbyterian Church, South, in a personal letter to me, (in which he laid it upon me, "in Christ's name, and with the authority in love, of such an one as Paul the aged" to pursue my studies and writings in this very direction), thus described what he characterized as the chiefest, if not the only hope of the Christian church: "The revival of a Sunday-school of Christ, as one of the services of the church, instituted by Christ and demanded by the very terms of his Commission, that all converted by the preaching of the gospel should be matriculated as disciples; that is as pupils or learners, in his school, on his holy day, with his Bible as their text-book, and with his taught as their teachers; there to be taught systematically all things whatsoever he hath commanded; that is, the 'all Scripture,' which is 'able to make . . . wise unto salvation through faith which is in Christ Jesus.'[1] This school ought, according to the Commission, to include all in the congregation, both old and young, as teachers or as learners, with the pastor as the assistant superintendent, Christ as the chief and infallible Superintendent, and the Holy Spirit as the glorious Monitor and Inspirer. Christ has in this [agency] provided for all that he promised, and at first bestowed, and all that the Church has by its neglect lost and is losing,— the restoration of belief, the divine authority of Scripture, the full efficiency of the ministry, and the gospel as the power of God, and the wisdom of God, to the salvation of innumerable souls."

---

[1] 2 Tim. 3 : 15, 16.

And no more than Dr. Archibald Alexander could Dr. Thomas Smyth be reckoned a Sunday-school enthusiast or specialist, because of his taking this enlarged view of the duty and the gain of systematic Bible-study by the entire membership of the Church of Christ, and by all who would come under the influence of the Church of Christ, in the school of Christ's appointing. Indeed, so conservative a body as the General Assembly of the Presbyterian Church has formally declared "that it is exceedingly desirable that the entire congregation, old and young, be permanently connected with the Sunday-school, either as scholars or teachers;"[1] and it has recommended to its local church authorities "to put forth practical and persistent efforts to enlist their entire congregations in systematic Bible-study and teaching in connection with the Sunday-school."[2]

Yet with all the emphasis thus laid by fathers in Israel and by Church Assemblies on the importance and the duty of congregational Bible-study, as a divinely appointed means of grace, how common it is for a church-member to feel that if he listens to pulpit preaching, in connection with the service of public worship, it matters little whether he has a part in social Bible-study, or not. And how much more frequently you hear expressed the fear that the service of Bible-study is deemed by its attendants a substitute for the preaching service, than the fear that the preaching service is deemed by its attendants a substitute for the service of Bible-study. Therefore it is that there is still need of repeated declarations of the truth that the service of interlocutory Bible-study, in

[1] Moore's *Presbyterian Digest*, 1886, p. 507 f.
[2] *Ibid.*, p. 840. See, also, p. 772.

connection with the public worship of God, is a service of primal importance in the Church of Christ; a service which cannot rightly be neglected by any disciple of the Lord Jesus Christ who is capable of bearing a part in it; a service which was given a foremost place in our Lord's plans of evangelizing, and which has never been assigned by him to a secondary place in the training agencies of his Church.

In many a community in America the true ideal of the church Bible-school is practically realized; the young and the old of the entire congregation being together in the social study of the Word of God, at one of the chief and regular services of the house of God.[1] In still more communities a goodly number of adults are found with the children in the Sunday-school; and these adults are always the more intelligent and responsive hearers of pulpit preaching because of their added knowledge through Bible-study.[2] Thirty years ago a superintendent

[1] In one instance I visited a Sunday-school having nearly two thousand members. It was the Sunday-school of a church of one hundred and fifty members; and absolutely every one of those church-members had a place in the Sunday-school, either as teacher or scholar. The Rev. Dr. Asa Bullard, of Massachusetts, told, in my hearing, of a church in his state, with a membership of five hundred and thirty-six, of which number five hundred and twelve had a place in the Sunday-school. "The minister in charge of this church," said Dr. Bullard, "would visit one of his members who absented himself from Sunday-school, to plead with him against this dereliction of duty, as if he had given up family worship."

[2] At a Sunday-school in Norwich, Connecticut, as I stood in the desk, on one occasion, I saw on one hand the governor of the state sitting as the teacher of a class; while, on the other hand, the mayor of the city was a scholar in a class composed of prominent business and professional men in his city. Again I saw, in a Fairfield County Sunday-school, the wife of the superintendent sitting as a scholar in a class, to the membership of which she had returned after being for twenty-five years a teacher in the school. Lacking now the strength to teach, she did not lack the heart to learn.

in a Connecticut Sunday-school pointed me with pride
to his "spectacle class;" every member of which was a
mother in Israel, old enough to require the aid of glasses
in reading.   At the present time, in a Bible-class which I
have the privilege of leading every week in my Philadelphia home, scholars of three generations from one family
often sit side by side in the social study of the same
Bible lesson; nor is the youngest of these scholars too
young, or the oldest too old, to enjoy and to profit by
the teachings of God's Word.

Apart, indeed, from the immediate advantage to the
adult Bible students, from their share in the service of
Bible-study in the Sunday-school, there is an obvious
gain to the character and standing of the Sunday-school,
in the estimation of children and youth, through its
being deemed the place for the study of the Bible by
those to whom they look up with loving reverence.
"How can we keep our young people from quitting
the Sunday-school when they have grown up?" was a
question proposed at a Sunday-school conference some
years ago.   Quickly there came the pertinent answer:
"Build a wall of old folks between them and the door, so
high that they'll never climb over it."   And that answer
covers an important truth concerning the method of having and holding a proper Sunday-school membership.

There is a power in numbers in the Sunday-school, not
only as promoting enthusiasm in the school as a whole,
but as quickening and aiding the mental perceptions and
the spiritual life of the individual scholar.   And just here
it is, as I have before suggested, that there is a positive
gain to the child who has choicest instruction at home,
from his attendance at a well-conducted Sunday-school.

At the best the teachings and the influence of parents are from above the child. They come down upon the child. The child must look up to take them in. In addition to all that can be done in this way for a child, there is room for both teachings and influence from alongside of the child; to be received by him while he is on his own plane of thought and feeling, and to enter his mind and heart through his sympathies. The best intentioned, the wisest, and the most loving parent in the world, cannot supply this lack as other children can supply it. Many a Christian parent has been surprised by a child's coming home from Sunday-school full of interest in an important thought which had been expressed to him by a fellow-scholar, or impressed upon him by a class-exercise or a school-service, when that very thought had been repeatedly emphasized to the child, by his parents, from above him, without being made a part of his mind-treasure, as now it had come to be through his companionship of feeling with its utterer, or its utterers. The very composition of the family forbids this massing of children of the same age to receive abiding impressions of truth through and by their massing; and here, it may be, is a reason why God ordained the Sunday-school as a complement of the family for the children's wise training.

Dr. Bushnell recognized the value of this sympathetic "taking-in exercise" by children in assemblies, when he urged the training of the little ones in services of sacred song and of Scripture recitation. "The Moravians," he said, "train their children largely by the singing of hymns that centre in Christ and true Christ-worship. So, dismissing partly the idea of a school, [for didactic teaching,] and organizing a discipleship in hosannas, we may put our children through songs of the Lamb,—chants, litanies, sonnets, holy madrigals, and doxologies,—such and so many, and full of Christ's dear love, that they will sing Christ into their very hearts, and be inwardly imbued and quickened by him. At the same time there will be rehearsed, with these, Scripture lessons that have the sense of God's authority and power and forgiveness and divine pastorship and child-cherishing friendship in them; everything, in short, that most appreciates God and the precious thoughts of God; everything that belongs to a penitent, adoring, tender, faithfully kept, patiently enduring, bravely steadfast, gloriously trustful character. And these rehearsed responsively, or by all together, and blended with high song, will make up a taking-in exercise, whereby Christ will be entered more and more deeply into the secret life of the children."[1]

Many, very many children have thus been helped into Christ-likeness by the influence of the united prayings and praisings and recitings of the Sunday-school. And very many more children ought to have the advantage of this kind of training service, in addition to all that can be done for them in the household. Nor is the gain of numbers as a means of promoting a sympathetic taking-in of truth by such a service limited to children, in the Sunday-school. Older persons are uplifted and swept along thereby, as has been shown in numberless instances. Hence it is that the Sunday-school has power for good hardly less through the collective influence of its class membership, and through its general exercises as led from the superintendent's desk, than through the

[1] Sermon on *God's Thoughts Fit Bread for Children*, pp. 32-34.

individual instruction secured to its every scholar. And this is why no Christian, young or old, can fail to be a loser through lacking a share in the exercises of the Sunday-school.

But it is never enough to have all the children of the church and of the congregation, and all of the older members of the church and of the congregation, in the Sunday-school. There ought always to be a goodly number of outside children in the membership of the Sunday-school, whether that Sunday-school be in city, or village, or country. The primary idea of the Sunday-school, as provided for in the Great Commission, as prosecuted by the Early Church, and as put into operation anew by Robert Raikes, is that of an agency for making scholars of the unevangelized; and that idea ought never to be lost sight of so long as there are any unevangelized persons to be made scholars of. The Church ought still, as in its earliest days, to make "the school the connecting link between herself and the world;" for on every side, peculiarly here in America, there are families unrepresented in the sanctuary, which can be reached easier, if not only, through winning their children into the Sunday-school. Perhaps the need and the possibilities of an increase of the Sunday-school membership by this kind of effort, can best be indicated by an illustration or two out of the Connecticut Sunday-school field, at a time when I had a closer knowledge than now of that particular field.

I will not name the localities, for the passing years may have changed the state of things in each of them. I will simply describe them as I was familiar with them. One of these Sunday-schools was in a manufacturing village, with a sweep of farming country about it.   It was one of four or five Sunday-schools in the village, and there were other Sunday-schools in the country beyond. It had a membership of about two hundred (which was fully up to the average for such a congregation as that with which it was connected), when a superintendent of some experience in city mission methods was put in charge of it.   At once he set himself at improving the Sunday-school, and at extending its membership.   He sought and secured the co-work of his scholars in his evangelizing.   He asked them to invite to their Sunday-school any child, or other person, who attended no Sunday-school or other church service elsewhere.   Each new comer thus brought in, received a certificate of membership in the school; while the scholar who had brought in the new comer received a certificate of that fact, not by way of reward, but as a simple recognition of the service rendered to the school.   The numbers in attendance increased steadily.

One Sunday a little girl scholar came to the superintendent asking if she could receive a certificate if she brought her father in.   "Certainly," was the prompt response; and the next Sunday the child led in her father, who received his certificate of membership, while she received hers of recognition.   The warm welcome given to the father so won his heart that he asked if he should have a certificate if he brought in his wife.   "Of course you shall," said the superintendent; and so both parents became scholars in that Sunday-school.   Nor did the ingathering stop there; for cousins and uncles and aunts were added from that family circle, until twelve in all were of the school membership.   At the close of a year that Sunday-school had three hundred members instead of two, while no other Sunday-school in or near the village had lost in numbers.

Non-church-goers came to be Sunday-school scholars there. New comers to the village were at once invited to the Sunday-school. In one instance a family which landed in New York from a foreign shore on Thursday, reached that village on Saturday evening; and the next day every member of that family was in the Sunday-school, led in by an enthusiastic and watchful scholar who was himself a foreigner. Parents and children from the country borders of the township were looked up and invited to the Sunday-school. As the Sunday-school hour, at the close of the forenoon service, approached, there would be a quiet gathering about the church door waiting for that Sunday-school to begin. Nor was *this* other than a gratifying sign; for there were some there who could not understand the language of the preacher, while they would be taught in their own tongue in the Sunday-school; others had walked three, four, and five miles,—mothers bringing their children in their arms, or leading them by their side,—unable to reach the earlier service, but ready to be in the Sunday-school and at the afternoon service which followed it; while still others were as yet interested only in the Sunday-school, but through it they were being led to an interest in all the services of the church. In fact, it may be said, just here, that a Sunday-school can hardly be doing its proper work unless it has more or fewer scholars who as yet have little love for any other service than the Sunday-school itself, which is so far their only linking with the services of the sanctuary, or with its religion. In this very way it is that a Sunday-school becomes a feeder to the congregation, and so also to the church.

The Sunday-school of which I am speaking grew to four hundred members, then to five hundred, then to more than even that. Many of those who were brought in from outside by its evangelistic work became active members of the church. The church of which that Sunday-school was a part grew in numbers and influence. Other Sunday-schools of the village and beyond were also the gainers by the new life in that school. The entire village and the entire township felt the impulse of this movement in the direction of a right use of the Sunday-school, as an evangelizing and as a training agency of the church. And what was done to extenc the membership of that Sunday-school might be doing, and ought to be doing, in lesser or larger measure, in every similar community to-day. Indeed, without some such work, no church, anywhere, can have its proper Sunday-school membership.

The second instance which I cite, is that of a Sunday-school in a purely country township, a township without a village in it. The superintendent of this Sunday-school had no city-mission experience; nor had he any special fitness for his place, save a quiet, earnest persistency of purpose. He was lacking in personal magnetism, and was slow and heavy in his manners. His Sunday-school was a small one, having, say, forty or fifty scholars, when he was chosen as its superintendent. He wanted the school membership increased; but he knew of no other way of bringing this about, except by going for one person at a time and sticking at him until he had him in as a scholar. He fastened his eyes, for example, on

'Squire Brown, who ought to be in Sunday-school on his own account, and as a means of bringing others in. He invited 'Squire Brown, accordingly, to join one of the Bible classes. Then he asked 'Squire Brown's wife to urge her husband to accept his invitation. If this was not sufficient, he had 'Squire Brown's children ask their father to come to their Sunday-school. Then, perhaps, he induced other members of the Bible-class to join in the same request; and he went to the pastor to have him say a word in that direction to 'Squire Brown. This work was followed up untiringly, as though the superintendent were really living only to the end of seeing 'Squire Brown in the Sunday-school. When 'Squire Brown finally came in, as he was pretty sure to do, there was at once another outsider—from the congregation or in the field beyond it—on whom the superintendent's eye was fixed; and the same process was repeated with him.

This was slow work, but it was sure work, and it was a work which any determined man can do. As the superintendent grew gray in the service, the membership of his Sunday-school was enlarged. At last he had one hundred and fifty persons in that school, a number equal to fully nine-tenths of the entire congregation; and the Sunday-school was called the "Banner Sunday-school" of the county. It had evangelized a large portion of the country population of its township, while it had quickened the life of the church of which it was a part; and it had illustrated a work which ought to be going on in every country township of America.

In all our country townships, peculiarly so in our Atlantic coast states, each church is a centre of light, illuminating the disk of a larger or smaller circle. Be-

yond the circumference of these circles, and in the inter-
stitial spaces between them, there are regions of moral
dimness, if not of absolute darkness, because of the lack
of direct influence from the church upon the dwellers
there.   Some of these neighborhoods are known by
such designations as "Hell Hollow," "Devil's Corner,"
"Sodom," and the like.   Still more of them are recognized simply as neglected or unevangelized districts.   In
wellnigh every such region, all our country over, there
are children and youth who ought to be of the Sunday-
school membership of their township, and who could be
secured to that membership if proper provision and effort
were made in their behalf by the churches near them.

In many an instance these little ones could not be expected to attend the Sunday-school at the church centre,
but they could easily be gathered into neighborhood or
branch Sunday-schools in their immediate vicinity.   The
Sunday-school membership of no church is in any sense
complete, unless it includes the children and youth of the
outside neighborhoods which are of its proper field of
labor,—that is of the entire field which can easier be
reached by it than by any other church; even though
from two to ten branch Sunday-schools have to be started
in order to secure this additional membership.   And
only by some such method of home evangelism as this,
can our American communities be brought under and
held by the training influence of the Church of Christ.
It is within bounds to say, that there are at least two or
three millions of children and youth now outside of the
Sunday-school, who could be added to its membership
within the current year by systematic and persistent
efforts in their behalf, by the churches of America already

professing an interest in Sunday-school work. And obviously there would be a better prospect of bringing into the church fold the parents of these children through their children's winsome leading, than of reaching the parents in such out-of-the-way places without the help of their children's potent influence.

Closely linked with this question of the proper membership of the Sunday-school, is the question of the Sunday-school's proper management. Because the Sunday-school is a department of the church, is in a peculiar sense one of the regular services of the church, the management of the Sunday-school naturally vests in the local church. The chief services of the church are worship, teaching, and preaching. There is no reason why one of these services more than another should be under the supervision and management of the local church. The immediate governing agency of the local church should be responsible for the management of the Sunday-school, as the church teaching service, as it is for the management of the church service of worship, and of the church preaching service. In the Protestant Episcopal Church, it is the rector who is responsible for the Sunday-school management. In the Presbyterian Church, this responsibility rests with the local session,—the pastor and the ruling elders. In the Methodist Episcopal Church it is vested in a Sunday-school board, as representing the quarterly conference; this board consisting of the preacher-in-charge, a committee of the quarterly conference, and the officers and teachers of the Sunday-schools. In the Baptist and in the Congregational churches the local church itself retains this responsibility. It matters less by what particular method the church discharges its responsibility of Sunday-school management, than that that responsibility be clearly recognized, and be in some way discharged by the church. By one method or another, the local church ought to perform its duty of rightly managing its Sunday-school.

If indeed, as is often the case, a Sunday-school exists quite apart from any local church, and connected with no particular religious denomination, the management of that Sunday-school cannot be from outside of its own membership. But that is no real departure from the principle of church management. Such a Sunday-school simply stands for a local church, for the time being. It is the germ of a church. Those who are in and of that Sunday-school must do the best they can of and by themselves until a local church organization is secured above them; and then the management of their Sunday-school should pass from themselves to the local church authorities.

And what does Sunday-school management involve and include? Sunday-school management involves and includes control, direction, and support; not one of these departments alone, nor two, but all three. Unless this be well understood by the church, the Sunday-school will not be properly managed, and trouble will be liable to follow.

The church ought to have control over the Sunday-school, although, of course, that necessary control is to be exercised with as little show and with as much considerateness as possible. While, as a rule, the selection of teachers may wisely be left with the superintendent, and the election of the superintendent and of other officers may wisely be left with the body of teachers, the church, directly or by its proper representatives, ought to have a controlling voice in approving or in disapproving the selection of teachers and the election of officers. And a like control of the lessons taught and of the moneys received and expended by the Sunday-school, ought to be exercised by the church in its official capacity. It is by no means necessary, nor is it ordinarily desirable, that the church should take the initiative in all these matters; but it is both desirable and important that the church should retain the determinative power concerning them all. Generally speaking, no representative committee of the church could better initiate and carry forward the details of Sunday-school management, than the corps of church-members already engaged in the active work of the Sunday-school; but the responsibility for and the control over this representative portion of its membership ought never to be lost sight of by the church; and whenever it is needful there ought to be an interposition, gently and firmly, by the church authorities accordingly.

The church ought to feel its responsibility for the direction of the Sunday-school; for the direction of its forms of classification, of its lines of teaching, of its methods of work, of its range of beneficences, of the nature and character of its special exercises—its missionary, or its anniversary, or its festival gatherings. It is not enough for the church to have control over the Sunday-school; the church ought to see to it that the Sunday-school moves on in right lines of progress continually. This oversight, by the church, of the Sunday-school in its ordinary and in its extraordinary activities, like the church control of the Sunday-school itself, should be without special show or unnecessary interference. It

should be exercised through, rather than upon, the
teachers and officers of the Sunday-school; but it should
be a practical reality, nevertheless. In the line of this
church oversight of the Sunday-school there might properly be formal examinations of the Sunday-school by the
church authorities, from time to time, and detailed reports
to the church of the doings of the Sunday-school at
stated seasons.

The church which controls and directs the Sunday-
school ought to make due provision for the support and
sustenance of the Sunday-school, including a provision
of time for its exercises, of rooms for its gathering, and
of money for its expenses. Indeed, until a church is
ready thus to provide for the children of its own household, its claim to control and direct those children would
hardly be recognized as a well-founded claim.[1]

The church should give all needed time, time enough
and at proper hours, to the Sunday-school exercises,
in the arrangement of its Lord's Day services. The
Sunday-school, as the church teaching agency, and as

---

[1] It will scarcely be questioned by any careful student of the history of the
modern Sunday-school movement, that the anomalous independency of the
modern Sunday-school is a natural consequence of the state of things which,
as a rule, made it necessary for the lovers of the church-school idea to force
their way into recognition against the active opposition, or the chilling indifference, of local church authorities generally. Now that the Sunday-school
has, in so many places, secured its prominence in spite of the local church,
there is small cause for wonder that it does not, in every case, put itself under
local church authority gracefully and with promptness. Where, indeed, a
church is ready to assume full control of its Sunday-school, it is important
that that church show its readiness to support as well as to control the object
of its new care. A child who has been compelled to shift for himself from his
very infancy, is not likely to be won to enthusiastic submissiveness by the
freshly put claim of his parents to govern him, without giving him board and
clothing.

the agency for the church care of the young, should not be ground between the upper and the nether mill-stones of what are called "regular services;" nor yet appended, as prefix or as suffix, to one of these services. It is itself a regular service,—as regular, as valid, and as important in its sphere, as any other divinely ordered service of the church. Dogs, not children, are to be fed with crumbs from the family table. That agency which is first in order in the requirements of the Great Commission, should not be assigned to a secondary place in the sanctuary plans of the church. Whatever portion of the day is best for the Sunday-school, all things considered, the Sunday-school ought to have; and this the Sunday-school can have, consistently with the interests of every department of church service; for there never is need of conflict between God's approved agencies and plans for the prosecution of his work on earth.

The church should see to it that the Sunday-school has proper accommodations for its gatherings. The Sunday-school ought not to be thrust into the "debasement" of the church—as the underground conference-room of some of our city and village churches has been fittingly designated. Neither should it be stowed away in a garret gallery. Nor yet should it be impenned in the stiff pews of the unsocial audience-room of the church. Fitly designed and appropriately finished and furnished rooms should be provided for its occupancy. If a new structure is needful to this end, then a new structure ought to be secured—at whatever cost be necessary. No house for worship can be called complete as a Christian sanctuary, which lacks a proper place in its appointments for the instruction and training of those whose presence was

14

always welcomed by our Lord, and whose hosannas in the temple he was pleased to approve as "perfected praise."[1]

The church should fully meet the legitimate expenses of the Sunday-school. The Sunday-school as an important department of regular church work should be provided for out of the common fund, or by the ordinary income, which is secured to meet the other fundamental expenses of the church. It is not enough for a church to put its Sunday-school on the list of missionary or charitable causes; nor is it defensible for a church to leave the officers and teachers of its Sunday-school to bear the expenses of necessary outlay in the ordinary running of the Sunday-school for the church. A reasonable sum for the support of the Sunday-school—in its supply of lesson-helps and record books and maps and music-books and library books and printed forms of various sorts, and other needful appliances—should be included in the annual estimate of church expenses, just as surely as should be the salary of the pastor, or of the organist or

---

[1] Sunday-school architecture is now a recognized feature of church architecture. It is no longer deemed sufficient to have a room prepared for purposes of social worship, or designed as a smaller auditorium for use on the occasion of mid-week lectures, which may be occupied by the Sunday-school at the hour of its Sunday sessions. A fitting Sunday-school building is designed primarily and chiefly for the Sunday-school itself. It includes an arrangement of rooms for the several departments of the Sunday-school, and often for separate classes in those several departments, all of which rooms can be thrown together, in sight of the superintendent's desk, at the time of the opening and closing exercises of the school, and again can be separated from one another during the time of the class teaching. There are Sunday-school buildings of this character, which include an arrangement of thirty or more rooms, on the radiating plan, capable of being thrown together or separated at the tap of the superintendent's bell; and improvements in the construction and arrangement of Sunday-school buildings are now the study of some of the foremost church architects in America.

chorister, or of the sexton or bell-ringer, or the sums required for warming and lighting the house of worship. Even the child of the bondwoman was provided with "bread and a bottle of water,"[1] when sent out into the wilderness by the father of the faithful; but these members of the Sunday-school "are not children of the bondwoman, but of the free."[2] Let them, therefore, be recognized and cared for accordingly.[3]

It need hardly be added, that when the Sunday-school is freely acknowledged as the first-born son of the church, —"no longer a bondservant, but a son; and if a son, then an heir;"[4]—watched over, sympathized with, and provided for by the parent whom it represents and whose hope of continued family life rests on it, there will no longer be any conflict of interest, of purpose, or of authority, between these senior and junior members of the

---

[1] Gen. 21 : 14.   [2] Gal. 4 : 31.

[3] A good Sunday-school costs something; and it ought to be worth all that it costs. In the early days of the modern Sunday-school, everything that the teachers had need of was provided for them, while they received a *per diem* allowance for their services. Nowadays there are Sunday-schools where the teachers, while working for nothing, are compelled to bear their own expenses in supplying needful helps to the children to whom they minister in the name of the church. There are, indeed, very few churches where the annual allowance for the entire Sunday-school expenses equals, or approaches, the allowance freely made for the organist and church choir. In the case of a church in the West that voted $8,000 a year to its pastor, $2,000 to its choir, and other outlays in proportion, without voting a single dollar for its Sunday-school expenses, it was pithily said that its Sunday-school might properly cry out with the prodigal: "How many hired servants of my father's have bread enough and to spare, and I perish with hunger!" The needful cost of a Sunday-school differs widely in different communities; but it may safely be said that an average of a dollar a year for every scholar under instruction is a very moderate outlay for ordinary expenses,—including such items as are suggested in the text above.

[4] Gal. 4 : 7.

household of faith. Having received the "adoption of sons,"[1] the membership of the Sunday-school will be ready to say with one voice to the church, "My father, thou art the guide of my youth."[2] And when the membership of the Sunday-school includes the entire membership of the church and of the congregation, all danger of competition in activities, or of jealousy in feeling, is removed beyond the pale of possibility. Harmony of action will come with a consciousness of unity of life. Family and school and pulpit will operate together "for the perfecting of the saints, unto the work of ministering, unto the building up of the body of Christ."[3] The church, of which these several agencies are members, will "grow up in all things into him, which is the head, even Christ; from whom all the body fitly framed and knit together by that which every joint supplieth, according to the working in due measure of each several part, maketh the increase of the body unto the building up of itself in love."[4]

[1] Gal. 4: 5. [2] Jer. 3: 4. [3] Eph. 4: 12. [4] Eph. 4: 15, 16.

LECTURE VI.

THE SUNDAY-SCHOOL: ITS TEACHERS AND THEIR TRAINING.

VI.

THE SUNDAY-SCHOOL: ITS TEACHERS AND THEIR TRAINING.

Class-grouping an Essential of the Sunday-school.— Available Teaching Material. — Child-likeness the True Standard.— Great Truths Best Apprehended in Childhood.—Young Teachers have an Advantage.—Wise Classifying of Teachers.—Supposed Lack of Good Teachers.—Where the Blame Rests.— How to Train Teachers.—Normal Classes.—Practice Classes. Preparation Classes.— Importance, Methods, and Feasibility of the Weekly Teachers'-Meeting.— Selection of Teachers.— Installing of Teachers.— Gain of Highest Standard.

It is, as has already been shown, an initial idea of the Sunday-school as an institution, or as a church agency, that its members be grouped in classes small enough to have every pupil reached individually by a competent teacher; these several classes being again brought together in a combined whole for general exercises of instruction and worship. Therefore it is that the supply of teachers is an important factor in Sunday-school work, and that the number of teachers in the Sunday-school must increase relatively with the increase of Sunday-school membership.

The practicability of securing competent teachers in sufficient numbers for the Sunday-school with even its present membership—to say nothing of the membership as it ought to be—is one of the serious questions in the minds of lovers of the word of truth and of the work of the church, when they contemplate the claims and the needs of the Sunday-school as the church teaching agency. In the settlement of this question, it is important to consider the essential qualifications of the Sunday-school teacher, and the feasibility of training for their teaching work those who are available for this service: in other words, it is necessary to look at the teaching material which is within reach of the church, and the methods of its improvement.

It needs no argument to show that not every teacher of the elementary truths of religion to children and youth has to be a master of all the higher truths of religion; that not every helper to the study of the Bible by children and youth has to be a trained exegete, able to read the Old Testament and the New in the original tongues, and qualified to expound the Scriptures in their deepest mysteries.   On the contrary, it is even true, whether generally known to be so or not, that a profound scholar in the realm of Bible knowledge is not *likely* to be—even if it were *possible* for him to be—so sympathetic and helpful a teacher of very young children, as a teacher to whom the primary truths of the Bible are as yet the chief treasures of his religious attainment.   It is much in this sphere of study as in any other.   It would hardly be thought either necessary or desirable to take an enthusiast in the history of English literature to teach a child his alphabet, or to set a great mathematician at helping a child learn his multiplication-table.   A brother or sister, or a fellow-pupil, who had more recently mastered these elements of knowledge, would have a sense of the difficulties to be met in their attaining, and a consciousness of the importance of their teaching, which the more learned teacher could hardly possess, as he turned away from his more advanced studies for such a simple service. The element of sympathy with a young learner in his lack and in his struggle, is an element of power in a teacher in any branch of knowledge; and in no branch of knowledge is this element of power more obviously important than in that of Bible-study. Peculiarly is it true that, in making clear the simplest facts of the gospel scheme, one to whom those facts have just been made clear has a decided advantage as a teacher.

It comes to pass, therefore, not only that there is no need to have trained theologians as the exclusive teachers of classes in the Sunday-school, but that such persons, if they were available, would not be likely to prove as competent and efficient teachers of the primary classes in the Sunday-school, as younger Christians to whom the elementary truths of the Bible are in a sense newer and so more immediately impressive. It is a peculiarity and a crowning glory of the gospel of our Lord Jesus Christ—a peculiarity and a glory also that are constantly being forgotten by the proclaimers of that gospel—that it is suited to and is best comprehended by the mind of a child; and that he who is the greater as a teacher of the truths of that gospel is he who is nearest to the child in his personal spirit and in his apprehension of the truths he is set to teach. It is easier, in fact, for a young person, than for one of maturer years, to be as a child, in the imparting to a child of those great fundamental truths of the Bible which are easiest received and best understood in childhood.

Rarely has the truth of a child's capability of comprehending, and so of declaring, the great cardinal doctrines of the religion of the Bible been more eloquently set forth and illustrated than in an utterance of the Rev. Dr. Charles Wadsworth, a son of Connecticut, which would seem worthy of quoting just here.

"We . . . maintain that, even intellectually received, or as forms of doctrine, the truths necessary to salvation are best apprehended in childhood; that the intellectual opinions or judgments little children form of high theological mysteries are nearer to the realities, and so truer, than the metaphysical elaborations of the ambitious rabbis of theology. For example, I come to one of these men of academic erudition, and I ask, '*What is God?*' and he answers 'God is a self-existent, independent, absolute, infinite Spirit; without emotions, for emotion implies succession; without dwelling-place, for pure spirit has no relations to position; without, indeed, any resemblances or analogies by which we can figure or conceive of him.' Now this may be all very profound and philosophic, but alas! not very comforting. God is what? An absolute and infinite *Spirit!* Ah me! that mysterious and awful word *Spirit!* No marvel that the disciples on Tiberias were troubled, as through the wild night came a wondrous form walking on the billows, and they thought it was '*a spirit.*' And so, when I look forth on the immensities of the universe, struggling to behold the invisible and to compass the incomprehensible, and, catching glimpses as it were of an absolute and infinite Spirit, am told that it is God, then I startle and stand back in the wild night, as the mighty seas roar around me, as from the forthgoing of some awful and incomprehensible Phantom.

But, sick of this vain searching to find out God unto perfection, I turn from the school of the rabbi, and find me a little child, happy and trustful in its unambitious and earnest instincts. And I say again, '*What is God?*' And the child answers, 'God is my heavenly Father.' And I know better now; for I know as much as I can know now. God the Spirit is my Father in heaven."[1]

And grand Dr. Bushnell gives added emphasis to this great truth, when he rebukes the prevailing assumption that children are not capable of knowing God in childhood. "The true knowledge of God, as in friendship," it is assumed, he says, "is possible to adults, but not to children; whereas the real fact is, that children are a great deal more capable of it. The boy child, Samuel, could hear the call when old Eli could not. . . . Ah! my friends, 'of these, of such is the kingdom of heaven:' so Christ says, and we make almost nothing of it. These children can make room for more gospel than we, and take in all most precious thoughts of God more easily. The very highest and most spiritual things are a great deal closer to them than to us. Let us not wonder, and not be offended, if they break out in hosannas on just looking in the face of Jesus, when the great multitude of priests and apostles are dumb, along the road, as the ass on which he rides."[2]

He who in child-mindedness has freely received the truths which are designed for children, is measurably qualified to impart those truths to others of like capacity and of greater need. This it is which is the method of true gospel teaching in all the centuries. It is Andrew

[1] Sermon on *Early Religious Culture*, p. 9 f.
[2] Sermon on *God's Thoughts Fit Bread for Children*, p. 24 f.

finding the Christ, and then finding his own brother and bringing him to Jesus.[1] It is Philip bringing Nathanael, without waiting for his own added growth in knowledge.[2] It is the Samaritan woman hurrying from the well to the village to repeat her first lesson from the Messiah to her friends and neighbors.[3] It is Priscilla and Aquila, who had learned one more lesson in truth than Apollos, taking him and instructing him accordingly.[4] It is the young men and women set as teachers of Bible truth in the catechetical school at Alexandria.[5] It is the Waldenses keeping up the standard of gospel knowledge in the centuries of moral darkness, by seeing to it, according to the testimony of their enemies, that " he who has been a disciple for seven days looks out some one whom he may teach in his turn, so that there is a continual increase" of them.[6] It is the revived activity of the lay membership of the church, preaching and teaching in the modern Sunday-school, in accordance with, and in improvement upon, the best methods of the early Christian Church;[7] and conformably to the injunction of our Lord to his disciples: "What I tell you in the darkness, speak ye in the light: and what ye hear in the ear, proclaim upon the house-tops."[8] It is, in short, the idea of John Wesley concerning the work of the membership of the church in the winning and training of souls, "At work, all at work, always at work."

A very frequent criticism of the Sunday-school as it now exists—a criticism that is indeed often made to

[1] John 1: 40-42.   [2] John 1: 45, 46.   [3] John 4: 28-30.

[4] Acts 18: 24-26.   [5] See p. 61, *ante.*   [6] See p. 66, *ante.*

[7] Acts 5: 42; 8: 4; Heb. 8: 10, 11.   [8] Matt. 10: 27.

appear as a main objection to the Sunday-school—is that a large proportion of its teachers are young persons; young men and women, without well-stored minds and a ripe experience in the Christian life. And it is probably true that a great many sensible persons are of the opinion that if the teachers in the Sunday-school were all of them men and women of mature years and of developed characters, full of knowledge as well as of love, the Sunday-school itself would be incomparably the gainer thereby. Yet, as a practical matter, if this change could be brought about, it would hardly fail to work to the serious injury of the Sunday-school, and to the loss and detriment of the scholars. Other things being equal, a godly young layman is preferable to a young clergyman, or to an older one, as a teacher of the average class of boys or girls in the Sunday-school; and a young girl of a right spirit can have a power over many a class of girls a little younger than herself, which a mother in Israel does not possess. If ministers and matrons were available for all the Sunday-school classes in America, it would be unwise to exchange for them the entire body of enthusiastic, earnest, and loving young believers, of both sexes, who are now doing God service in that field of effort.

It is not that there is no place for ministers and matrons, for men and women who are full of years and of knowledge, as teachers in the Sunday-school,—for there is a place and a work for them all in that service; but it is that *they* can never hope to fill the place and do the work as Sunday-school teachers, of the best of the young men and women who are now speaking words of loving counsel and entreaty, or are pointing the fittest truths of the Bible story to their younger fellows in Sunday-school membership. This truth is one which was found difficult of acceptance on the original introduction of the modern Sunday-school into Scotland and into America; and it is something of a stumbling-block to the Christians on the continent of Europe, who now are asked, in connection with the Sunday-school movement, to bring into the active teaching force of the church young men and women hitherto deemed in place only as passive listeners to pastoral instructions. Yet it is on this very truth that the Sunday-school agency is established, and on which it must rest. And it is in recognition of this truth—a truth that is involved in the very idea of the Incarnation—that intelligent workers in the field of college evangelism find a gain to the cause in sending on an inter-collegiate mission under-graduate Christian athletes in preference to learned and godly college professors. And so it is that it ought never to be forgotten, that among the best available teachers in the Sunday-school are young persons, of both sexes, who are not very far removed in years, in tastes, or in attainments, from those over whom, or alongside of whom, they are set, in the Lord.

Persons of different ages and of different degrees of knowledge and experience are desirable, as teachers, for different classes and grades of scholars in the Sunday-school; and this without the possibility of an unvarying assignment of certain sorts of teachers to certain sorts of scholars. A motherly body, for example, often has peculiar power at the head of the infant-class or primary department; yet one of the most winsome and efficient infant-class teachers I ever knew was a bachelor. A great deal depends on the native characteristics and the peculiar personal experiences of the teacher in such a case. There is more of true motherliness of heart in some bachelors than in some mothers; and children are quick to recognize this fact. In almost every case, however, there is a gain in having young helpers of the primary department set to reach the scholars of that department individually.

Ordinarily, young men do best as teachers of boys, and young women as teachers of girls. Yet in some cases a refined young lady can control a class of ruder boys, by an unconscious appeal to their native gallantry, when a man could do little as their teacher; and, on the other hand, a class of frivolous girls will be awed into a respectful attitude before a gentleman teacher, as they would not before a teacher of their own sex. Yet, again, there are women who could never teach girls as well as they can teach boys; and other women who can teach only girls successfully. Meanwhile, men and women of education and character and experience can do a work in the leading of adults in Bible-study, or in counseling and guiding adults in their personal lives, which could not be done by a younger teacher. In short, there is a need in the Sunday-school of teachers of various ages and grades of attainment; but, withal, the larger part of the work of teaching young children and youth—including the work both of instruction and of influence—must be done, if it is well done, by young Christian teachers.

No person, however, whether younger or older, or of whichever sex, can be a true teacher in the Sunday-school without knowing what to teach, be it much or little, and how to teach it. And this necessity of knowledge so far on the teacher's part, carries with it a corresponding responsibility, on the part of the church, to secure that measure of fitness of the teacher to be a teaching representative of the church in the church Bible-school. Even if a bright young person be not expected, as among the Waldenses of olden time, to be fitted by merely " seven days " of Christian instruction for the duty of communicating some religious truth to one less informed than himself,[1] he might reasonably be expected—especially if he be of more than average capacity—to learn enough in seven years of wise church teaching to qualify him for a share in bringing others up to his measure of attainment in Bible knowledge. Hence every well-filled church which has been prosecuting its work of discipling and training the members of its charge, by its own chosen methods, for a generation or more, ought to have a fair proportion of its entire membership already fully competent to declare the great truths of the gospel of Christ to the young and the ignorant, and to aid beginners in Bible-study in their earliest truth-seeking. If there is a lack at this point, the church is manifestly to blame for it, either because of a neglect of right effort at instruction, or because of a mistake in the methods of instruction employed. And it need hardly be added that it is the latter cause, rather than the former, to which the lack in almost every case should be ascribed.

A still favorite idea in the church is, that it is what is sometimes called the "teaching pulpit" which should be relied on as a chief means of instructing the membership of the church in religious truth; and where that agency is clearly at its best without satisfactory results,—in the

---

[1] See page 66, *ante.*

growth of the young church-members in Bible knowledge, —the ministerial habit is to ascribe the failure to the poor material worked on, rather than to the poor method made use of.[1] It is a very common thing—I speak out of my personal experience and observation, when I say it is a *very* common thing—for a good pastor to say in substance : "My difficulty with the Sunday-school is, that the teachers in it are so incompetent. Here and there, in my Sunday-school, for example, there is a well-informed Bible-teacher; but the most of them are wretchedly incompetent. Some of them seem actually ignorant of the very first principles of religious truth. And I am afraid it is so elsewhere, very generally."

[1] To rely on pulpit preaching as a primary means of religious *instruction*, is to act counter to God's plan and to the lessons of all human experience. Persons who have had the benefit of the best pulpit preaching possible, under the best conditions imaginable, without the preceding or the accompanying help of interlocutory teaching, must inevitably be lacking in the knowledge of the truths presented by the preacher. Many a good preacher has given emphasis to this truth in his teachings (see pages 89-93, *ante*). Thomas Doolittel, a friend of Richard Baxter, writing on this subject in 1700, said : "Alas! how many hear practical sermons as riddles which they cannot understand, because they were never taught catechetical doctrines and terms in a familiar way, adapted to their weak capacities. The one ought to be done, but the other should not be left undone. Why then doth the one abound from day to day, and the other (tho' an ordinance of God) in too many places is not to be found any day? It is undeniable that a plain, familiar way of interloqutory (which is proper) catechizing, is a more speedy and easie way to cure the ignorance of people than preaching or common-placing upon an answer in the catechism by a set continued speech (however profitable to the knowing) can pretend to be. For a catechist, without vain boasting, (as experience proves,) might say that he (rightly managing this work) can help ignorant persons to more knowledge in ten months, than multitudes that never learn'd the first principles, by following of sermons have obtained in ten [or] in forty years. If so, and we be dying, and people dying, and our and their lives be short, why do we take the longest and not the shortest way? and that which is more difficult before that which must be confessed to such people to be the more easie?" (*A Plain Method of Catechizing*, p. 2 f.) Sure enough, why do we?

It does not seem to occur to such a man that he is practically passing condemnation on his method of work, if not on himself as a worker, in his endeavor to fulfill his Lord's injunction to teach—not to try to teach, but to teach—all the great truths of the gospel to the young disciples of his charge. He fails to realize that he is in fact confessing: "The poor creatures whose only religious instruction is my sermonizing are wretchedly ignorant. After they have sat under my preaching for, say, ten or twenty years, they seem to know next to nothing about the Bible and its teachings. And I am afraid that it is much the same with all those everywhere who depend on pulpit discourses for religious instruction." Granted that the minister himself in such a case is honest and earnest and competent in his sphere, and correct as to the results of his effort, and it remains that his method of work is proved eminently unsatisfactory. If the principal of a preparatory school were to admit that not one pupil in fifty who passed a series of years under his instruction had any considerable measure of knowledge to show for his schooling, a sensible parent would naturally conclude that either a different teacher or a different method of teaching was a necessity in that school. Similarly it is fair to conclude, from the lack of Bible knowledge on the part of those who depend on the "teaching pulpit" for their instruction, that the *methods* of the "teaching pulpit" (since the *men* in the pulpit are above fair question) are by no means sufficient for the teaching and training of those who ought to be teachers in the church Bible-school.

Those who are to teach by the teaching process must be taught by the teaching process; taught what to teach and how to teach it, by the interlocutory method of teaching,—the only method of elementary teaching which is worthy of the name of teaching. Every church ought to have, what many a church does have, a normal class, or training class, of intending teachers; a class in which those who are candidates for the teaching office, or who are likely to become such, are under instruction, in both the matter and methods of Bible teaching. The studies of this class should include the origin, nature, structure, scope, and general contents of the Bible; the main features of Bible chronology, Bible geography, and Oriental manners and customs; the methods of using, of studying, and of teaching the Bible; and whatever else may be fairly within the range of the Sunday-school teacher's mission and labors. Its exercises should include the handling of the Bible as a book of study and of reference; the exhibit of approved methods of explaining and applying Bible truth; and a measure of practice in various lines of wise teaching.

Such a training class may be held on a week-day evening especially devoted to it; or at the close of, or just before, the regular mid-week meeting of the church; or yet, again, in a room by itself at the hour of the regular Sunday-school session. In the latter case, the illustrative study and teaching of the Bible in the exercises of this class may properly be in the line of the lesson of the day in the Sunday-school curriculum. When such a class is recognized as a necessity, the time and place for its holding will easily be decided on—and secured. And such a class, in one form or another, *is* a necessity in the field of every local church.

A class of this kind must be taught; not lectured to or harangued, but *taught;* and in order to its teaching it

must be under a *teacher*,—one who realizes the difference
between lecturing or haranguing and teaching, and who
will be content with nothing short of teaching, in his
endeavors with his class.   The very idea of a class of
this sort is the securing of effective teaching to those who
have not gained needful instruction through pulpit sermonizing on Sundays, and conference room desk lecturing
on week-days.   Hence the method here must be radically
different from the methods there.   Most pastors would
be amazed to know how ignorant are many of their
hearers concerning the very truths which the pastors
take for granted in their simpler ordinary pulpit discourses.[1]   He who is a true teacher of a class of intending

---

[1] Thomas Doolittel, before cited (in his *Plain Method of Catechizing*, pp.
106-109), gives many illustrations of the ignorance of persons who, in his day,
had been preached to, but not taught.   Thus he says: " Now you are a dying,
whether are you going? a question I did propose, lately, to one of about
seventy years of age, upon that which proved the man's death-bed.   The
answer was, To heaven, sir, I hope.   I asked, By whom must you, a sinner,
get to heaven ?   [He] said, By my Saviour Jesus Christ.   I enquired, Who
is Christ ?   This person did not know.   What hath Christ done or suffered
to save sinners ?   [He] could to this make no answer.   I enquired, Was
Christ God or man ?   [He] could not tell.   I asked, What offices Christ had ?
The person was an utter stranger to all this.   I found all that was known of
Christ by this person was Christ's name, and nothing else.   Lord, my bowels
did yearn, my soul was astonished.   I stood amazed to see one so near to
dying, and so confident of heaven, and yet so ignorant of Jesus Christ.   Lord,
thought I, can a sinner be saved without a Saviour, by an unknown Christ !
Can a soul go blind to heaven !   What pity, oh what pity was it, that this
person was not catechized before death drew so nigh, and then had not time
to learn ; for death soon separated the soul from the body, and the body is
now in the grave and the soul is gone into the other world."

Nor is the state of things so different now from the days of Baxter and
Doolittel.   A New England clergyman told me of his conversion to a hearty
interest in the Sunday-school through finding the ignorance of gospel truth
in the mind of one of the attentive hearers of his preaching for a series of
years, when he conversed with her on her death-bed.   " To my amazement,"

teachers will, however, make it his business to ascertain the ignorance as well as the intelligence of his every pupil at any point which is for the time being under consideration; and he will never take it for granted that he has taught any one thing to a pupil of his charge until he has proof that his pupil now knows that thing. It may be that the best available teacher for the training class is

---

he said, " I found her hardly less ignorant of the great fundamental truths of the gospel than if she had been brought up in a heathen land. I tell you, that as I stood by her bedside, trying to make plain to her, in that late hour of her probation, those simple truths which I had repeated to her from the pulpit over and over again, and which I had supposed she knew all about, I had a new sense of the fact that to say a thing explicitly and repeatedly is not necessarily to make that thing the possession of those who hear it " (see the Lecturer's *Teaching and Teachers*, p. 11 f.). In other words, that preacher had found that preaching is not teaching.

Dr. Steel (in his *Christian Teacher in Sunday-schools*, p. 120 f.) cites the testimony of an intelligent missionary worker in London as to the ignorance of fundamental truth on the part of those who have been preached to, but not taught. A young assistant of this missionary was telling to a sick man the truths of the gospel, without any thought that the hearer was ignorant of the meaning of the terms employed in the discourse. " The poor man listened with every appearance of attention, and when my young friend said, 'You know,' or any other interrogative, he replied, 'Certainly, sir,' or 'In course, sir.' My companion appeared pleased with the man's attention to instruction, and I thought it time to undeceive him. 'Mr. ——,' said I, 'my friend has been taking much pains to instruct you, and now I will ask you a few questions. Do you know who Jesus Christ was?' 'Well, no,' said he, after a pause, 'I should say that's werry hard to tell.' 'Do you know whether he was St. John's brother?' 'No, that I don't.' 'Can you tell me who the Trinity are?' 'No, sir.' 'Are you a sinner?' 'Oh, certainly, sir, we are all sinners.' A pause. 'Have you ever done wrong?' 'Why, no; I don't consider as ever I have.' 'Did you ever commit sin?' 'Why, no; I don't know as ever I did.' 'But do you think you're a sinner?' 'Oh, certainly, sir, we're all sinners.' 'What is a sinner?' 'Well I'm *blest* if I know rightly; I never had no head-piece!'" There are more men of that measure of religious intelligence in the much-preached-to and still untaught hearers in the average American, as well as in the English, congregation to-day, than most persons suppose.

a clergyman, and it may be that he is a layman; but in either case his effectiveness at the head of that class must depend, not on his being a minister nor yet on his being a layman, but on his being a teacher and on his doing the work of a teacher.

In addition to the normal class or training class for intending teachers, and as a step beyond it in the line of teacher training, a Bible-class in the regular Sunday-school, taught by a teacher who is a teacher, and not a lecturer, may be a means of fitting young persons for the work of Sunday-school teaching, by its illustration of wise methods of Sunday-school teaching. In such a class the lesson is taught not merely as a specimen exercise, but in all seriousness and from a sincere desire to learn the truths of the lesson, while a member of the class, in bearing an active part in its exercises, is learning how the lesson should be taught, as well as what the lesson teaches; and thus the Bible-class becomes, in a sense, a practice class for intending teachers. One who is in such a class can be occasionally called on, for a single Sunday, as a substitute teacher over a younger class, and so be practiced and tested. In some instances, a Bible-class of this character pursues the ordinary curriculum of the Sunday-school of which it is a part, but takes its lesson a week in advance of the rest of the school. In other words, its lesson for to-day is the lesson which the other classes will have next Sunday. This is in order to fit the members of the Bible-class to teach to-day's lesson next Sunday with some preparation, in case they are called on for substitute service accordingly. And so, in one way or in another, the training of scholars in the Sunday-school for the work of Sunday-school teaching can be going on, and should be going on, coincidently with the ordinary work of the Sunday-school as the Bible teaching agency of the church.

But whatever be done by way of training intending teachers for the station and duties of a Sunday-school teacher, by means of a normal class or of a practice class, the work of training and teaching in and for their service as teachers those who already are teachers in the Sunday-school, must be done in and by means of a weekly teachers'-meeting as a preparation class for each next following Sunday's lesson.   Indeed, without a weekly meeting of teachers as a preparation class, a Sunday-school is hardly deserving of the name of Sunday-school. It certainly cannot do properly the work of a Sunday-school in the Sunday-school sphere.   This truth needs to be recognized as of invariable application.

As was pointed out at the opening of this discussion of the Sunday-school theme,[1] the true Sunday-school idea includes the grouping of children and the child-like into separate classes under particular teachers for specific Bible-study; and the combining of these classes, or separate groups, into a school-whole for common influences and mutual co-work.   Without the grouping into separate classes there is no opportunity of reaching the pupils individually.   Without the combining of the separate groups into a school-whole there is no opportunity of securing a unity of impression on the entire assembly. There must be both class-work and school-work; class-instruction and school-instruction; class-influence and school-influence.   To make sure of all this the teachers

---

[1] Lecture I., p. 3.

must be brought together, and together helped to a unity of plan, of purpose, of spirit, and of endeavor, in their separate class-work and in their combined school-work.

If the teachers of the Sunday-school are not thus gathered, to compare the results of their separate study, and to help each other by an interchange of thoughts and opinions, they are not likely to be in agreement in their understanding, and so in their teaching, of the lesson before them. Nor is there any prospect, without this agency, of bringing up the poorer teachers to the standard of the best qualified, and of giving to every teacher the benefit of the best thought and the most careful preparation of all the teachers, in the study of a given lesson. Moreover, it is only by some such means as this that he who leads and oversees the school as a whole can measure and impress and train his teachers as teachers, both individually and collectively, and can sift out those who cannot be trained by him. With the best superintendent in the world, a Sunday-school without a weekly teachers'-meeting is rather an aggregation of schools than a unified school; each class being in a sense a school by itself, without special benefit from or special sympathy with the labors and attainments, the experiences and needs, of other classes in the same room. There is in that assemblage no one school current of thought and feeling, no one school standard of teaching; nor has the superintendent a possibility of securing this. Unless, therefore, a Sunday-school has a weekly teachers'-meeting, it lacks an essential feature of the true Sunday-school; and its teachers can neither be at their best, nor do their best, as Sunday-school teachers in connection with that Sunday-school.

The time and place of holding the weekly teachers'-meeting will necessarily be different in different communities; yet there are advantages in having its sessions late in the week, in order that all who come to it can bring the results of their lesson-study, and can go from it to their classes with its promptings and impressions fresh in their minds. To have it, according to the practice in some places, as a supplemental exercise at the close of the regular session of the Sunday-school, with a view to a brief survey of the next Sunday's lesson; or as following the mid-week church prayer-meeting; or as a preliminary exercise just before the Sunday-school session, or before the morning church service,—is certainly better than not to have it at all; but it is obvious that a still better way, the proper way indeed, is to take an evening for it, or an afternoon if, as in some country communities, the afternoon rather than the evening be preferred for such a gathering. If there is a comfortable church parlor, or a teachers'-meeting room at the church, that is a good place for it. But in most communities a private house is more attractive. Ordinarily it is better to have the meeting continuously at one house, in order that all may know where to find it, even after a temporary absence; but in widely scattered communities a change from house to house, in order to equalize the travel for all, is sometimes deemed important.

There is no one method of conduct which is best for all teachers'-meetings. But, as already suggested, there is one method of conduct which is never best for a teachers'-meeting, and that is for the leader to lecture the teachers; to give them an address on the lesson before them; to tell them, in continuous discourse, what he thinks, or what he knows, or what he thinks he knows, about the lesson. Lecturing the teachers is very well in its time and place, as preaching to them is in its time and place; but neither lecturing nor preaching is, in any degree or in any sense, a substitute, on the one hand, for a mutual examination of the lesson by the teachers under a skilled leader; or, on the other hand, for a careful testing and training, by a skilled leader, of those teachers for the work of teaching that lesson.

The leader of the teachers'-meeting ought to find out what the teachers already know, or think, or think they know, about the lesson before them; also the points and measure of their chiefest ignorance in the line of their needs for the teaching of that lesson. In neither direction will a leader be helped in the slightest degree by a lecture from himself. The teachers, on the other hand, ought to be made to realize where their own knowledge concerning the lesson is imperfect or is at fault, and they ought to be helped to an accurate knowledge and to a correct understanding of the lesson and its teachings. A lecture from the leader would be likely to fail in giving just the information and aid most needed by the most needy teachers; and the better the lecture the greater its liability to fail just here; for rarely would a lecturer think it necessary to state those elemental facts, or make those simpler explanations, in his lecture, which a questioning of the teachers would indicate to be all-essential to the right informing of some one of them.

Four things concerning the lesson under examination are to be looked at in the conduct of every teachers'-meeting; namely, the text, the teachings, the applications, and the methods of using.

The *text* includes all of the context which is necessary to make the text clear as it stands. Its examination covers the meaning of the very words of Scripture here employed. That examination will frequently disclose some startling misconception, by a relatively intelligent teacher, of the meaning of a familiar word; while it will enable the competent leader to supply the results of his fullest knowledge of the text to those who are in want of it to a degree before unsuspected by him.

The *teachings* cover the truths taught by the words as they stand, extending to the central truth of the passage, and to its subordinate or incidental truths. An examination of these teachings, by and with the teachers, will enable the leader to know the bent of mind and character, and the doctrinal strength and weakness, of his teachers severally, as would otherwise be impossible to him. And ten wise words from the leader at the right time in the course of such an examination, would be likely to effect more for the correction of a teacher's error, or for the supply of a teacher's lack, than ten lectures delivered by him without his knowledge of the teacher's particular need now disclosed to him.

The *applications* are the practical bearings of the lesson truths on character and life and duty. Here it is, peculiarly, that there is a gain in bringing out the views of different teachers, rather than attempting to give to all the views of one. No teacher or leader is so bright that his mind would see all the applications of a lesson truth which might be brought out by ten or twenty bright teachers of different modes of life and thought. Any correction or improvement of these for which the leader is competent, is timely just here.

The *methods of using* the lesson and its teachings are the ways by which the teachers are to present and apply and illustrate those teachings to their scholars. This covers the whole range of the teaching process as applicable to all grades and kinds of scholars. Valuable hints and suggestions in this line are likely to be brought out by different teachers, as a result of their skill and experience in teaching; and if the leader be a better teacher than any of those whom he leads, he can make his superiority a benefit to all by his supplemental hints and suggestions.

The aim and purpose of the teachers'-meeting should be, in fact, to prepare the teachers for the immediate teaching of the lesson before them. The meeting is not for the teachers' first *study* of the lesson, but for a comparison and correction of the *results* of such study. All its methods should, therefore, be directed to the testing and training of the individual teachers, under the oversight and guidance of a skilled leader—be he pastor, or superintendent, or duly qualified teacher.

The feasibility of a teachers'-meeting in any community pivots on a recognition of its necessity. In a city or town or village, there is no practical barrier to such a gathering in the remoteness of the teachers from one another and from the school centre. If the teachers in such a place feel that they cannot properly be ready to teach on Sunday without attending a teachers'-meeting before Sunday, and if the superintendent agrees with them at this point, a teachers'-meeting will be kept up there as a matter of course. In any country community, also, where the people find a way of getting to church on Sundays, or to a voting-place on an election day, or to a funeral when a prominent person is to be buried, or to a circus, or other "great moral show" on its occasional appearance, the difficulty of gathering the teachers at a teachers'-meeting will be recognized as surmountable, as soon as all see that a teachers'-meeting must be had.

In illustration of what is practicable in the line of a teachers'-meeting in the country, a Sunday-school in a New England community can be pointed to, where, while its seventeen teachers are scattered over a field of from three to five miles' sweep, a teachers'-meeting has been maintained by it for nearly twenty years. As to the method of getting together those of its lady teachers who are dependent on others for means of conveyance, or for an escort, the superintendent of this Sunday-school reports: "Our pastor has a team, and he takes all who will accompany him from his section. The superintendent, living a mile and a half distant from his pastor, is always glad to take a full load from his neighborhood; he having had a large spring-wagon fitted up for the purpose, which will accommodate nine. A lantern is carried by him in dark nights, as he goes from house to house to get the party together. Teachers who have teams call at various residences along the route; and thus they are gathered."[1] What has been done in that New England community might be done in many another. At all events, in some way a teachers'-meeting, as a preparation class for the teachers, ought to be secured, every week, in every Sunday-school. So far there would seem to be no room for discussion.

Of course, it must be understood that no training of a teacher in a normal class, in a practice class, or in a

---

[1] See *The Sunday School Times* for February 6, 1886, p. 82.

preparation class, can in itself secure to a teacher that
discernment of spiritual truth, that supreme love for
Christ, and that devoted love for souls, which are the
chiefest and the most important power of one who would
open and apply the lessons of God's Word to children and
to the child-like.[1]   But he who leads any one of these
training-classes ought himself to be so imbued with the
spirit of Christ, and with a sense of the beauty, the preciousness, and the sufficiency, of the truths of the gospel
of Christ, that his words and ways will tend to impress
upon all its members the conviction that only as they are
taught and guided by the Spirit of God can they be true
teachers of the Word of God, or faithful guides of those
whom God has given into their charge.

Moreover, outside of these training-classes for teachers,
whatever is calculated to emphasize in the mind of a Sunday-school teacher the peculiar importance and sacredness
of his teaching-office, and the special responsibility of his
position as a representative of the Church of Christ in
that teaching-office, has its obvious value in the proper
training of the Sunday-school teacher, and in the holding
him to a high standard in the performance of his duty as
a teacher.   Hence it is that every person who enters
upon the office of a Sunday-school teacher ought to
be helped to realize that in so doing he assumes an
important responsibility, and occupies a representative

[1] It would hardly be claimed, however, that a teacher would have less of
spiritual-mindedness through having a larger measure of intelligent fitness for
the *teaching* work of a teacher.   He ought to be able to *influence* his scholars
by his personal character, while he *instructs* them by means of his knowledge
of the truth and of wise methods of its imparting and fixing.   There is no
superior sanctity in slovenliness, and a teacher might have all the more zeal
through having more knowledge.

position, in the realm of a sacred calling. To this end, a formal covenanting of the teacher to be faithful in his new sphere and duties is wisely practiced in many a Sunday-school; and, again, a formal installing of teachers, with appropriate religious services, is a custom which grows in favor.[1]

Sunday-school teachers should be *selected* for their important work, not taken at hap-hazard, nor merely as they proffer their services, but selected with care by the church or its duly appointed representative. If, indeed, it be said that, in a given community, there is a lack of teaching material, and that the Sunday-school must take the best that offers, it will still be clear that even *there* there is a duty of selecting "the *best* that offers," rather than the worst. Every Sunday-school must have some standard of fitness for its teachers; if, indeed, it be no higher a standard than that of a good moral character and of an intelligent belief in the divine authority of the Holy Scriptures. The standard being recognized, the teachers should be selected accordingly.

And, be it remembered, the higher the standard in such a matter as fitness for the Sunday-school teacher's

[1] Various forms of installation for officers and teachers in the Sunday-school have been arranged and published from time to time. One of these forms, as prepared for and as used in the Grace Methodist Episcopal Church Sunday-school of Jacksonville, Illinois, is given in full in *The Sunday School Times* for April 28, 1877. It includes an order of worship, with appropriate responsive readings from the Bible; a series of questions to the officers-elect by the pastor; another series of questions to the teachers-elect; and a vow of consecration to be repeated aloud by all the installed officers and teachers. This subject is treated by Bishop John H. Vincent in *The Modern Sunday-school* (p. 156 f.). A form for the public reception of Sunday-school teachers, including the teachers' covenant, is given by him in Appendix A of that work (p. 291 f.).

office, the easier it will be, in the long run, to secure
persons who are conformed, or who desire to be conformed, to that standard. It is a principle of human
nature to be influenced in one's estimate of the value of
an object by the price which is set upon it by its holder.
If he who knows it best deems it of little worth, others
less acquainted with its value are not likely to think more
of it than he does. The higher *he* holds it, the more
worth it is liable to have in *their* sight. This principle
shows itself in spheres of mental and spiritual attainment,
as well as in the sphere of material objects of possession.
A business establishment which is more select than its
rivals in the choice of workers in its several departments
has more good seekers for position there, because of the
very stimulus and incentive thus given to competing applicants. To raise the standard of admission to a public
school, to an academy, to a college, or to a university,
tends to increase the number of those who intelligently
strive to be fitted for entrance there.[1] The position of

[1] Frequent illustrations of this principle have been furnished in the management of mission-schools in our American cities. So long as the doors
were open to all indiscriminate comers and goers, the attendance at such a
school would be irregular, and the estimate put upon its advantages would
be comparatively a low one. But no sooner were fair qualifications for admission required at its doors than the estimate of its advantages began to rise in
its vicinity, and the attendance on its exercises began to improve in regularity
as well as in quality.

Some years ago an experiment in this line was made in connection with the
Sunday-school of Olivet Chapel, New York, an undenominational mission, of
which the Rev. Dr. A. F. Schauffler was pastor and superintendent, and Mr.
Franklin Allen was general secretary. To guard against the evils of an indefinite membership of roving scholars, a stricter classification of those in regular
attendance at the school was undertaken, and greater care was exercised in
the admission of new members. All applicants for admission to the primary,
or to the intermediate, department, were assigned to a reception-room, where

teacher in any institution of learning is likely to be sought after, by competent candidates, in proportion to the acquirements which are understood to be the possession of him to whom it will be awarded. And this prevailing principle has its application in the sphere of the Sunday-school teacher's work, as elsewhere.

To say that any person is fitted to be a Sunday-school teacher is to deprive the Sunday-school teacher's position

they were to await a vacancy in classes for which they might be fitted. On their admission to this reception-room, the name, the address, and the date of entry of each person were taken ; and to each was given a certificate of connection with this scholars' preparatory class, including a specification of certain duties of a scholar in the Sunday-school. Regular attendance at this preparatory class—under provisional instruction—until the time of a transfer to a permanent class, was made a condition of such transfer. Meanwhile the homes of these intending-scholars, or candidate-scholars, were visited by the missionary visitor of the school, in order to the obtaining of such facts as would promote an intelligent judgment as to the wise assignment of the children to the regular classes. Moreover, even after full admission to a regular class, a scholar was liable to be dropped from the rolls if he were absent four consecutive Sundays without a satisfactory written excuse.

The working of this plan abundantly justified its wisdom. Children of the neighborhood became desirous of finding a place in a school so carefully guarded as this, and parents had a new interest in the admission of their children to such an institution. Soon the reception-room was overflowing with patient waiters; and then another step was taken in an upward direction, by the announcement that only when a vacancy occurred in the reception-room could a child come in there. This induced competition in well-doing outside of the school, as a means to securing the first vacancy in the reception-room. And by thus raising the standard of admission to that Sunday-school, a larger average of earnest and well-disposed scholars was secured in its attendance throughout the year. Thus, in 1875, the year before this plan was introduced, the average weekly attendance at the school was 514, that number being forty-five per cent. of the total number on the rolls. In 1878, when the plan had been working for three years, the average weekly attendance was 574, which was more than seventy-eight per cent of the total membership. And this is but a single item in the many proofs of the substantial gain to that school membership through raising its standards of admission. (For details of this plan, see *Olivet Chapel Year Book* for 1877, for 1878, and for 1879.)

16

of that honor and dignity and sacredness, and even of
that identity, which would make it a place worthy of a
true and devoted Christian's reverent striving after. To
define the special qualifications for that position, which
must be insisted on as its prerequisite, and to indicate
the special duties which are inseparable from its occupancy, at once lift it before the mind of an earnest and
an intelligent Christian worker as a sphere to be sought
and to be filled, understandingly. One of the commonest
difficulties, indeed, in the securing of competent and
faithful Sunday-school teachers is the lack of a clear
knowledge, on the part both of him who seeks such
teachers and of those who are sought as such teachers,
of the duties and responsibilities of the position in question. Hence, to mark out the scope and limits of the
competent and worthy Sunday-school teacher's sphere is
to present that sphere more distinctly as an object of
consideration before those who are invited to enter it;
and to uplift a high standard of attainment and of performance as the ideal in that sphere is to arouse a new
conception of its importance, and of its desirableness, in
the mind of those before whom it is held as a field of
good service for Christ, with the opportunities, the enjoy-
ments, and the rewards of such service. If, therefore, the
Church of Christ would have capable and faithful teachers
in its Sunday-school, let the Church of Christ know and
show what is the standard of capable and faithful Sunday-school teaching.

It may, it is true, be necessary, in a particular school,
to make use of temporary substitutes, or candidates,
for the office of teacher; but even that should be done
with carefulness and deliberation, and with the explicit

understanding, by the temporary incumbent of the teacher's position, that he holds it but tentatively. Until one is fully conformed in his qualifications and attainments to the recognized standard of the teaching-office in his Sunday-school, he ought not to be counted a full teacher there. And when the time comes for one to enter formally upon the office of Sunday-school teacher, it is right and fitting—as before suggested—that he sign a covenant obligation to be faithful in the specific duties of his important and responsible sphere.

The Sunday-school teacher being a representative of the church, and the church being responsible for its representatives in the Sunday-school teaching-office, it is important that the recognition of this representative and responsible position of the Sunday-school teacher be made manifest on the part of both the church and the Sunday-school teacher. It is quite proper that the superintendent of the Sunday-school, as the duly empowered representative of the church, should select and appoint new teachers; but the approval of the church ought to be deemed essential to the confirming of new teachers in their office. And it is in view of this fact that the suggested mode of publicly installing new teachers, and of their covenanting for their duties, has an added value.

In short, we see that there is a need, a great and growing need, of good teachers for the church Bible-school; that the material for good teachers is not as abundant as it might be, and that what there is of the material is not as satisfactory as could be desired. And we see also that the best available teaching material can be taken as it is, and by wise methods be brought to what it ought to be. We see that the church must have a standard for its Sunday-school teachers, and must feel a responsibility for bringing its teachers up to that standard. We see that it is not for the church to complain of the lack of good teachers in its Sunday-school, as though the blame rested on the Sunday-school or on the teachers; but that it is for the church to recognize its own fault in permitting this deficiency to continue in the sphere of its own responsibility and privilege, and to take steps for the meeting and supplying of this deficiency.

LECTURE VII.

THE PASTOR AND THE SUNDAY-SCHOOL.

VII.

THE PASTOR AND THE SUNDAY-SCHOOL.

Meaning of the Term "Pastor."—The True Pastor's Sphere and Duties.—A Pastor's Responsibility for his Sunday-school.—Gain of Setting Others at Work.—Dr. Stephen H. Tyng's Pastoral Work in his Sunday-school.—A Scene in Plymouth Church.—A Specimen Church-school and its Pastor.—Dr. Constans L. Goodell as a Sunday-school Pastor.—No One Way for All Pastors.—Suggested Ways of Working.—Making the Closing Impression in the Desk.—Recognizing the Place and Work of Others.—Getting and Giving Due Credit.

In speaking of the pastor and the Sunday-school, I use the term "pastor" in its primitive sense of "shepherd," or overseer and guardian of a specific flock, and not in its more limited meaning of a clergyman visiting from house to house in religious conversation with the people of his charge. In the apostolic days, while the local church was a less prominent factor than afterwards in the community of which it formed a part, the Lord, as we are told, "gave some to be apostles; and some, prophets; and some, evangelists; and some, pastors and teachers; for the perfecting of the saints, unto the work of ministering, unto the building up of the body of Christ."[1] But with the local church as it is to-day, not merely in the Baptist and Congregational polity, but in every branch of

[1] Eph. 4: 11, 12.

247

the Church of Christ, the clergyman in charge has, within limits, the responsibility of securing to his people the ministry covered by the idea of apostle, and of prophet, and of evangelist, and of pastor, and of teacher; and all this ministry is included in the term "pastor," or "shepherd," of the local church flock. It is of the relation of the pastor, in this sense of the term "pastor," to the Sunday-school as the chief teaching agency of his charge, that I am to speak to you to-day.

It is by no forced figure of speech that a clergyman as the head, under Christ, of a local church, may be likened to the president of a university; his Sunday-school representing the undergraduate department; his pulpit representing the agency of sermons and lectures and addresses, whereby graduates and undergraduates are told of their duties, are guided in their studies, and are inspired to their labors; his pastoral work, in its more restricted sense, representing his personal intercourse, in all its possibilities of magnetic influence, with those under him and those about him; his evangelistic labors representing his winsome exhibit of all that which he lives for, and which he loves, in his occasional addresses at outside gatherings of those whom he could not reach within the walls of the institution over which he presides,—all these lines of varied and important work being given their chiefest power by that administrative ability and that weight of personal character which enables him to be over them all, and to keep them severally at their highest and at their best. Happy, happy, that university which, like Yale, has a president signally and felicitously successful alike in each and all these various departments of university work and of university influence! Let such a university president be the ideal pattern of completeness of service, in his smaller sphere, before the mind of every pastor of a local church.

By virtue of his office, a clergyman as pastor in charge of a local church and congregation is responsible for the oversight and guidance of all the departments of formal religious worship and of representative Christian work in his church and congregation. The services of public worship in the sanctuary, the proclamations of truth from the pulpit, the interlocutory teaching of God's Word in the Sunday-school, the exercises of social prayer and of Christian conference in the mid-week prayer-meeting, and the general religious activities of his people in the direction of the various beneficent associations in which, as members of his church-fold, they bear a representative part,—each and all of these lines of action and of influence come within the scope of his official oversight and of his personal responsibility. The Sunday-school of his church is, therefore, *his* Sunday-school in the same sense that the pulpit of his church is *his* pulpit. This being so, it follows that if a pastor is what he ought to be—or what he needs to be—in knowledge, in ability, in spirit, and in purpose,—his Sunday-school will be what it ought it to be,—in plan, in scope, in organization, and in methods of working. It *will be* all this before he is through with it, even if it *is not* all this when he takes hold of it.

But because a pastor is responsible for the oversight and guidance of his Sunday-school, it is not to be understood that he has all the work of the Sunday-school to do, nor even that its main details are to be immediately directed by him. A pastor may be quite as wisely and quite as fully responsible for the pulpit of his church when it is occupied by another clergyman, of his selection, as when he occupies it himself. Many a pastor even prefers to have his mid-week prayer-meeting led by lay members of his church, rather than by their pastor; and this without the thought that he is less responsible for its wise direction in the one case than in the other. In most cases a pastor desires that the service of song in the sanctuary, for the character and scope of which he recognizes his responsibility, be in the immediate charge of a skilled musical leader. And as it is in these services of preaching, and of social prayer, and of sacred song, so it is in the Sunday-school teaching service,—the pastor's responsibility of oversight and guidance may be, and ordinarily is, best met and discharged through the wisely watched and the wisely aided labors of a skilled superintendent, who is the immediate selecter and director of the teachers, and leader of the Sunday-school exercises.

Under the old Jewish law, the religious teacher of the children, who was in charge of the synagogue Bible-school, was not the chief ruler of the synagogue, although he was subject to the local sanhedrin of which that ruler was the head. The early catechumenical schools of the Christian Church were not always immediately presided over by an ordained clergyman,—as is illustrated by the distinguished case of Origen at Alexandria. All the way down the centuries, it has been more customary for a layman than for a clergyman to be at the head of the church-school teaching service; and if, indeed, a pastor superintends his own Sunday-school, he does so by taking the place, for the time being, of a subordinate official of the church, in addition to the performance of his duties as the chief official of the local church and congregation. Thus for lack of a competent man to serve as superintendent, or to be put in training for that position, a pastor may deem it best to superintend his Sunday-school; as, under similar circumstances, he might feel it his duty to lead his church choir, or to act as church organist. But in such a case it behooves the pastor to bear in mind that his church is not so well furnished, while it has a pastor who is a good superintendent, as it would be if it had a pastor *and* a good superintendent; for in this field of Christian work, as in every other, "it is better to set ten men at work than it is to do the work of ten men."[1]

Those illustrations, which abound, of good pastors who have superintended their own Sunday-schools with rare efficiency and with excellent results, simply go to show the worth and importance of wise Sunday-school super-intendence—by whomsoever performed. They do not tend to prove that it is better for a pastor to be without the help of a trained superintendent of his Sunday-school. On the contrary, they suggest the desirableness of a good superintendent for every church Sunday-school, in addi-tion to the best pastor possible. These illustrations are, in fact, marks of progress toward a better state of things; and, as such, some of them are well worth noting by those who would learn what a pastor himself could do for his Sunday-school, and what he ought to see to it that some one else does do for his Sunday-school.

[1] The Rev. Dr. William M. Taylor says on this point: " In my opinion that minister is the best organizer who follows the advice given by a wise old pastor to a young brother in the ministry,—' Young man, never do yourself what you can get another to do for you as well.' " Even if the work could be better done by one's self than by another, it would be well to set the poorer worker at learning how to do it, by doing it as well as he can.

Dr. Stephen H. Tyng, Senior, is perhaps as good an illustration as could be named of an American pastor who, as a rule, preferred to superintend his own Sunday-school, and who continued to do so with rare ability and effectiveness for a series of years. His first pastorate was begun, in 1829, over St. Paul's Protestant Episcopal Church in Philadelphia; a church in which Sunday-schools, in a somewhat primitive form, had been conducted since 1816. To those schools, as reorganized by himself, Dr. Tyng devoted much time and attention, and with gratifying results. But it was when he was called to have charge of the Church of the Epiphany, in the same city, at the time of its founding, in 1834, that Dr. Tyng was first enabled to give to the Sunday-school the place to which he deemed it entitled in the plans of the church, and in the affections of the pastor. "That church," he says, "was founded upon the Sunday-school. Its energy and strength were given to the [Sunday-] school. Previously, the Sunday-school had been [generally] considered an appendage to the church, and by some ministers and members a troublesome appendage. We founded *this* church with the distinct understanding and plan, that the Sunday-school should be the main and prominent object of regard, and its convenience and successful operation thoroughly provided for; and we carried out this principle completely." [1]

A half-century's history of the church thus founded has given evidence of the wisdom of its primary methods of evangelism and of Christian training, through the divinely appointed church-school agency. During the

[1] Dr. Tyng's *Forty Years' Experience in Sunday-schools*, pp. 10-12.

eleven years of his continuance with this church, Dr. Tyng devoted one evening in the week to the instruction of his Sunday-school teachers; he was always present at the morning session of his Sunday-school (the school having two sessions every Sunday); he taught a Bible-class composed of women; and he gave a monthly address to the Sunday-school, at the time of one of its sessions. When he left Philadelphia, for New York, in 1845, this Sunday-school had nearly thirty-folded under his super-vision; and in looking back upon his Philadelphia min-istry, he could say that no part of it seemed to him "to have been so remunerative and happy" as that in con-nection with the Sunday-schools of his charge there.[1]

In St. George's Church, New York, to which Dr. Tyng was called from Philadelphia, the Sunday-school had been prominent under the Rev. Dr. Milnor. But when the church organization was removed up-town, from Beekman Street, soon after Dr. Tyng's assuming its charge, a new start was taken with it, with the Sunday-school as its basis rather than as an appendage to it. "Our new enterprise," he says, "was in its very founda-tion and purpose, like the Epiphany, a Sunday-school church." In five years the Sunday-school, which was begun with about thirty children, had increased to a membership of more than a thousand. A mission-school was started by it, which soon numbered about five hundred. The aggregate of these schools continued much the same for years, even though ten other Sunday-schools were meantime gathered by other churches in the neighborhood of these. For a while, Dr. Tyng had a

[1] Dr. Tyng's *Forty Years' Experience in Sunday-schools*, p. 13 f.

layman as the superintendent of his church Sunday-school. Later, he was its superintendent as well as its pastor.

Thirteen years after the up-town Sunday-school of St. George's Church was organized, Dr. Tyng said, of his pastoral connection with it: "From the commencement of this school, I have never failed to go through all these rooms and classes [weekly], and to maintain a personal inspection and oversight of the whole operation in all its branches and its practical details. For the last three years I have given my whole time and presence to their actual personal management, during the whole period of the session. If you should be disposed to ask why I have undertaken this additional labor, I can only say, because my whole experience of the operation has so enlarged my sense of its importance, and my affectionate interest therein, that I have felt it a vast pleasure and enjoyment to be myself personally and constantly engaged in its duties and its success. I have around me valued laymen whom I should be glad to see earnestly at work, and very faithful teachers who are constantly so. But thus far, neither the amount of actual toil, nor the importance of keeping the lay power of the church engaged, has been sufficient to overcome my own selfish delight in the occupation, or my unwillingness to relinquish it. Perhaps in this I have been wrong, But I have seen some very blessed and valuable results arising from the labors thus pursued." [1]

I am not citing these experiences and opinions of Dr. Tyng as illustrating the ideal pastor in his relation to the

[1] Dr. Tyng's *Forty Years' Experience in Sunday-schools*, pp. 16-22.

Sunday-school work; but I refer to them as indicative of an estimate of the Sunday-school in its relation to church life and to church progress which was the basis of Dr. Tyng's pastoral work, an estimate which I deem justified by Scripture, by experience, and by reason. Holding that estimate of the Sunday-school, a wise pastor could, with things as they now are, improve on Dr. Tyng's method of pastoral supervision of the Sunday-school work, by securing the doing of that work by trained laymen, where Dr. Tyng preferred to do it all himself. But Dr. Tyng obviously did better for his church while he was its pastor, by giving such prominence to his Sunday-school, even though he failed to train laymen for its chief direction, than he could have done by leaving that Sunday-school without the personal sympathy and oversight of its pastor, whoever might have superintended it.

As I stood with him, on one occasion, twenty years or so ago, looking in at the door of his main Sunday-school room at St. George's, Dr. Tyng said to me with honest pride, as his eye swept over all the classes of that busy throng: "Every teacher in this room started under my eye as a scholar in the infant-class. I have trained them all, myself; and I know them all; and they know me. They are my children in the faith." And again he told me that he knew of more than fifty ministers of Christ who had been under his oversight as scholars in that infant class. There is an element of pastoral power in that kind of Sunday-school training work, which every pastor would do well to make available in his field by one method or by another. That is the truth I would emphasize from Dr. Tyng's experience and opinions. He practically covered the ground of his philosophy of pastoral work in connection with the Sunday-school, when he said in a public address, on one occasion: "For years, if the choice before me in my work as a pastor, has been between one child and two adults, I have always been ready to take the child."

Indeed, it may be worth while just here to give more fully the circumstances of the address in which this remark of Dr. Tyng's was made. It was at an annual convention of the Sunday-school teachers of New York State, held in Brooklyn, in the autumn of 1858, now nearly thirty years ago. The closing evening of the convention was given to a public meeting in Plymouth Church, to be addressed by the Rev. Henry Ward Beecher, the Rev. Dr. Stephen H. Tyng, and the Rev. Dr. Richard S. Storrs. The house was packed to its utmost capacity. Dr. Tyng was delayed in his reaching the house, so that Mr. Beecher was well into his address before Dr. Tyng took a seat behind him as a listener. Mr. Beecher said that the longer he lived the more he valued those sermons preached where one man was the minister and one man was the congregation; where the preaching was face to face and eye to eye, with a "Thou art the man!" as its unmistakable application; and it was the opportunity of such preaching as this that gave the Sunday-school teacher a peculiar power, which he, as a pulpit preacher to a large congregation, often envied. But Mr. Beecher went on to say that, as things were, his work was in the pulpit, and with adults; therefore he was compelled to leave this face-to-face work with children to other persons in the field of his church and congregation. All of this was said by Mr. Beecher before Dr. Tyng arrived. Then Mr. Beecher proceeded to give an admirable exhibit of the Sunday-school teacher's spirit and work, to which Dr. Tyng listened with interest.

At the opening of his immediately following address, Dr. Tyng referred, in his stately and graceful way, to the genius and eloquence of the speaker who had preceded him, and who, as he expressed it, had, in his remarks, not only touched the entire circumference of the evening's theme, but filled the whole disk within. Then he launched out upon the subject for himself, telling of his uniform preference for one child rather than for two adults, as already mentioned. "It seems to me," said Dr. Tyng, "that the Devil would never ask anything more of a minister than to have him feel that his mission was chiefly to the grown-up members of his congregation, while some one else was to look after the children." The patness of this thrust, at the admission made by Mr. Beecher before Dr. Tyng's arrival, was palpable to the audience, and it was greeted with a ripple of involuntary laughter. Stimulated by this responsiveness, while unsuspicious of its cause, Dr. Tyng followed up his hit with his wonted vigor. Pointing down to the main entrance door before him, of the Plymouth Church auditorium, he hissed out his satirical sentences with that peculiar intensity of his: "I can see the Devil looking in at that door, and saying to the minister on this platform, 'Now you just stand there and fire away at the old folks, and I'll go around and steal away the little ones—as the Indians steal ducks, swimming under them, catching them by the legs, and pulling them under.'"

Sitting by Mr. Beecher's side, while this speech was making, I saw that for once he felt that the laugh was fairly on him, in his own church. He met the case

17

gracefully, by coming forward, at the close of Dr. Tyng's address, and admitting that the hit was a fair one. "I wondered," he said, "what Dr. Tyng was up to, when he covered me all over with 'soft soap,' to begin with; but I found out before he was through. He was only doing as the anaconda does, when it licks its victim all over, from head to foot, in order to swallow the poor creature down at a single gulp." But aside from any question of the pertinency of those remarks of Dr. Tyng to Mr. Beecher personally, as a pastor, they certainly cover a truth which ought not to be overlooked by pastors generally.

Another illustration of a Sunday-school made the centre of the pastor's church work, and superintended by the pastor himself with rare success, is worthy of note in this connection. The pastor's name I withhold at his own request; but I will say that, before he was a pastor, he had that training as a school teacher which Luther wished for every pastor. His school I describe as I saw it some years ago; for I understand that its methods have not been changed materially since that time.

The church Sunday-school, in this instance, is distinctively a *church* Sunday-school, for the training of the children and of the child-like in the church and congregation. Mission work among the young in the community about this Sunday-school is carried on by itself; but that work is not deemed the work of the church Sunday-school. Scholars are admitted as full members of this Sunday-school only on passing a required examination; and they retain their membership only by faithfulness in the discharge of recognized duties in the Sunday-school. Although the denomination of this church is one that would be classed as non-liturgical, the examination prescribed in this school is on an arranged liturgy, or series of recitative exercises, including the Ten Commandments, the Beatitudes, the Prodigal Son, the Judgment, the Apostles' Creed, the Lord's Prayer, and other kindred selections; all of which must be accurately memorized, ready for use in public recitation whenever called for. Until new scholars are proficient in these exercises, and have shown by a satisfactory probation, for a specified term, that they are willing to conform to the school regulations, they are counted as visitors, receiving attention from the teachers, but not being sharers in all the privileges of the school.

The lessons of the Sunday-school are arranged by the pastor, according to his own preference, in the line of a systematic study of the Scriptures. With each Sunday's lesson, brief explanatory or illustrative passages of Scripture are noted for reading in the household. A hymn for the month is also selected by the pastor, to be printed with the list of lessons and home-readings; and this hymn, together with the lesson-text, must be memorized by teachers and scholars alike, as one of the conditions of continued membership in the Sunday-school. The lesson-hymn for the month is, by the way, used in the weekly prayer-meeting of the church, as well as in the Sunday-school exercises; for the Sunday-school in that church is vitally connected with every department of church work and church worship.

On Friday evening of each week the pastor-superintendent meets his teachers, to lead them in their mutual preparation for their Sunday teaching service. Here it is that his peculiar power as a teacher, and as a teacher

of teachers, shows itself at its best. It is no lecture on
the lesson that he gives them in this teachers'-meeting.
On the contrary, he finds out what they know, and what
they need to know, individually, in the line of their teaching work. Then he helps them to learn, and he shows
them how to teach. He, as a teacher, trains them to be
teachers. This work of his they appreciate, and they
avail themselves of it gratefully. For a series of years
the average attendance at this meeting has been considerably more than a majority of the entire number of
teachers in the Sunday-school.

The theme of the day's lesson, which has been the
theme of the week's home study, is often made the theme
of the pastor's Sunday morning discourse, following the
chief service of worship in the sanctuary. Then, after an
intermission, the Sunday-school gathers under the pastor's lead. Selections from the school liturgy are recited
by teachers and scholars in unison, at the pastor's call—
all from memory. The pastor's prayer is repeated after
him by the school, sentence by sentence, in its offering;
and it is followed by the Lord's Prayer, in concert. At
the close of the period of class lesson-study, a call is made
for the perfect classes to rise. "Perfectness" here indi-
cates conformity to a specified standard, in attendance,
conduct, recitation, and an offering to the Lord's treasury.
The perfect classes, having been commended, retire from
the room, leaving the imperfect classes there. Individually perfect scholars, out of imperfect classes, are then
asked to rise, and are permitted to retire. Finally, the
imperfect scholars are conversed with individually according to their several needs, and then dismissed.

A close system of marking is kept up in this Sunday-school, and a careful record of the results is disclosed at the end of each year. If a scholar seems needlessly imperfect, without a spirit of reformation, he loses the privileges of the school in whole or in part. The full term of a school course in this Sunday-school is six years. Its close receives recognition, and the due reward of scholars, by the church. As the Sunday-school has recently concluded its fourth term of six years, with its numbers and its interest well sustained, its history furnishes added proof of the truth already noted, that under good leadership a Sunday-school can more surely, if not more easily, be held to a high standard than to a lower one.

With all that the pastor, in this instance, does for his Sunday-school by his personal presence and labors, he does not forget to set and train others at work in various departments of its management and conduct. The chief value of this Sunday-school as an illustration, in my present reference to it, is, however, as showing that a pastor can, if he has the will and the ability, make the Sunday-school the central agency for the church training of the children and youth of his charge, and for the improvement and unifying of household religious instruction and influence in their behalf.

If, in such a lecture as this, I were merely to tell of what a pastor ought to do, or of what he might do, for his Sunday-school, as though I were presenting my own ideal of a pastor's work in this line, a very natural criticism upon my course would be—especially on the part of those whose experiences were farthest from the standard thus held up: "Oh! that is all very well in theory, but it is not practicable. A minister who would attempt to do for his Sunday-school all that you propose for him, would have to neglect his other more important duties as a preacher and as a pastor, and his charge would suffer in consequence." To forestall this objection I give illustrations of the successful working in actual practice of every plan which I suggest as a desirable one; and I cite in its favor the testimony of a pastor who while using it has been more than ordinarily efficient in the general work of the ministry. I go farther than this; I even claim that no pastor can be pointed to, who, in the neglect of all work in this line, has been the means of bringing a church to such a degree of efficiency, and of securing to it such permanence of church life, as are the result of work of this character by the pastors to whom I refer thus illustratively.

Take, for example, the life-record of the Rev. Dr. Constans L. Goodell, whose biography has recently been given to the world.[1] Dr. Goodell was pastor first of a Congregational church in New Britain, Connecticut, then of one in St. Louis, Missouri. In both fields he was singularly successful in bringing his churches to a high standard of living and giving, and of growing and doing. He has been called "the model pastor,"[2] "an ideal minister,"[3] "a remarkable preacher."[4] The Rev. Dr. William M. Taylor says[5] that Dr. Goodell was "worthy to be called the Great-heart of our Western pulpit," where he passed the later years of his life; and that "his two churches [East and West] were admirably managed, realizing, more nearly than most, work for all, and a department for each. He

---

[1] *The Life of Constans L. Goodell, D.D.*, by A. H. Currier, D.D.

[2] *Ibid.*, p. 196.   [3] *Ibid.*, p. 371.   [4] *Ibid.*, p. 192.   [5] *Ibid.*, pp. ix, xi.

found for 'every man his work.'"[1] This "Christian pastor, to whom was granted a rare success in the gospel ministry,"[2] gave large prominence in the plans of his ministerial life to the Sunday-school as the church agency for discipling and training the children and the child-like; and he recognized no duties as standing in the way of his presence in and his personal ministry to and through his church Sunday-school; even though he preferred to be there only as its pastor, rather than as both pastor and superintendent—according to the plan of Dr. Tyng and the other pastor instanced by me.

On this point I speak from my personal acquaintance with Dr. Goodell in his ministerial work in both his fields. I recall, for example, a rainy Sunday when I attended the forenoon service at his church in New Britain, and was surprised at the large congregation present on such a day. At the close of the service the Sunday-school assembled. The number in attendance was fully as large as that of the forenoon congregation; only a few persons of any age going away from the sanctuary without a part in the service of Bible-study, while the number of those who did leave was more than made good by new comers. The pastor was in the Sunday-school on that occasion as always, hardly less the life of the school than he was the life of the pulpit. Years after, I found a similar state of things in his church and Sunday-school in St. Louis. His

[1] Joseph Cook, in the Prelude to his lecture on "Phillips, Gough, and Beecher," at St. Louis, April 17, 1888, said of Dr. Goodell: "He . . . was called, early in life, the model preacher of Connecticut; he should now and always be called the model preacher and pastor of the Mississippi Valley." (*The Advance*, May 24, 1888.)

[2] *The Life of Constans L. Goodell, D. D.,* p. 3.

biographer, indeed, says of this sphere of Dr. Goodell's work: "Probably his labors among, and for, the young of his pastoral charge, were as remarkable and important as any part of his ministerial work. To them was due no small portion of his success in building up his own churches, and making them the centres of power and influence which they became in the communities about them."[1]   He adds that "Dr. Goodell was as constant in his attendance upon his Sunday-school as the superintendent himself." And he says that so closely was Dr. Goodell identified with the children of his charge, that "when he died, a little boy, of another church and Sunday-school, ran home, and said to his mother, 'O mamma! the children's friend is dead.'"[2]

But Dr. Goodell can declare his own views of the importance of a pastor's work in and through the church Bible-school even better than his biographer or any outside observer can declare it for him.   In a little volume, entitled "How to Build a Church," Dr. Goodell makes clear his opinions on this point.   He says emphatically: "He who builds the Church of Christ must save the children. If we save the children, we save the world.   The world is most easily and effectively saved in childhood. . . . Life and death are in the training of children.   The generation which takes the most children along with it for Christ will do most to build his kingdom, and to thin the ranks of the opposition. . . . Shepherds increase their flocks by carefully nursing the lambs; so pastors enlarge their folds by caring for the young.   The question is being earnestly asked, 'How can we bring the men to

---

[1] *The Life of Constans L. Goodell, D. D.*, p. 407.   [2] *Ibid.*, p. 412 f.

Christ?' Bring in the boys, then you will have the men. . . . Seek the children early, seek them faithfully. The pastor's best work will be in giving direction to their life at the start. The pointing of the gun determines the entire course of the ball. There is no escape from these truths." [1]

In describing the methods of a pastor's work for the young, in accordance with the principles thus announced by him, Dr. Goodell says: "The pastor will reach the children through the Bible-school. That is not the children's church, but it is the church and pastor mingling with the children, and laying out all their experience and wisdom and spiritual power on them for their instruction in righteousness. The pastor is always in the Bible-school. He thus brings the adults and youth together, retaining the older scholars in the school, . . . all bound together by mutual interest. That great and widening gulf between adults and children, so harmful to each, is in this way prevented. The Bible-school places an acting-pastor in the person of the teacher over each [class] circle of youth. It affords a work to do which blesses both teacher and pupil. It keeps the heart warm in service, and prepares the whole church for usefulness. It prevents any gap occurring in the services of the church. The young worship with the parents, the adults study God's Word with the young, and all grow up together, homogeneous. The Sabbath-school becomes a constant feeder of the church; the church becomes a garden enclosed about the children. Is not this God's order?" [2]

It certainly cannot be wondered at, that a pastor holding

---

[1] *How to Build a Church*, p. 35 f.

[2] *Ibid.*, p. 37 f.

these views and acting on these principles should have been so eminently successful in church building and in church training as was Dr. Goodell. It would be a cause for wonder if any pastor were equally successful with Dr. Goodell in church building and church training, while giving less prominence than Dr. Goodell to God's order in work for souls.

One good pastor will work in one way, and another in another way, to promote the welfare of his Sunday-school, or of his Sunday-schools. It matters less that he works in this way or in that way, than that he works in some way, and this with a sense of the need and value of his working accordingly. Says the Rev. Dr. Abbott E. Kittredge, formerly of Chicago and now of New York City: "I regard my relation to the children of the schools connected with my church as a *pastoral* relation, and I therefore visit one, at least, of my schools every Sabbath; for I feel that I must *know* the children if I would do them good spiritually, and they must know me, and have confidence in me. I love to take their hands, look into their happy faces, and say a kind word, which may be as seed in good soil. I should feel guilty if I neglected my Sunday-schools, and my own experience is like that of all pastors who love the children, that their hearts respond quickly to the gospel invitation, and that the grand vineyard for the sowing and the reaping is the Sunday-school. During my eighteen years in Chicago, I received hundreds of children to the church, and they grew up to be my most earnest and consecrated members."[1]

In suggesting another line of work in and for the Sun-

---

[1] In a personal letter to the Lecturer.

day-school by the pastor, one of the more prominent Methodist clergymen in our country, whose name I withhold at his request, says: "My theory is that the pastor should conduct the teachers'-meeting, acting as the 'superintendent of instruction,' the teachers being his assistants. Thus he begins the instruction, and gives the key-note to it. He then, as I think, should conduct the [lesson] review in the Sunday-school [at the close of the school session], thus concluding the work by the direct application of the lesson. For all this he should make an elaborate preparation; almost, if not quite, equal to that which he makes for his pulpit work. If it be claimed that this is too much for a pastor to do, then let it be replied that in some other department he should be relieved, that he may do this; for certainly no sermon can reach so many minds to so important and far-reaching results as such a use of a minister's power through the Sunday-school. One weakness of the practical policy in the average church is to take the principal teacher [the pastor] away from the young and susceptible minds of his flock, and keep him in contact with only the older and more fixed people, upon whom he can exert but a comparatively limited influence. Better one sermon a day in the general congregation, and thorough work with the children, youth, and other *students* in the church."

Referring to his varying methods of work for his Sunday-school in the different fields to which as a Methodist minister he is assigned from year to year, this clergyman says: "When I have the time, and the work seems to need my special attention, I am invariably beside the superintendent on the platform throughout the entire [school] session. I preside at the meetings of the Sun-

day-school Board, and offer suggestions when they are, or
are not, asked for, as to the arrangements of classes and
teachers.   I send to teachers personal circulars and tracts
concerning their work; talk and pray with them about
their responsibility, etc.   Where I can carry out my ideas
concerning the teachers'-meeting and the review, without
much friction, I do so.   And I constantly seek to discover methods by which I can secure the most successful
carrying on of that department [of church work], and to
impress the whole church with its superior importance.
Of course, I am sometimes restricted by some fellow-
workers who say my business is in the *pulpit*, and not in
the Sunday-school.   But I manage to push the work as
best I can even under such circumstances; seeking to
bring the teachers to high standards by normal teaching
and other means, encouraging them towards high ideals,
and to be satisfied only with high results.   This I do
with conscientious persistency."[1]   And so I might go on
with these testimonies of earnest and judicious pastors
who cultivate their Sunday-school fields with the most
gratifying results.

It would, indeed, be well if every pastor could, as suggested by the last-cited clergyman, personally conduct
the training and teaching of his Sunday-school teachers,
in a regular normal class, and in the weekly teachers'-
meeting.   But unfortunately not every pastor is specifically qualified for this work.   In very many cases the
pastor's fitting for the ministry has not included a study
of teaching methods, as distinct from preaching methods;
hence, while he can easily tell his Sunday-school teachers

---

[1] In a personal letter to the Lecturer.

what he knows, he does not understand how to test their knowledge, and to cause them individually to know what they individually need to know; nor does he understand how to train them to do for others a service which he is not able to do for them. But, even as things are, every pastor can do something towards securing this training and teaching of his teachers by the best person available for it within the limits of his pastoral charge. And God speed the day when every pastor shall be qualified to do this for himself!

A pastor can, at least, be always, or generally, present in his Sunday-school at its regular sessions, and so be identified with its work and influence, in the minds of both teachers and scholars. I have known pastors who were particular to have their names, as pastors, at the head of the Sunday-school roll, and who were rarely absent from roll-call at the opening of their Sunday-school sessions. Again, I know many pastors who usually bear some part in the Sunday-school at its opening or at its closing, coming thereby into a closer personal and pastoral relation with the membership of the Sunday-school as such, than would otherwise be possible. The pastor whose absence from a Sunday-school session would be regretted as an exception, has a hold upon the hearts of those who attend that Sunday-school, unattainable by a pastor whose presence there would be a matter of surprise, if not a cause of constraint.

To a pastor who has any measure of teaching power, the closing exercises of the Sunday-school hour certainly offer a fine opportunity of pointing out and impressing a lesson truth for the week, as the Methodist pastor just cited has suggested; and many a pastor recognizes and improves this opportunity, as I have had frequent occasion to observe. I recall the pastor of a large city Sunday-school who was peculiarly effective in this line. He was not the superintendent of his Sunday-school, but he was unmistakably its pastor. During the latter part of the Sunday-school hour he would be in the Sunday-school, passing from room to room, with a pleasant word or a pleasant look to the teachers and scholars on this side and on that. At a fitting time in the closing exercises, he would rise in the superintendent's desk, and with a few quickly spoken, clean-cut questions he would bring out a point in the day's lesson, which he would press home as a final thought of the hour, rarely taking more than from three to five minutes in this part of the service. I give an example of his work of this sort, from my memory; not as a model, but as an illustration of method.

The lesson of the day was the story of Esau's sale of his birthright. As the school hushed to silence at the tap of the superintendent's bell, the pastor's voice rang out: "Our lesson to-day"—not *your* lesson, mark you, but *our* lesson—"our lesson to-day is about two brothers. The elder brother's name was ——?" "Esau" came back from five hundred voices at once. And the questioning and answering went on. "The younger brother's name was ——?" "Jacob." "Esau was a hunter. Jacob was a ——?" "Shepherd." "They made a bargain with each other. What did Esau sell?" "His birthright." "What did he get for it?" "A mess of pottage." "Was the gratification to Esau, of that mess of pottage, short-lived or permanent?" "Short-lived." "Would the gain of his birthright have been short-lived or permanent?" "Permanent." "Was Esau's bargain a good

one, or a bad one?" "A bad one." "Wise, or foolish?"
"Foolish." "Yes, that's so. It was a bad and foolish
bargain to barter a permanent gain for a short-lived
gratification. Such a bargain as that is always bad, is
always foolish. Remember that. Never, never barter
your good name, or your bright hopes, for the gratification of your appetite, or for any present indulgence.
And the worst and foolishest bargain of all is to barter
your eternal future for anything that this life can give
you." That was all. But was not that a great deal?

In a small country Sunday-school, again, I found a
somewhat different method from this, pursued by the
pastor in his closing exercise of the Sunday-school hour.
He knew the measure of his teachers from his acquaintance with them in the teachers'-meeting. Standing
before the blackboard, with chalk in hand, he asked one
teacher after another what practical point he, or she, had
emphasized in the day's lesson teaching. As the answer
came back from the teacher, that pastor wrote it down
on the blackboard. When eight or ten different points
had been brought out in this way, the pastor read them
aloud to the attentive school. Then *he* added a point
which to his mind was a fitting climax of the series,
writing it on the blackboard as he stated it. The series
of practical points thus recorded was read aloud by
the entire school in concert. The pastor pressed his
climax-point in a single sentence, and the lesson of the
day stood in a new light before all the school of his
charge. And so in the small Sunday-school as in the
large one, in the country as in the city, the pastor can
do a work of teaching and of preaching, in a few minutes
well used in his Sunday-school, in addition to and beyond

all that he can do elsewhere. The pastor who neglects this opportunity neglects it to his own loss, to the loss of his Sunday-school, and to the loss of the church of which he is the pastor.

Many a pastor shows his interest in the Sunday-school by teaching a Bible-class. This is well as far as it goes. It certainly is better than for the pastor to have no immediate connection with the Sunday-school. But, at the best, a pastor as the teacher of a single class is in the Sunday-school as a teacher rather than as the pastor; just as he is in the Sunday-school as the superintendent, rather than as the pastor, when he superintends his Sunday-school. It is well for a pastor to be able and to be willing, if need be, to act as superintendent, as teacher, or as singing-leader, in his Sunday-school, or even to fill all three of these offices at the same time. But it is obviously better for a pastor, when he has the will, the ability, and the training thereto, to be the recognized pastor of the Sunday-school, over the teachers, over the singing-leader, and over the superintendent, with competent and trustworthy persons under him in all these stations; he giving added efficiency to them all, in and through his official relation and his personal work, as their pastor. Indeed, the less a pastor has to do for a Sunday-school in any other sphere than that of the pastor, the more he can do effectively for his Sunday-school in the pastor's sphere. Hence the chief practical present question for the average pastor is, How can I do most and best for my Sunday-school, while working in and for it toward this higher ideal?

So long as a pastor is only the pastor in his Sunday-school, not immediately filling any subordinate office, he will, of course, as a wise pastor, have due regard to those who hold other offices in his Sunday-school. Although he is over the superintendent, he is not the superintendent; nor is it for him to direct the details of the work committed to the superintendent, nor to control the action of those who are under the superintendent, except through, or by arrangement with, the superintendent. There is no surer way of getting good work from one in any subordinate position of authority than by laying upon that subordinate the fullest responsibility within his sphere, and showing confidence in him as thus responsible; even while watching his work with a sense of larger responsibility for him and for his work as his superior. A good commander, on land or on sea, is always careful to avoid any seeming ignoring or overriding of the authority of a subordinate, within the command of that subordinate; and a good pastor ought to have, so far, the qualities of a good commander in his sphere. What he desires to have done in the realm of the superintendent's authority, the pastor will seek to do through the superintendent himself, or with his cordial assent.

If, indeed, the pastor finds that the superintendent of his Sunday-school is not fitted for his place, or is not willing to co-work heartily with and in recognition of the authority of his pastor, it is for the pastor to decide whether he shall, as a matter of wise expediency, continue to bear with the superintendent in that incompetency, or in that bad spirit; or shall at once set himself to get a better man in the position of superintendent of his Sunday-school. Meanwhile, however, whatever be his decision on this point, the pastor will bear in mind,

18

religiously, that while the superintendent is superintendent he is just as truly the superintendent as the pastor is pastor while he is the pastor. With this understanding of the proper relation of things, there is little danger of unpleasant clashing between a pastor and his superintendent, however much patient doing or enduring there may be on the pastor's part in bringing the Sunday-school management to where it ought to be.

As a matter of fact, the better fitted a pastor is for his place and work as the pastor of his Sunday-school, the more likely he is to be in both right and pleasant relations to all who are connected with his Sunday-school, and to have under him those who co-work heartily with him, while they look up to him with loving confidence and honor. On this point I speak in view of a somewhat extended and varied personal observation in the Sunday-school field generally. A good illustration of the truth may, indeed, be given from one of the Sunday-schools to which I have already referred in this lecture, as showing a wise pastor's wise work; a school which stands out in my memory as one of the best managed country Sunday-schools I ever saw.

When I spoke with warmth, to the superintendent of that Sunday-school, of its methods and their working, he responded in all heartiness: "Our *pastor* has done all this. He deserves the whole credit. He has trained our teachers. He made our song-roll for us. He leads our singing. He is always in the school. He presses home the lesson at the close of the study hour. He brings the church to see its duty to the Sunday-school. In fact, he does pretty much everything." That sounded very pleasantly. But the very next day, when I spoke to that pastor about his Sunday-school, without his knowing what had been said to me of his part in it, he said warmly: "Our *superintendent* is everything in our Sunday-school. He spares neither time nor money to help it along. He is earnest and faithful. He is full of expedients. I could do nothing without our superintendent. In fact, he *is* the Sunday-school." That also sounded pleasantly. Those two views of that one Sunday-school were in a sense one and the same view. Each view was a half-truth essential to the completeness of the other half. And so it will be, always, where pastor and superintendent are competent to and are faithful in their work. They are "fellow-workers with the truth," "in honor preferring one another," "each counting [the] other better than himself," as they labor together in one spirit toward a common end.

It appears, indeed, that the pastor of a local church as a pastor, as a shepherd of the Master's flock, ought to recognize the place and part of the Sunday-school in the organization and plans of the church, for the shepherding of the sheep and for the feeding of the lambs in the church-fold. Through the church he ought to secure to the Sunday-school its proper church control and its due membership, together with needful time and fitting accommodations for its exercises. As the head of the church, he should feel his responsibility for the wise conduct of the Sunday-school, and for the nature, character, and measure of its instructions. His persistent endeavor should be to have the Sunday-school well officered, and to have its teachers carefully selected and faithfully and efficiently trained. He should be personally familiar with the workings of his Sunday-school, frequently, if not generally, present at its sessions, and unfailingly ready in counsel, suggestion, and sympathy, with those who are in immediate charge of its every department of activity. If all is at present as it should be, in the organization and workings of his Sunday-school, it is for the pastor to keep them at that standard. If change is needed, it is for the pastor to bring about the needful change, without unnecessary delay or unnecessary friction. This should be the ideal and the aim of the pastor, toward which his thoughts and his labors should tend. Until his Sunday-school is all that it ought to be, a pastor ought to deem himself on trial as its pastor.

LECTURE VIII.

THE SUNDAY–SCHOOL: ITS AUXILIARY
TRAINING AGENCIES.

VIII.

THE SUNDAY-SCHOOL: ITS AUXILIARY TRAINING AGENCIES.

Threefold Training Work in Every Sphere.— Enlistment, Instruction, and Drill.—Pulpit, School, and Gymnasia.—Gain through Practice Methods.— Loss through their Lack.— Ancient and Modern Illustrations of this.— Juvenile Missionary Societies. — Juvenile Temperance Societies.— Church Guilds.— Young Christian Bands.— Young People's Society of Christian Endeavor.— Gain to the Workers the Primary Aim.— A Pastor's Place in such Work.— Many Members, but One Body.

In every process of training to service, there is the threefold work of winning to the service, of informing concerning the service, and of exercising in the service; of enlistment, of instruction, and of drill. In the lack of any one of these three factors, the training process is incomplete; whether it be in the sphere of mechanical, of mental, or of moral service.

A carpenter's apprentice, a farm hand, a sailor boy, or a young soldier, must first be won, or attracted, or in some way secured, to his new line of service; then he must be informed concerning his particular duties in his sphere; after that he must be exercised, or practiced, or drilled, in those duties. It is not enough for him to want to do, nor yet for him to want to do and to know how to do; in order to his full training, he must evidence his ability to do that which he has been instructed to do, and which he has undertaken to do. A pupil in the elementary branches of knowledge, a student in any branch of art, a novice in any one of the learned professions, must not only be aroused to an interest in the sphere he has entered; he must also have instruction in its principles and details, and then he must acquire by actual experiment, or practice, some measure of proficiency in the exercise of his powers as thus directed, before he can be said to be trained for service in his chosen sphere. In the moral realm, as in the mechanical and in the mental, the work of attracting the individual to right service, and of informing him concerning its details, must be complemented by his practice in that line, or he is yet untrained, morally. A child who is told of the pleasures and the gain of Bible-reading and of prayer, and of the benefits which come from self-denying beneficence, and who has received specific instruction concerning the methods of such well-doing, cannot be counted as trained in such well-doing, until he has been induced to read the Bible, and to pray, and to give to and to do for others at a real cost to himself. As, so far, it is in every other sphere of training, so pre-eminently it is in the training of the young in and by the Church of Christ.

Exercise, or practice, or drill, being an essential factor in the training process, and the Church being divinely set to the work of training, the Church must, as a matter of course, be ready to provide exercise, or practice, or drill, in the direction of its training, for those persons whose formal training it has undertaken. From of old there can have been no other way than this. The three hundred and eighteen "trained" men whom Abraham took with him in pursuit of Chedorlaomer[1] could never have done the brilliant work they did in that campaign, unless they were already practiced in the line of campaigning and of the use of weapons of war. The seven hundred Benjamites, in the days of the Judges, "every one [of whom] could sling stones at an hair-breadth and not miss,"[2] never acquired their efficiency without practice, whoever enlisted or whoever instructed them. In that much misused injunction in Proverbs,[3] "Train up a child in the way he should go," the suggestion is that a child ought to be started upon, and exercised or practiced in, the line of conduct or action which is peculiarly his own, or for which he individually is adapted, if you would have him adhere to that line when he is grown up.[4] The Rabbis, in their application of this inspired injunction, say: "At nine or ten years of age the child is to be habituated [practiced] to perform his religious duties [in order] to make habit [the habit of right action] the second nature."[5] It is not enough that he is already in the religious community, and that he is instructed concerning his religious duties,—without practice in those duties he is yet untrained in religion.

Plato, as representing the best classic thought on this

---

[1] Gen. 14 : 14.   [2] Judg. 20 : 16.   [3] Prov. 22 : 6.

[4] "The Hebrew, 'according to the tenor of his way,' means the path specially belonging to, specially fitted for, the individual's character. Instead of sanctioning a rigorous monotony of discipline under the notion that it is 'the right way,' the proverb enjoins the closest possible study of each child's temperament, and the adaptation of 'his way of life' to that" (*The Speaker's Comm.*, in loco). It is not, Train up a child in *your* way ; but it is, Train up a child in *his* way,—the way which befits him,—if you would have him keep in that way, when he is old enough to choose for himself.   [5] Yoma, 82.

point, seems to paraphrase and illustrate the injunction
in Proverbs when he says: "He who would be good at
anything must practice that thing from his youth upwards, both in sport and earnest, in the particular manner
which the work requires. For example, he who is to be
a good builder should play at building children's houses,
and he who is to be a good husbandman, at tilling the
ground. Those who have the care of their education
should provide them when young with mimic tools
[accordingly]. And they should learn beforehand the
knowledge which they will afterwards require for their
art. For example, the future carpenter should learn to
measure or apply the line in play; and the future warrior
should learn riding, or some other exercise for amusement; and the teacher should endeavor to direct the
children's inclinations and pleasures by the help of their
amusements, to their final aim in life. . . . The soul of
the child in his play should be trained to that sort of
excellence in which, when he grows up to manhood, he
will have to be perfected."[1] Or as a wiser than Plato
had said: "Train up a child in the [particular] way he
should go: and [if you do this, then] when he is old, he
will not depart from it."

So prominent in the Jewish mind was this idea of
practice as an essential factor in the training process,
that even the highest members of the priestly order are
said to have been kept in practice, under special instructors, in the line of their priestly duties. It is even
said that the High Priest himself was taken in charge by
Rabbinical experts, for seven days before the great Day

---

[1] Laws, Bk. i., in Jowett's *Dialogues of Plato*, IV., 164 f.

of Atonement, in order that he might practice himself under their scrutiny in the details of his peculiar duties in the rites and ceremonies of that day.[1]

Our Lord in training his band of apostles first enlisted them as his followers;[2] then he instructed them in the principles[3] and methods of the service to which they were called; after this he sent them out to practice in the line of his instructions to them.[4] This was and is the one true method in right training, and of course it was adopted by our Lord in his work.

The threefold work of winning, of informing, and of exercising,—of enlistment, of instruction, and of drill,— must proceed, wherever the training process is made practical, to the completion of the religious life of young disciples of Christ, to-day. The first factor in this work we may say is represented by the pulpit; the second, by the Sunday-school; the third, by those auxiliary agencies of guilds and bands and associations and societies and orders and leagues and circles, for the prosecution of particular lines of effort, or for the cultivation of particular virtues, which for lack of a better name may be counted as the "gymnasia" of the church, (using that term in its classical signification,) in which the young membership is to have practice in moral and spiritual athletics.

There is, indeed, a certain appropriateness in the designation "gymnasia," as applied to this class of practice

[1] See Geikie's *Life and Words of Christ*, I., 549 f., note *e;* with citations from Jost and Cohen.

[2] Matt. 10: 2-4; Mark 3: 13-19; Luke 6: 12-16; John 1: 35-51.

[3] Matt. 5: 1-48; 6: 1-34; 7: 1-29.

[4] Matt. 10: 1-42; Mark 6: 7-13; Luke 9: 1-6.

agencies of the church, in view of the fact that the ancient gymnasium made provision for the development of the physical, the mental, and the moral powers of its pupils, under the control of carefully framed laws, and under the direction and watch of skilled and judicious gymnasiarchs.[1] This was one of the chief agencies by which the ancient Greeks sought to bring their youth to the standard of the highest and completest manhood of which they had any conception.[2] It would be truly a pity if Christians were less ready than the classic heathen to employ every well-devised means for the promoting of the growth of each individual disciple of Jesus "unto a full-grown man, unto the measure of the stature of the fullness of Christ."[3] It is seemingly in recognition of this duty of the Church, that in Germany, where the Church is represented in the State, the term "gymnasia" is still applied to those schools where exercise and practice in the various branches of preparatory study are secured to those who are in training for the highest duties of a Christian manhood.

Without the results of church gymnasium exercising, the church-membership can never be at its best. So long as the church devotes its energies chiefly to securing new recruits, and telling them what they ought to

[1] See art. "Gymnasium," in *Encyc. Brit.;* also Mahaffy's *Social Life in Greece*, pp. 332-334.

[2] Professor Mahaffy, in his *Social Life in Greece* (p. 330 f.), says that the "extraordinary attention to which Greek boys were liable, made their moral training, when successful, more perfect than any now aimed at, even by the strictest parents. In fact, the higher education of a Greek boy combined, with the best physical and intellectual training then attainable, a moral supervision as strict as that which we practice in bringing up our daughters."

[3] Eph. 4: 11-13.

do, without setting them at work, and guiding and overseeing their work, the church will never be brought to
that degree of effectiveness which is its duty and its
privilege in the plan of its Founder. Force and efficiency in any organization as an organization are always
to be measured by that skill which comes through discipline and practice, rather than by mere numbers. A
thousand men thoroughly trained as soldiers are more
than a match for ten thousand men in a mob, as truly in
our day as in the days of Abraham and of the Judges.[1]
An army is not made an army by successful recruiting
agents, nor yet by well-informed military instructors.
The drill and exercise of the soldiers personally go far
to settle the practical value of an army as an army. This
is as true of the Christian host as of any other. If one-
tenth of its members were what they might become by
wise training, the power of this host as a host would be
mightier by far than it is to-day; for a trained soldier is
more than ten times the measure of a new recruit.

"Herein is my Father glorified," says our Lord, "that
ye bear much fruit; and so shall ye be my disciples."[2]
Not more branches, but more on each branch, is the
longing of the great Husbandman; not more of the disciples, but more *in* the disciples. Any plan of church
work which promotes the fruitage of the several branches
is quite as sure to have our Lord's approval as is any
plan which merely multiplies the branches. Yet this
does not, by any means, seem to be the controlling idea
of pastors and teachers generally in their direction of
church work. They are more likely to find satisfaction

---

[1] See p. 280 f., *ante.*   [2] John 15 : 8.

in those lines of effort which multiply souls, than in those which improve souls.

Just here I recall an illustration, however, of one Connecticut pastor who entertained the less common opinion of the true measure of church efficiency. He was over one of the largest and most prominent churches in the state; but he was by no means satisfied with the spiritual attainments of its membership. He was in conference with several of his ministerial brethren over a proposal to invite a well-known evangelist to labor in their immediate field. He expressed a readiness to co-operate in any such effort to promote the religious welfare of the community. "Well," said one of the ministers, "I hope the evangelist will come; for even if the time is not quite ripe for him, he may be the means of bringing in a few additions to our church-membership." "Oh! that's not what I'm hoping for," said this pastor earnestly. "It's not any more members that I want; but it's improvement in those I have. Why, I'd refuse an offer to-day of two hundred more of the average sort now in my church. But if an evangelist can stir up a few of those I have, and bring them to a fair standard of Christian activity, I'll hold up both hands for his coming, and will sit up nights to pray for him." Even though that view of the case is a somewhat distorted one, it is quite as near the truth as one which sees the chief gain of a church in additions to its membership, rather than in its enlarged measure of spiritual efficiency.

Like all other good agencies of the Church of Christ, these practice agencies, or the church gymnasia as I have called them, have had new prominence and added power in Protestant Christendom since the modern revival and expansion of the church teaching agency. They have never been lost sight of in the Church of Rome, where they have been represented—and too often misrepresented—by societies, and orders, and fraternities for the promotion of the spiritual life of their members, and for the prosecution of various kinds of Christian service—apart from the great missionary societies of that church. But it is only within the last century or so that Protestant Christians generally have made extensive or systematic use of these agencies. They were not unknown in the Moravian Church, in connection with its class-training system, at a much earlier date. It was in 1717 that Baron Watteville, a fellow-student of Count Zinzendorf, started one of these helps to Christian exercise under the name of "The Order of the Grain of Mustard Seed;"[1] and it is even clear that it was through the example of the Moravians that John Wesley made the class-meeting as a practice agency for young converts an essential feature of his new organization.[2] Those Methodist class-meetings have certainly done much to practice their members in social prayer, and in Christian testimony and exhortation, and so far to promote their personal religious training.

It was in the form of juvenile missionary societies that this complemental factor in the training process first gained a hold on Sunday-school workers generally. The children and youth of a Sunday-school were associated into a formal missionary organization, each class being made a separate branch of the main school society, and all were practiced in giving to the missionary cause, and

---

[1] See Tyerman's *Life of Wesley*, I., 196.　　　[2] See p. 106 f., *ante*.

in hearing and telling of its importance and its progress, and in managing the details of plans for its furthering. The results of this kind of effort were an illustration of its surpassing value. The sums of money contributed by the young givers were a surprise to those who had been most sanguine of liberal offerings by the children.[1] They put to shame the gifts of many a wealthy church, and their magnitude tended directly to raise the standard of missionary giving in the churches which they indirectly represented, especially when the children thus trained to giving and doing in behalf of missions grew up to take the place of those who had not been similarly trained in childhood. And now these juvenile missionary societies and bands are a prominent feature in the training work of Protestant churches generally.

It is by practice, not by hearsay merely, that children learn the truth that "it is more blessed to give than to receive;"[2] and they can hardly begin too early in the

---

[1] One of the earlier successful experiments in this line was made, in 1847, by the Rev. Dr. Richard Newton, in the Sunday-school of St. Paul's (Episcopal) Church, Philadelphia, which was then in his charge. Describing this experiment and its results before the National Sunday-school Convention in Philadelphia, February 22-24, 1859, (as reported in *The Sunday School Times* for March 5, 1859, p. 7,) Dr. Newton said: "It is about twelve years since we commenced, in the church with which I am connected, the system of connecting an offering with our Sunday-school anniversaries. It was commenced in great feebleness and great trembling. When the matter was about to be undertaken, one of the teachers thought, ' Well, perhaps, with great effort, we may be able to roll up as much as $25 !' The first offering amounted to $100. From that day the system has continued, the interest increasing every year. There is no forcing : it is a spontaneous work ; it comes up like water from the fountain ; it gushes out freely and fully. It has kept rolling on, rolling on ; and last year the offering was $2,600, from a school of five hundred children and fifty or sixty teachers,—not children in wealthy position, but many of them children of the poor, most of them children of those in ordinary circumstances."   [2] Acts 20 : 35.

line of this practice. I heard the Rev. Dr. Titus Coan, the veteran missionary to the Sandwich Islands, tell of seeing the Christian mothers among the native Hawaiians bring their infants in arms up to the church contribution box, and practice them there in giving money into the Lord's treasury. The mother would put a piece of money into her child's hand. With the instinct of nature —not of grace—the little fingers would close tightly over the money, and hold it fast. Then the mother would take the child's arm by the wrist, and hold the little hand over the contribution box, and with gentle firmness would shake the hand until its grasp on the money was loosened, and the coin dropped into the box. The mother's loving smile and words of approval were the child's reward for its submissiveness; and the frequent repetition of this process brought the child to a certain enjoyment of winning his mother's commendation in this way, and of performing an act to which he was urged. Thus it was that, before the child was able to go alone, he was in the habit of bearing a part in missionary giving; and by the whole course of his training, of which this was a portion, he found the blessedness of being a giver in behalf of the Lord's cause.

It is by methods of practice in the line of Christian giving that children of the poorer classes in the mission-schools of city and of country have so generally been brought to enjoy giving, to an extent unknown in many a rich man's home. It is not merely because they are asked to give, nor yet because they are instructed in their duty to give, but it is by their being exercised in giving, that children become familiar with the delights of giving, and that they form the habit of giving gladly.

It is likewise by the test of practice that, in so many Sunday-schools, children have found more enjoyment in bringing in their offerings for others at Christmas, than ever they found in the receiving of gifts from the Sunday-school, when *that* was the custom.[1]   Indeed, the missionary cause in its every aspect owes much, at the present time, to the missionary spirit which has been developed by its exercising in giving and doing, as a part of the training process in and through the Sunday-school and its co-operative agencies.

Next, perhaps, in early prominence, after the juvenile missionary societies, as a practice agency in conjunction with the Sunday-school, there came the juvenile total-abstinence societies.   It was forty-six years ago that I became a member of an organization of this nature, known as the " Cold Water Army," which had its companies in most of the towns and villages of my native

---

[1] In 1869, Mr. Henry P. Haven, of New London, Connecticut, introduced into the Sunday-school of the Second Congregational Church, of which he was superintendent, the plan of having the teachers and scholars bring Christmas gifts to the Lord, instead of receiving them, as formerly, in the name of the Lord.   This plan worked admirably in his field, and it has been widely adopted in other Sunday-schools elsewhere.   An account of this method and of its workings is to be found in *A Model Superintendent* (pp. 33, 84 f.). Illustrations of the successful working of this plan are to be found, also, in *The Sunday School Times* for January 21, 1882; for November 24, and for December 1, 1883; and for December 27, 1884.   In 1879 this plan was introduced into the Sunday-school of the Walnut Street Presbyterian Church of Philadelphia.   In advance of its adoption it was laid before the scholars in the Sunday-school, in order that they might decide for themselves whether they should receive Christmas gifts as was the custom there until then, or should bring Christmas gifts into the Lord's treasury for the benefit of the Lord's dear ones.   They voted twenty to one in favor of the change.   From that time to the present the plan has grown in favor with both scholars and teachers in that Sunday-school, and it has done not a little to promote the spirit of Christian giving in the entire church and congregation.

state. It was by means of the special training which I received in that organization, and as a result of the reflex influence of my activities in connection with it, that my personal opinions and habits in the line of total abstinence became fixed and abiding, and subsequently proved, under God, a means of my preservation from utter ruin; and I am confident that I am only an illustration of its widespread work, so far. An expansion of the Cold Water Army idea was later found in what is known as the Band of Hope; an organization which has been extended throughout the English-speaking world, and which now numbers millions in its membership, with a history, a literature, and a sphere of its own; its purpose being the promotion of total-abstinence and other virtues. It is in a similar line of effort and method of work that the Blue Ribbon Army, and the White Ribbon Army, and the White Cross Army, and the Boys' Brigade, and many other organizations, have done and are doing a good work in training the young by exercising them in special lines of well-doing.

A reviving, in the Church of England, of the old church guilds, for the oversight and exercise and guidance of young persons associated in them for common effort in a given direction, followed these other popular practice agencies in conjunction with the Sunday-school movement of the past century. In their present form they seem to have had a new beginning in England in 1851;[1] yet they claim a descent from the organizations of the same designation in the Middle Ages and earlier.[2] From

---

[1] See art. "Guilds," in Benham's *Dictionary of Religion*

[2] See art. "Guilds," in *Encyc. Brit.*

England they were brought to this country. An American Episcopal writer says concerning them:[1] "Church guilds, in the ages of their fullest development, always seemed to flourish especially in England. They are therefore a part of the traditional life of the Anglican Communion. And the atmosphere of American society and institutions would seem to be wonderfully adapted to perpetuate this tradition." Of the purpose and value of such an agency this writer says: "The object proposed in these guilds is the maintenance of the spiritual life, fidelity to religious obligations, and deepening of devotion. Boys and girls, young men and young women, are most simply and easily influenced and retained in attachment to the church through instrumentalities of this sort. When the period of adolescence is reached, it is often found difficult, especially in the case of boys, to keep them true to their religious duties. Here the spiritual guild comes in, and through the sanctified power of association supplies a very timely agency to fortify young persons against worldly and evil companionships, and to invigorate their constancy to God and Holy Church. It reinforces moral courage at that uncertain age when it is most prone to falter. . . . The guild will put nerve and sinew into Sunday-school work, and standing ready will take boys and girls, and mould and shape them, as the Sunday-school from its nature can hardly do." These church guilds are now numerous and flourishing in the American Episcopal Church; and they are effective in the line of work for which they are designed.

A mere enumeration of the various organizations which

---

1 See art. " Church Guilds," in *The Church Cyclopædia.*

have more or less prominence as auxiliary training agencies in the work of the Christian Church with and for the young would be no slight task, even apart from any attempt to indicate their particular lines of effort severally, and the main facts of their origin and history. Included in these are the Young Men's Christian Associations, the Young Women's Christian Associations, the Bible-reading and Prayer Alliances, the Bible Correspondence Schools, the Chautauqua Circles, the Kitchen Gardens, the Ministering Children's Leagues, and Bands and Clubs for special service in endless variety.[1] It is sufficient, in this connection, merely to refer to their extended sweep and scope, calling farther particular attention only to that class of organizations among them which aims at bringing the young converts, or young communicants, in a local church, immediately under the oversight of their pastor, for guidance in the duties and activities of the Christian life.

In the Church of England and in the American Episcopal Church, the Young Communicants' Class has long been a favorite agency for the nurture and exercise of young believers, under pastoral watch and guidance. In the Methodist churches, the class-meeting system has made similar provision for probationers and young communicants. In the Congregational and Presbyterian and Baptist churches, the Young People's Prayer Meeting has been employed widely to the same end.[2] There are local churches in New England in which a meeting of this sort has been continued with good results for a half-

---

[1] See, in this line, Stall's *Methods of Church Work*.
[2] See, on this subject, Clark's *Young People's Prayer Meetings*.

century or more, having under its influence generation after generation of young people.

In addition to these more generally known agencies, there have been special agencies devised by particular pastors and superintendents to accomplish a similar work in their local sphere. Thus Mr. Henry P. Haven, of New London, a model superintendent in his way, as early as 1842 formed what he called a Religious Class, in connection with a neighborhood Sunday-school super-intended by him.[1] Its object was "the religious improve-ment and growth in grace of the professed followers of Jesus in that vicinity." Members of the class were ex-pected to attend, if possible, its every meeting, and "to answer in turn the questions of the superintendent on religious subjects, particularly respecting the state of their own hearts." If necessarily absent, a member was "to remember in secret or silent prayer those who were assembled together." Each member of the class was at liberty to invite in any friends who were seriously inter-ested in their personal religious state; with the under-standing that these new comers should be also ready to answer any questions propounded by the superintendent —who in this case stood in the place of a pastor, the Sunday-school being connected with no local church. This Religious Class was a means of starting similar classes, in a variety of forms, in churches and Sunday-schools near and more remote.

Under the name of the Boys' Circle, and of the Girls' Circle, classes for the fuller religious training of the young have been conducted by many a pastor, with exercises

---

[1] See the Lecturer's *A Model Superintendent*, p. 66.

calculated to develop the Christian activity of the individual members.   There are, indeed, pastors of no mean
power as preachers who have made more of an impress
on the people of their charge and in the community about
them, through their work in such circles as these in their
own fields, than through all their preaching, for the whole
period of their ministry; or than they could have hoped
to make had they been ten times more eloquent preachers
than they are.   And so far these preachers illustrate the
need and the value of a complemental training agency,
to make effective the best work of the pulpit and of the
school for the upbuilding of the young Christian believer.[1]

A remarkable exhibit of the increasing sense of this
truth in the community at large is found in the rapid
growth and extension of the organization known as The
Young People's Society of Christian Endeavor; started
in 1881 by the Rev. F. E. Clark, then of Portland, Maine;
now of Boston.[2]   Its plan is not unlike that of some forms
of the church guild.   Its object is "to promote an earnest
Christian life among its members, to increase their mutual
acquaintance, and to make them more useful in the service of God."   From a single local society of sixty

[1] The Rev. Dr. Constans L. Goodell, whose good work as a pastor has
already been referred to, says on this subject (in *How to Build a Church*, p.
39 f.): "The pastor will wish to have young people's meetings and gatherings for Christian endeavor where workers may be trained for special lines of
usefulness, the study of missions, the practice of benevolent giving, and the
art of gathering in the straying.   He will give them printed matter to read.
He will guide them to habits of usefulness.   He will enlist every young person's service in some fit way, where a responsibility will develop the character
by sound and healthful growth.   His motto will be, 'A work for every boy,
and a boy for every work.'"

[2] See Clark's *The Children and the Church;* also his *Young People's
Prayer Meetings*, pp. 100-117.

members, this organization has, in seven years, grown to thirty-five hundred societies, and a membership of, say, two hundred and fifty thousand. It has extended into various denominations, and into wellnigh every state in the United States. It has now its national organization; and with the true American instinct it multiplies its conventions, local and general, as a means of extending its influence and of developing its power.

According to the plans of its founder, this organization aims "to make religion child religion, a natural, rational, permanent part of the child's life; to make the Lord Jesus Christ to appear the children's friend, and his active, acknowledged service something to be entered into and enjoyed by all young persons as heartily, zealously, and constantly as their studies and their games." It is not claimed by him that the method he employs "is the only way, or the best way, to train young Christians;" but "only that it is one way which has received some signal marks of the divine approval." As such a means, this organization has been found effective by many a wise pastor in the work of giving new interest and zest to the Christian activity of the young people of his charge, and of supplying them with added practice in various directions of desirable service. And so far it is eminently worthy of the attention of pastors generally. Nor is there any lack of literature to make its details clear to those who would become acquainted with its workings.

It is noticeable that the growing interest in plans and methods for the Christian training of children and youth, under the direction of the church, is by no means confined to any one branch of the Church of Christ, but that it is showing itself on every side, among thinkers and workers of the most diverse views in the matter of religious doctrine and of ecclesiastical organization. Within the past year, for example, a series of suggestive papers on this subject has appeared in successive numbers of The Church Sunday School Magazine, of London, from the pen of the Rev. E. T. Vaughan, an Honorary Canon of St. Albans, as representing the estimate of work in this line from the standpoint of a Church of England clergyman: and the spirit and thought of these papers seem much the same as the spirit and thought of an admirable treatise on the same general subject, from the standpoint of a New England Congregational clergyman, under the title of "The Culture of Child Piety," by the Rev. Dr. Amos S. Chesebrough, of Connecticut; and these two works are but illustrations of an extensive range of literature in the same direction.

Says Canon Vaughan, speaking of the comparative lack, in his branch of the Church, of other agencies than the Sunday-school for the Christian training of the young: "We must avail ourselves as largely as possible of two engines largely used by others, especially by the Wesleyan body, but hitherto very imperfectly understood and used by the English Church. The first of these is that of association for mutual support and help in Christian living. The other is that of useful employment in the active service of the Church of which they are members." In explanation and emphasis of his meaning in this reference to the twofold training to Christian living and Christian working Canon Vaughan adds: "Those who have been confirmed and become communicants should at once, if possible, be formed into guilds or (under whatsoever name and form) societies for mutual edification,

sympathy, encouragement.   They must not be left iso-
lated, each to fight his own battle with temptation, and
to carry on his own life of service to the one Lord, by
himself, and with no assistance from those similarly cir-
cumstanced with himself.   They must be united together
under some systematic guidance, in societies as simply
organized, and encumbered with as few rules and forms
as possible, and not too large to allow a strong sense of
mutual fellowship in the Christian life to grow up between the members."   And in addition to this association
for mutual help in Christian living, there must be association for help in Christian working.   "The members
of our societies for the benefit of the younger members
of the church," continues Canon Vaughan, "must be
taught and accustomed to remember in practice that they
are called as Christ's servants not merely to keep their
own souls, but to be workers for others.   Their Christian
life must be a life of active service for the good of the
body to which they belong, and of the world around
them.   Definite church work of some kind must, if
possible, be found for them."[1]

Dr. Chesebrough has treated this whole subject with
more of fullness of detail, and in a more comprehensive
view of the principles involved in it.   The point at which
he is in contact with Canon Vaughan, and with other
thoughtful writers in the same line, is where he recommends as a hopeful agency of Christian training for the
young, "class instruction to bands or circles of children
meeting regularly, with a direct view to their training for
and in Christian discipleship;"[2] and where he names, as

[1] *The Church Sunday School Magazine*, July, 1887, pp. 550-553.
[2] *The Culture of Child Piety*, p. 171.

one line of instruction for such a class, the showing a young person "how best to live a consecrated Christian life, intelligent, steadfast, fruitful, progressive,"[1] and as another line of instruction, the giving of "practical lessons" in "the ministries of love and Christian service."[2]

Out of his own experience as a pastor, he says: "When I stand in my pulpit and present, as God gives me ability, the gospel message to adult men and women, I do it in the earnest hope that I may win some of them to Christ. But I see many in my audience to whom this same gospel has been faithfully preached for years. They are, it may be, respectful listeners, kind and generous parishioners, and excellent neighbors and citizens. But they have grown up in unbelief, and have become more and more hardened in their unbelief from year to year. And of these, there are some who sit as undisturbed under the most moving appeals of the gospel, even in times of revival, as an impregnable castle wall, defying all the best aimed missiles. Oh, at what a terrible disadvantage do I seek to save these parishioners! The best time to save them —the only time, perhaps, in which they could have been saved—has gone by forever. To what a fearful waste are all efforts and all prayers in their behalf consigned at this late hour! I go now from my pulpit into my children's training class. What a change! Every eye glistens with attention and responsive interest. The eager, hungry souls feed on the living bread. The plastic characters yield to the moulding hands of truth and love. And I cry out, 'Oh! that those men and women who have encased their hearts in an adamant of a third or a half [of a] century of unbelief could have been subjected

---

[1] *The Culture of Child Piety*, p. 188.

[2] *Ibid.*, p. 206.

to a discreet and faithful Christian training in childhood! It might not have been with them as it is now.'"[1]   In the line of this thought of Dr. Chesebrough, a Baptist pastor of New Haven who told me, while I was preparing this very lecture, of a training class of this character which he conducts on a Tuesday evening, said emphatically, " My Tuesday evening scholars are my best Sunday morning hearers." And why, indeed, should not this be so? Certainly, it requires good training to make one a good hearer ; and the better the preacher, the greater the need of training, in order to gain most from his best discourses.

In considering the twofold work of the church practice agencies for the young, as a help in the Christian training of the young,—the work of training to a right Christian life, and the work of training to right Christian service,—the truth ought not to be lost sight of, that in both these lines of training the immediate gain sought after is a gain to the young person who is under special training, rather than a gain to those with whom he is under training, or to those to whom he is sent in a line of particular service. The main purpose of what I have spoken of as the church gymnasium, is obviously the developing and directing of the Christian manhood of the youth there set at the testing and practice of his spiritual powers; not the ministering to those with whom he may be associated in the course of his careful training. And just here it is that a misconception of the truth has long stood in the way of the proper training of young communicants in the Christian Church.

The Rev. F. E. Clark, who has been so prominent in

[1] *The Culture of Child Piety*, p. 33 f.

connection with the Society of Christian Endeavor, has stigmatized the idea of "edification" as "the prayer-meeting fetich;" because that idea has kept back from a part in the prayer-meeting so many who needed the help of participation in it, but who were not supposed to be capable of such a participation to the *edifying* of those who were present in the prayer-meeting. Yet the Apostle recommends that "all things be done unto edifying;" [1] and the Apostle's recommendation ought not to be disregarded, although it may be perverted by insisting that it is always the *hearer*, rather than the *speaker*, who is to be edified through one's speaking. In the Christian practice class for young people, all things should be done unto the edifying of those who do them. If a young person in one of those meetings raises his voice in prayer, or in personal testimony, or in Bible recitation, the important practical question is not, "Does this tend to the edifying of those who hear him?" but it is, "Does this tend to *his* edifying?" So, again, his giving and his doing as a means of practice to him, in connection with membership in such a class, is to be judged by the standard of its helpfulness to him, rather than by the standard of its immediate helpfulness to others.

It is sometimes suggested as an objection to such an organization as the Young People's Society of Christian Endeavor, that no immediate practical benefit to others is directly aimed at in its activities; that, in its exercises, its members spend their strength for themselves rather than for others. But this objection would have force against all gymnastic exercises. The pulling of chest-weights uses strength that might be used in pumping

[1] 1 Cor. 14: 26.

water. The muscle given to a rowing machine might run a treadmill, or saw firewood. So, again, the practice exercises of linguistics and mathematics in the college class-room employ time and brain power that would suffice to keep a set of bank books, or fill the editorial columns of a daily newspaper. But without this unpractical exercising in these physical and mental spheres, the men who are exercised thereby would never be fitted for their best work elsewhere.

Nor is this principle less applicable to the moral than to the mental and physical spheres. Exercising one's self unto godliness is an important process in the development of a symmetrical Christian character—which shall afterwards manifest itself in good to others also. Practicing in the examining of the Bible for words of promise, of counsel, and of warning; practicing in the study of particular mission-fields, in order to secure an understanding of and an interest in them; practicing in the expressing of one's thoughts concerning some theme of religious interest; practicing in prayer with and for others,—the value of all this is primarily a subjective value, and its immediate gain is to the individual who performs the part assigned to him; but it is by just such practice as this that a young Christian can best be fitted for an intelligent and efficient ministry of good to others, by means of Bible reading, of Christian counsel and sympathy, of helpful fervent prayer, and of participation in the great missionary movements of the Church of Christ.

Yet it is to be borne ever in mind that practice as a factor in the training process of Christian workers is valuable only as it prepares for activity in Christian work with and for others; hence this practice should be kept within its proper limits, and wisely directed even there. Just so far as there are openings for Christian service by the young people, in each particular community, should those openings be pointed out as avenues of usefulness for the young people who can enter them. Visiting the poor, carrying flowers to the sick, looking up new scholars for the Sunday-school, distributing religious reading, having a part in a sewing-school, or in a kitchen-garden, sharing in the missionary movements of the local church, and many another mode of well-doing, will be among the ways which thus present themselves. And it is important that those who are trained for work be, as soon as is practicable, set at the work for which they are trained.

Like every other department of work in the local church, every guild, or band, or society, or circle, which is an approved auxiliary agency of the church-school for the practice and exercise and drill of the children and youth of the church and congregation in the direction of their wise training, ought to be under the oversight and the general control of the pastor of the local church, in all its plans and methods of activity. And just here there are two extremes to be guarded against. On the one hand, the pastor ought not to hinder the fullest and freest development of the personal power of his young people, by any undue checking, or restraining, or overshadowing of them in their proper activities within the scope and field of such legitimate associations. On the other hand, the pastor ought to see to it that no other overseer or director than himself, outside of these local associations, is given the place which is properly his own, as the head of the local church, in watching and guiding the church training of his young people.

Although the pastor is over all these associations of his young people, his best work in and through them all is obviously by means of the wisely fostered and the wisely directed activities of their members severally, not by his own activity as their chiefest member. In this matter, it is for the pastor to show his young people what *they* can do; not for the pastor to show his young people what *he* can do. *His* power is to be evidenced by their evidencing *their* power—under his direction. *His* importance is to be realized, in his bringing them to realize *their* importance—as his co-workers. In the pulpit, the pastor has all the work to do. In the Sunday-school, the pastor has a portion of the work to do, while the teachers and the scholars have a larger portion of the work to do. In the church gymnasium, the young people have all the work to do, while the pastor has the responsibility of seeing that they do the work they ought to do in the way they ought to do it.

While, however, the members of a young people's association of any local church ought to be free from the hindering, or the cramping, of any unnecessary pastoral constraint, they ought to be guarded quite as carefully against a feeling of any responsibility to an organization outside of their own church; or of any dependence on a guide or overseer beyond themselves, other than their pastor. A peculiarity, and an advantage, of the American Sunday-school system, is, that the Sunday-school of a local church in America is looked upon as a department of that local church, having no dependence upon, and no organic connection with, a Sunday-school of any other church. Hereby the American Sunday-school is made to appear more distinctively and exclusively a portion of the local church organization—a sharer in the very life of that organization—than is the average English Sunday-school.[1] There is no more reason why the young people's association of a local church should be in immediate connection with, or should make its reports to, or should look for directions or suggestions from, a county, or a state, or a national organization of young people's associations, than there is why the Sunday-school, or indeed the prayer-meeting, of that church should be in like relations with an outside organization of Sunday-schools or of prayer-meetings.

It is quite proper that those who are interested in Sunday-school work, or in prayer-meeting work, or in the work of young people's associations, as such, should come together in conference, or in convention, for the purpose of counseling and quickening one another in the line of their common endeavors. It may even be well for individuals to associate themselves in an organization for the purpose of sending out and of sustaining experts in any such line of work, in order to the extension and improvement of work of that sort; but all this should be wholly apart from any combining or overseeing of the Sunday-schools, or the prayer-meetings, or the young people's associations, which are established in connection

---

[1] The London Sunday-school Union is a union of Sunday-schools. The American Sunday School Union is an association of individuals for the promotion of Sunday-school interests. In the former case, the local Sunday-schools retain their connection with the national society. In the latter case, the local Sunday-schools have no immediate connection with the national society. The difference in these two systems was discussed quite fully between Secretary Hartley, of the London Sunday-school Union, and the Lecturer, in *The Sunday School Times*, for December 6, 1873, April 25, 1874, and May 9, 1874.

with local churches.   The pastor of a local church is the head, under Christ, of all the departments of Christian work in the field of his charge; and he should guard jealously the oversight of his pulpit, of his Sunday-school, and of the various practice agencies which are co-working with the pulpit and the Sunday-school for the training of the children and of the child-like of his pastorship.

The Church of Christ is the body of Christ. In this body there are various members.   The pulpit is as the head, by means of which the truth is perceived for, and is indicated to, the other members.   The Sunday-school is as the hands, by means of which the truth thus made known is laid hold of, and is made a permanent possession, for the benefit of the other members.   The auxiliary practice agencies are the feet, by means of which the other members are started in the path of duty, according to the truth which the head discloses, and which the hands lay hold on.   The head cannot say to the hands, I have no need of you; nor again the head to the feet, I have no need of you.   Nay, much rather, those members of the body which we have thought to be less honorable, upon these we ought to bestow more abundant honor; for all these are of the body of Christ, and severally members thereof.   And while in and through these members there are diversities of ministrations, there is the same Lord; while there are diversities of workings, it is the same God who worketh all things in all.

LECTURE IX.

PREACHING TO CHILDREN: ITS IMPORTANCE
AND ITS DIFFICULTIES.

IX.

PREACHING TO CHILDREN: ITS IMPORTANCE AND ITS DIFFICULTIES.

Threefold Meaning of the Term "Preaching."—Preaching Possible in the Sunday-school Class.—Gain to Children from Pulpit Sermonizing.—Danger of their Neglect by the Preacher.—Impressibility of Children.—The Children's Crusade.—Separate Services for Children.—Five-Minute Sermons. Antiquity of this Plan.—Modern Preachers to Children.—Preaching to Children not an Easy Matter.—Its Influence on the Preacher.—Stimulus to Success in the Fact of the Difficulties.

"Preaching" is a term employed in our English Bible in three distinct senses; the same word being given as the translation of at least three Greek words with clearly different meanings. *Kērussō* [1] is to herald the message of one who has authority—whether the message be welcome or unwelcome, a message of good or a message of ill. *Euanggelizō* [2] is to proclaim good tidings; to an-

---

[1] See Thayer's *Greek-Eng. Lex.*, s. v. Comp. Matt. 3 : 1-3; 10: 7, 27; Mark 1 : 4, 7; 3 : 14; Luke 3 : 3, 4; Acts 8 : 5; 9 : 20; 10 : 42; 15 : 21; 19 : 13; Rom. 10 : 15; 1 Cor. 1 : 23, 24; 2 Cor. 4 : 5; 11 : 4; 1 Tim. 2 : 7 (see R. V. marg.); 2 Tim. 1 : 11 (see R. V. marg.). Comp., also, Gen. 41 : 43; Dan. 3 : 4, in LXX.

[2] See Thayer's *Greek-Eng. Lex.*, s. v. Comp. Matt. 11 : 5; Luke 3 : 18 (R. V.); 4 : 18; 4 : 43 (R. V.); 7 : 22; 16 : 16 (R. V.); Acts 10 : 36 (R. V.); 14 : 15 (R. V.); 16 : 10; Rom. 10 : 15; 1 Cor. 15 : 1; 2 Cor. 11 : 7; Gal. 1 : 8, 11; Eph. 2 : 17; 3 : 8; Heb. 4 : 2, 6 (R. V.); 1 Peter 1 : 12, 25 (R.V.). Comp.,

nounce a truth which should bring gladness to its hearer. *Katanggellō*[1] is primarily to treat a subject thoroughly, to make clear a truth; or, as the Revisers have indicated, in their rendering of this term by "proclaim," it is to make known that which is in itself worth knowing.[2]

As applied to religious truth, the first of these words finds its emphasis in the *sender* of the message; the second finds its emphasis in the *receivers* of the message; the third finds its emphasis in the *substance* of the message. In the first case, the preacher realizes *for whom* he stands; in the second, *to whom* he is sent; in the third, the importance of the *truth* which he is set to declare. This is the threefold Bible view of preaching. In our modern popular phrasing, "preaching" practically includes all three of these ideas, with a compression, or a limitation, of their scope to the pulpit declarations of religious truth; or, as Webster defines it, "preaching" is "to utter in a sermon, or a formal religious harangue." It is in the modern and popular sense of the term, rather than in any one of its biblical senses, that I now speak of preaching; as I call attention to the importance and the difficulties, and again to the principles and the methods, of preaching to children.

It is true that all three of the phases of preaching which are presented in the Bible words translated by that term can be—and practically they often are—secured in and through the Sunday-school, as the divinely com-

also, 1 Sam. 31 : 9; 2 Sam. 1 : 9; Psa. 40 : 10 (39 : 10); 96 : 2 (95 : 2); Isa. 40 : 9, in LXX.

[1] See Thayer's *Greek-Eng. Lex.*, s. v. Comp. Acts 4 : 2; 13 : 5; 17 : 10-13; 1 Cor. 9 : 14; Phil. 1 : 15-18; Col. 1 : 24-28.

[2] See Crabb's *English Synonymes*, s. v. "Declare."

manded agency for the ministry of the church to children and to the child-like; apart from the later developed and the not distinctively enjoined agency of pulpit sermonizing. But it is also true that pulpit sermonizing has its abundant justification in the needs of the human mind, and in the intimations and the illustrations of the Bible narrative; and it will not be questioned that pulpit sermonizing—preaching in its modern popular signification —has been, and is, and in the nature of things must continue to be, a pre-eminent agency for the heralding of God's truth, for the declaring of the good tidings of salvation, and for the intelligent and discriminating exhibit of themes of eternal moment. Hence it is unmistakably needful that the advantages of pulpit sermonizing be secured to the most important, to the most impressible, and to the most hopeful, class of hearers; and who will say that that class does not include—if, indeed, it be not wholly composed of—the *children?*

He who is a teacher in the Sunday-school can be, as I have said, a herald preacher to his scholars, giving them God's message as from God; he can be a gospel preacher to those scholars, declaring to them the good news of a Saviour who died and who lives for them; he can be a disclosing, a proclaiming, or an enlightening, preacher, in his conferences with those scholars over the truths he would bring to their understanding and attention. The true teacher is all this. As Richard Baxter says on this point: "I hope there is none so silly as to think this [personal] conference [as between teacher and pupil] is not preaching. What, doth the number we speak to make it preaching? Or doth interlocution make it none? Surely, a man may as truly preach to one as to a thou-

sand." [1] But in addition to all the preaching thus done
by the teacher in the Sunday-school, there is a preaching
work to be done by the pastor in and from the pulpit, in
announcing and impressing and enforcing the truths of
God's word, by means of that form of continuous discourse, which came after a season to take the place of
the earlier form of homily, or conference, or conversation, which was the chief method of preaching in the first
two centuries of our Christian era.[2]

As a rule, however, pulpit preaching is not addressed
to children as children ; nor are children included in the
number of those to whom it is supposed, or designed, to
be intelligible.   Children are indeed expected to attend
the church services where preaching is a prominent feature, and where it is even counted a means of grace; but
the pulpit preacher does not, ordinarily, recognize, as a
corollary of this expectation, his corresponding duty to
adapt his preaching to the capacities and needs of his
children hearers.   Claiming, to start with, that God's appointed agency for the winning and training of souls is
pulpit preaching rather than Bible-school teaching, and
that therefore children ought to attend on that appointed
agency, the modern church practically deprives those
children who do thus attend, of the chief advantage of
that agency, by couching the addresses of the pulpit in
language which is to the children an unknown tongue.[3]

---

[1] " The Reformed Pastor," in *Practical Works*, XIV., 246-354.

[2] See Broadus's *Lectures on the History of Preaching*, p. 46; also Smith's
Dict. of Christian Antiq., art. " Homily ; " also pp. 53-56, *ante*.

[3] It is a very common thing to hear a Christian minister say, that if a child
must choose between attending church or attending Sunday-school, he ought
to attend church and let the Sunday-school go ; when the practical meaning

It would, to be sure, be practicable to have the words of the preacher such as children and adults could together understand and profit by; but that would necessitate the bringing down those words to the comprehension of the children, as the common plane of intelligence for all; and *that* is the very opposite of ordinary pulpit practice. The emphatic and specific declaration of our Lord to adults was: "Except ye turn [not *be converted*, as our old version mis-rendered it, but *turn*] and become as little children, ye shall in no wise enter into the kingdom of heaven;"[1] and, "Whosoever shall not receive the kingdom of God as a little child, he shall in no wise enter therein."[2] The seeming rendering of these words, as applied to children, by the modern pulpit, is: "Except ye push on and become as grown folks, ye shall in no wise share in the lessons about the kingdom of heaven;" and "Whosoever cannot understand the kingdom of God as a full-grown person, he shall in no wise partake of its privileges." Is it too much to say that this suggests a new application of those other words of our Lord to religious teachers: "Ye have [so far] made void the word of God because of your tradition"?[3]

There is even good ground for questioning the wisdom of an enforced, or a voluntary, habitual regular attendance of children upon religious services which are not

---

of that minister is, that if a child must choose between attending on services which are beyond his intelligence, or attending on services which are adapted to his intelligence, he ought to choose the former, in spite of the unreasonableness of a course like this. Such a minister, whoever he may be, makes the twofold mistake of supposing that modern pulpit sermonizing is one of God's ordained agencies for the religious training of the young, and that interlocutory Bible teaching is not.

[1] Matt. 18: 3.

[2] Mark 10: 15; Luke 18: 17.

[3] Matt. 15: 6; Mark 7: 13.

designed for the comprehension and the participation of children. Said President Barnas Sears, on one occasion, in my hearing: "I am by no means sure of the good effect, on children, of sitting in listlessness, and acquiring habits of inattention in the house of God, when nothing is offered them from the pulpit, and they are not expected to understand, or to have a part in, the exercises of worship."[1] And this is a doubt which has also been in the mind of many another thoughtful educator.

The Rev. Dr. Thomas H. Gallaudet, who was an exceptionally intelligent student of the child mind, would not consent to train his children to mental inattention, by having them sit, in their younger years, without occupation, through long services which were obviously above their understanding. He allowed them to take seats on the crickets, or footstools, in the family pew at church; there to read their Bibles or their Sunday-school books, while the service went on; and, as occasion offered, he would call them up to listen to the singing, or to a portion of Bible reading, or to some statement or illustration in the preacher's discourse, which was within the scope of their comprehension. In this way, all of Dr. Gallaudet's children were guarded from habits of wearisome listlessness in church, and ultimately became intelligent sharers in the forms and spirit of sanctuary services. On the other hand, there is reason for believing that the old-time co-partnership of the preacher and the tithing-man, in the work of making the Lord's house a place of undeserved penance to children, huddled together in the galleries as they were, was an important factor in diminishing the

---

[1] In an address at Newport, heard by the Lecturer.

interest of successive generations in the services of that house,—as we know was the case prior to the introduction of the Sunday-school.[1]

While, however, it would be better, if the choice must be made, to have children attend the Sunday-school and be faithfully cared for there, without attending on those pulpit ministrations which are specifically not designed for their benefit, than to have them attend on such pulpit ministrations without having the aid of intelligent Sunday-school instruction;[2] yet, obviously, a better way still is for children to have the incalculable advantage of pulpit ministrations suited to their capacity and needs, in addition to all that could be secured to them by the best Sunday-school training imaginable. And just this better way it is to which I am now calling attention.

The importance of preaching to children pivots on the relative numbers and impressibility of children in comparison with adults, in the community at large, and on the place assigned to them, as the charge of his disciples, by our Lord. Because childhood is pre-eminently the season for an intelligent choice of a lifetime course of good or of evil, and because children, far more than adults, are open to impressions and influences of an abiding nature, therefore the herald of God's word, the bearer of the gospel message, the exponent of all-important religious truths, has a duty to address himself directly to children, as the most numerous and the most hopeful

---

[1] See note at p. 174, *ante.*

[2] The Jews held that the place of study was superior to the place of worship; and that while a synagogue might be turned into a school, a school must not be given up for a synagogue. (See Maimonides' *Yad Ha-chazaqa,* Part I., ₴ 3 ; also Addenda to *Shulchan Arukh.*)

class of persons in the field of his labors; the more especially because He in whose name the preacher stands
has given such emphasis to the sin and the peril of de-
spising the little ones, or of being the means of their
stumbling in, or of their turning from, the path of right.

On what plea, indeed, can a preacher justify himself in
addressing his words of invitation and counsel chiefly to
the comparatively hopeless minority of comparatively unimpressible adults, to the neglect of an obviously more
hopeful majority of unquestionably impressible children,
when both these classes are within his reach? By what
right does he locate his evangelizing pulpit hard by the
very gate of perdition, to enable him to cry out to a few
of those who are hurrying toward that dark portal under
the accelerating impulse of their long years of sinful de-
scending, while he leaves unwarned and unguided the
great masses of children who are yet far up the road at
the foot of which he is stationed, but who are in danger
of the very perils against which he is uttering his warning cry to the remnant of their parents' generation? If,
indeed, he were to say that our Lord taught that those
who enter his service at the eleventh hour are to be welcomed as cordially as if they came earlier, it would be
well for him to be reminded that the householder, in the
parable, " went out early in the morning to hire laborers
into his vineyard,"[1] and that it was only after those whom
he secured at that time had been ten hours at their work,
that he gave his invitation to those who had been idlers
until then.   There is nothing in the Bible, in history, or
in sound reason, that will justify a man of God in waiting

---

[1] Matt. 20 : 1-7.

until the mid-life of his hearers before he makes his direct call on them to enter the service of Him whom he represents. Nor is there any such justification for his delay in giving needful Christian counsel to those who already are in his Master's service. Whether looked upon as out of Christ or as in Christ, a child has a stronger claim than an adult on the preaching service of a minister of Christ, when the two are brought into practical comparison.

Incidental proof of the importance of preaching to children is found in the illustrations of its effectiveness on memorable occasions—whether the preaching on those occasions was wisely or unwisely directed. Look, for example, at that wonderful uprising of the children for the rescue of the Holy Sepulchre from the followers of the False Prophet, in the beginning of the thirteenth century! It was after five crusades, under the lead of kings and knights, had proved a failure, that a Christian youth in France was moved to follow in the steps of Peter the Hermit and of St. Bernard, as a preacher of a crusade; but he to the children, instead of, as they, to adults. And this young Stephen of Cloyes, with the co-work of young Nicholas of Cologne, and of Peter of Burgundy, and others, appealed to the children to come forward and "win a victory which soldiers and nobles had failed to gain." The text of these preachers was the startlingly significant words of David, as interpreted by David's greater Son: "Out of the mouth of babes and sucklings hast thou ordained strength because of thine enemies, that thou mightest still the enemy and the avenger." [1] Under this appeal children, by the thousand, left their

---

[1] Comp. Psa. 8 : 2 ; Matt. 21 : 16.

homes and enlisted for the crusade. They were from eight years old and upward. The efforts of parents and of the civil authorities were powerless against the influence of the preachers who had the children's ear.

Fifty thousand or more of these children set out from their homes in southern and central Europe. Some thirty thousand of them perished in, or fell from, the way. The few thousands who finally reached the East were betrayed and sold into slavery by those who had professed to be their friends and guides.[1] This incident in mediæval story it is of which Longfellow sings in wondering praise:

> " What is this I read in history,
> Full of marvel, full of mystery,
> Difficult to understand?
> Is it fiction? is it truth?
> Children in the flower of youth,
> Heart in heart, and hand in hand,
> Ignorant of what helps or harms,
> Without armor, without arms,
> Journeying to the Holy Land!

> " Who shall answer or divine?
> Never since the world was made
> Such a wonderful crusade
> Started forth for Palestine.
> .   .   .   .   .
> " Like a shower of blossoms blown
> From the parent trees were they;
> Like a flock of birds that fly
> Through the unfrequented sky,
> Holding nothing as their own,
> Passed they into lands unknown,
> Passed to suffer and to die.

[1] See Michaud's *History of the Crusades*, II., 202; III., 441-446; Mills's *History of the Crusades*, note at p. 245, Note Gg, p. 272; Lea's *History of the Inquisition*, I., 147 f.; Gray's *The Children's Crusade*, passim.

" O the simple, child-like trust!
  O the faith that could believe
  What the harnessed, iron-mailed
  Knights of Christendom had failed
  By their prowess to achieve,
  They, the children, could and must!"[1]

Nor can we say that these children, thus marvelously swayed by the power of the living preacher, were not moved in the innermost depths of their spiritual being by the influences which impelled them to their acts of heroic—even though most unwise—daring and doing. The record stands that when a number of these child crusaders were captives in Bagdad, an attempt was made, under the direction of a council of Saracen princes, to win them to the creed of the False Prophet. On the one hand, they were tempted with rewards if they would yield; and, on the other hand, they were threatened with torture and with death if they remained firm. And of the entire number thus brought to the test, not one failed or faltered, even in the face of the cruel martyrdom to which eighteen of them were successively subjected in the presence of the others.[2] All were as true to their God as were the young Hebrew captives in the same region of the world in the days of Nebuchadnezzar.[3] And who will doubt that the fidelity of these, as of those, was the firmer because they had been brought into the service of their divine Master in the early morning of their days, instead of being left uncared for until their life's noonday?

In the middle of the eighteenth century, there were

---

[1] " The Children's Crusade (A Fragment)," in *Poems* (Household Edition), p. 406.

[2] Gray's *Children's Crusade*, pp. 203-206.

[3] Dan. 3 : 1-30.

wonderful revivals of religion among children in Germany, under the preaching of Count Zinzendorf and his fellow Moravian preachers.[1] Nothing in the work of John Wesley seemed to be more of a surprise to him than the effect of his preaching on those children who heard him; and because of what he saw was the influence on them of sermons not directly designed for their benefit, he was led to prepare sermons suited to their tastes and understanding.[2] Jonathan Edwards bore testimony to the remarkable results of pulpit preaching on the children of New England in the great revival of a hundred and fifty years ago.[3] So, again, in our day, many a conservative clergyman in England, Scotland, and America, has been brought to realize anew the power of preaching to children by witnessing the unmistakably good results of sermons to children by special evangelists, whose style and methods of working could not have the approval of those clergymen.[4] And so a sense of the importance of this ministry to the little ones has been growing in the minds of thoughtful observers of the means and agencies of promoting God's work in the world.

One of the foremost difficulties in the way of securing fitting and timely preaching to children in these later days is encountered in the question of when and where and how this preaching should be conducted. And this question is differently answered in different communities, according to the preference of different pastors.

[1] See note 1, at p. 106, *ante.*   [2] See pp. 106-108, *ante.*

[3] See Edwards's reports of this revival in Prince's *Christian History* for 1743, pp. 115-128.

[4] The "Children's Special Service Mission," of London, grew out of the interest excited by the evangelistic services for children, conducted by the

A plan which has had large prominence in England, and which is not without its illustrations in America, is that of a separate service of worship and of preaching for the children on the Lord's Day, either at the same hour with the general service for adults or at a later hour in the day. In many cases, in England, where the Sunday-school session precedes the ordinary forenoon church service, the children from the Sunday-school assemble in a room by themselves, at the hour when the larger congregation gathers in the main auditorium of the church, and are there led in a service of worship adapted to their comprehension and needs; that service being followed by a sermon or address peculiarly designed for their hearing and profit. This, of course, involves the necessity of an assistant clergyman, or of a duly empowered layman, to conduct this service, while the chief pastor conducts the service for the congregation generally.[1] Services of this character are numbered by the hundred in metropolitan and in rural communities in England, where they are no longer deemed an experiment, but are counted an approved feature of pastoral work in churches of the Establishment, and even yet more commonly in the churches of non-conformists generally.[2] Services very

Rev. E. P. Hammond, of America, during his visit to Great Britain, in 1867. See, on this point, T. B. Bishop's *A Plea for Children's Services*, p. 13 f.

[1] See the Rev. Samuel Martin's "Separate Services for Sunday School Children," in *Papers for Teachers;* also Sir Charles Reed's *The Infant Class in the Sunday School*, pp. 81-101.

[2] As long ago as 1866, Mr. Fountain J. Hartley, an honorary secretary of the London Sunday School Union, writing on this subject, said : "Three hundred and eleven separate morning services are now reported by the London schools ; and as some of the schools do not meet in the morning at all, while many others do not possess school-rooms in which services can be held apart from the usual public engagements, a large majority may be said to

much like these were quite a feature in Christian work in Boston, more than half a century ago.[1]

This form of separate service bears much the same relation to the ordinary church-service that the primary class bears to the main Sunday-school. Its tendency is to interest the children in both public worship and pulpit preaching, and to train them for an intelligent part in the one, and for an intelligent apprehension of the other. So far from leading them away from church attendance, it brings them to an enjoyment of that measure of it which is now permitted them, and to a pleasant looking forward to the time when they can be advanced to a share in all of its privileges, for an appreciation of which they are now preparing. The united testimony of those who have had experience of the separate service for children on this plan, seems to be unqualifiedly in its favor, in view of its practical working and of its manifest tendency.

More than forty years ago, a prize essay on the religious training of children, published by the London Sunday School Union, protested against the enforced attendance of children at services expressly designed for adults, and advocated the plan of separate services for children. Said the writer of this essay: "It would be

have embraced the plan of endeavoring to conduct juvenile worship in a style and manner suitable to the age and capacity of the worshipers" ("Sunday School Statistics, and the Lesson they Teach," p. 27, in *Papers for Teachers*). Yet earlier, Sir (then Mr.) Charles Reed, in advocating this agency, said: "The author of this book has collected, from all the principal towns in England and Wales, the statistics upon this subject, the result of which is to prove, that almost everywhere objections have been overcome, and the experiment having been successful, the new scheme of infant service has become a fixed institution in every school" (*The Infant Class in the Sunday School*, p. 84, note).

[1] See *Report of the Ministers at Large* for 1835.

no greater absurdity for an Englishman who knew nothing but his mother-tongue to attend a sanctuary where
the entire service was conducted in Latin, than for children ignorant of the first principles of Christianity to be
taken to our churches and chapels, and told that merely
sitting quiet there, without in the least degree entering
into the spirit of what is going forward, is 'to keep *holy*
the sabbath day.' It is a perfect mockery; and God,
who looketh at the heart, seeth multitudes of children
trained thus to desecrate his house and profane his day."
Therefore, " in lieu of the adult public service, it would
be well to hold, at the same time, every sabbath morning, a separate religious service for children, adapted to
their tender capacities. The children should have a sermon preached to them by a regularly appointed party ;
a text should be taken and a discourse delivered ; matter,
manner, and style suited to their infantile minds." [1]

A quarter of a century and more after this suggestion,
from a non-conformist source, the subject of separate services for children was a theme of prominent discussion
in the Church [of England] Congress at Brighton,—as
indeed it had and has been in many another religious
conference,—and on this occasion a speaker, who testified
from a wide field of observation, said emphatically: " I
have never known a separate service, when conducted
with any spirit, to fail. The children appreciate it because it is their service, and [they] joining in it with heart
and lips, their worship comes up with acceptance before
Him who deigns out of the mouths of babes and sucklings to perfect praise." And yet more recently Bishop

[1] Louisa Davids's *The Sunday School*, p. 224 f.

W. Walsham How, the Suffragan of [East] London, said : " Children's services [and he included both ' separate ' and ' special '[1] services in this designation] are becoming more and more a recognized feature in our church [of England] system." And he added pertinently : " It is strange how completely the children, who always form an important element in our congregations, were neglected in past times."[2]   Children's services in Westminster Abbey, with preaching by the Dean, have now had prominence for years ; and they were never more admirably and profitably conducted than under the administration of Dean Bradley, who was a teacher before he was in this place as a preacher.

A plan for a weekly separate service for children which has been more widely followed in America, and which is by no means an uncommon plan in England, is for the pastor to give to that service the place of a regular service in the order of the Lord's Day arrangement for the sanctuary. In other words, the pastor conducts one service for the benefit of the adult members of his congregation, and one for the benefit of the children and youth of his congregation. Even this gives an advantage in the division of the services to the adult membership ; for there are comparatively few adults in the average congregation who do not know enough to understand a service which is within the scope of a child's comprehension, if they choose to attend it ; while there are, on the other hand, but few children who can comprehend the meaning of services distinctly intended for

---

[1] See T. B. Bishop's *A Plea for Children's Services.*

[2] *Plain Words to Children*, Preface, p. v.

the adult ear and mind. It would indeed be an ungracious spirit for an adult to object to a service in the Lord's house, simply on the ground that the Lord's dearest ones could understand it.

For at least a quarter of a century, the Rev. Dr. Tyng "made the sermon of every Sunday afternoon a sermon to the young." Referring to this service, after eleven years of its testing, he said: "The Lord has been pleased very graciously and mercifully to own this [pulpit] teaching in many cases of conversion to himself, and in much real edification of youth in his service. I have considered no part of my work more valuable and important than this. And certainly no portion of it has seemed so popular and acceptable to others."[1] Emphasizing the value of pulpit services of this character, Dr. Tyng added: "If every pastor would give one sermon on every Sunday especially addressed to the young, and designed and prepared to teach them, he would find himself enlarging his direct usefulness in this particular work, and equally advancing the value and benefit of every other class of his public and private labors in religious instruction also. The parents and [other] adults of his flock will learn as much, and love as much the teaching for themselves, when he speaks to the youth directly and simply, as when he addresses them in a deeper and more mature discourse."[2] On one occasion I heard good Dr. Tyng give added force to this latter thought by saying: "If more ministers would preach to the children of their congregation, more of the grown people would understand their ministers." Dr. Broadus says, similarly: "One

---

[1] *Forty Years' Experience in Sunday-schools*, p. 24 f.   [2] *Ibid.*, p. 210.

great benefit of frequently preaching to children is that a minister thus learns better how to preach to grown folks, both in the way of *simplifying* and *enlivening* the religious instruction." [1]

Another clergyman, whose weekly sermons to children were continued with profit for a series of years, was the Rev. Dr. J. L. McKee, of Kentucky, a Presbyterian pastor, and later a college professor. In looking back upon this phase of his ministerial work, after an experiment with it of seven years, this was his testimony concerning it: " I have no question in saying that if I have any way of estimating my work, this [preaching to children] is by far the most favorable part of all that I have done." And, as expressive of his view of the relative importance and value of this kind of ministerial work, he said of efforts to hasten a preparedness for the millennium: " In order to reach it the sooner, instead of giving two sermons a day to grown people and one to children, we should at least reverse this and give children two, while we give the grown people one. If what we say about the memory and the early impressions be true, and if it is of the greatest importance to give the right direction to the young heart, and if what we state about the mind being unoccupied in childhood, and that you can write upon it impressions that can never be blotted out—if this be true, then I say the logic of the case compels us to give the children two sermons where we give the grown people one. And I tell you if the children had the money to pay the salaries of the ministers this would be done." Dr. McKee, like Dr. Tyng, found that in preaching to the

[1] In the Introduction to Eaton's *Talks to Children*, p. 10 f.

children ne was for the first time making the truth intelligible to many of his adult hearers; and as an added advantage in preaching of this character he said : " It is very often the case that there is something you want to say to the grown people that is somehow at outs with the dignity, or propriety, or spirit of a sermon to them ; but you can give them ' Hail, Columbia' over the heads of the children; and they can't say a word about it." '

Twenty-five years ago, the Rev. Edward Spooner, a Church of England clergyman, in a little book entitled Parson and People, which was introduced to American readers by the Rev. Dr. Leonard Woolsey Bacon, told of his gratifying experience with weekly services for children, including a sermon, or a " sermonette" as he called it. And he gave the testimony of other clergymen, both of " High Church " and of " Evangelical " affinities, who had tried the same plan with excellent results for a series of years.[2] Thus it will be seen that this is by no means a novelty, nor a practice confined to one class of ministers.

Still another method of securing a weekly service of preaching to children, which has found favor on both sides of the ocean, is that of giving to the children a brief and distinct portion of the regular forenoon service, every Sunday morning. In some churches the children's portion is given to them at the opening of the forenoon service, and they are then permitted to retire from the sanctuary. In other churches, they receive their portion just before the sermon to the adults is given by the preacher, and then they remain through the entire service.

[1] *Report of the Fifth National Sunday School Convention* (1872), pp. 74-77.

[2] *Parson and People*, pp. 137-141.

An earnest plea for this recognition of the children by the preacher, was made at the Pan-Presbyterian Council in Philadelphia, in 1880, by the Rev. Dr. Alexander Macleod, of Birkenhead, England. Speaking of his own branch of the Church of Christ, as he might, indeed, have spoken of wellnigh every other branch, also, he said: " Who can think of the immense number of children scattered over our Presbyterian churches, who come up to the public service Sunday after Sunday, with eager hope of finding some interest for their young souls, with that hope growing smaller and smaller as the brief years of childhood run out, until at last the pathetic habit is formed of expecting nothing—who can think of this, and not sympathize with the desire to provide for them also a portion in the service which they shall look forward to, and by which their spiritual lives shall be fed?" In explaining a method by which the children should have a portion of every forenoon service he said: " I am not advocating an untried proposal. Many congregations in England and Scotland have had happy experience of it for years." Dr. Macleod's recommendation was: "At every morning service, for one ten minutes out of the ninety, let the minister be in direct contact with the souls of the children. Let never a [Lord's] day pass in which he shall not give wings to a story of God's love, or [of] Christian life. . . . Doing this, we shall whet and keep whole the appetite of the children for the services of the sanctuary. Doing this, we shall open [to them] the windows of heaven, and give them also glimpses of the vision of God. And in that golden place, in those so consecrated minutes, we shall bring back for the children, and it may be for their parents as well, the days when Jesus spoke to his disciples in parables, and taught those children of his love, as they were able to receive his words."[1]

Before this appeal of Dr. Macleod was made, there were American pastors who employed much the same method as that which he advocated, as a means of pulpit provision for children. Perhaps the earliest collection of "five-minute sermons" to children, given to the public on this side of the water, was one (in 1878) by the Rev. J. G. Merrill, a Congregational clergyman, then of Davenport, Iowa, and now of St. Louis, Missouri. A later collection of similar character (in 1882) was from the pen of the Rev. John C. Hill, a Presbyterian clergyman, of Fayetteville, New York, who estimated that at that time some two hundred pastors in the United States were in the habit of preaching such sermons to the children of their congregations.[2] A more recent collection of the same sort has been sent out by the Rev. William Armstrong, a well-known Methodist Episcopal clergyman.[3]

In favor of the plan of providing for the children first, and then permitting them to retire from the house, it can be said that that was practically the custom in the Christian Church for the first four or five centuries of our era; when the catechumens were expected to leave the house at the close of the Bible reading and the familiar homilizing, without even having a share in the public prayers or in the recitation of the Creed.[4] As an excuse, on the other hand, for retaining the children through the remain-

---

[1] *Report of Proceedings of the Second General Council of the Presbyterian Alliance*, pp. 441-447.

[2] *The Children's Sermon.*

[3] *Five-Minute Sermons to Children.*

[4] See Bingham's *Antiquities of the Christian Church*, Bk. xiv., ch. 5, § 2.

der of the services, which they cannot understand, it can be said that a child who has already been given, by his pastor, something to think of during the morning hour, will sit patiently, and without listlessness, while his parents are receiving their portion for the day. If, indeed, a child has received a single fresh thought, which he grasps as his own, or a single earnest impression which makes itself felt for the hour, from his pastor's Sunday morning sermon, he has made a larger gain than that of the average adult sermon hearer, week by week, all the world over.

And this thought suggests yet another method which has found favor with some, for meeting the difficulty of giving the children their portion from the pulpit, without the necessity of separating them for the time being from the great congregation. I describe it, by an illustration, as it is practiced by some pastors, more or less regularly, in their pulpit ministrations. A pastor is preaching to his adult congregation in his ordinary style. At a fitting and a well-considered point in his discourse, he pauses, looks down into the faces of those children who are before him, and says familiarly: "I want these children who are here this morning to understand what I am preaching about." By that time the preacher has the ears of every child in the congregation; and he has caught the fresh attention of not a few of the adults whose thoughts were wandering. He repeats his text, and tells its meaning in a few simple words. He gives a carefully chosen illustration, calculated to make the main truth of his text clearer to a child's mind. He adds an application of the text and its truth to the daily life and to the life purpose of a child. Then he says: "Now, children, *that* is what

I am preaching about; and I want to see if you can understand what I am saying about it to these older persons;" and he resumes the thread of his discourse, after a digression, or after a re-impression, of this sort, of perhaps three or four minutes.

Every child in that congregation feels that that sermon is preached to *him*. He listens to *his* preacher with a new interest in what is being said, even though he cannot understand it fully.[1] And more than a majority of the older members of that congregation—wherever the church may be—are enabled to have a better understanding of the point and purport of that sermon than *they* could have gained without some such mode as this of its illustration and enforcement.

Nor does this method of interrupting the main current of a religious discourse to adults, in order to speak helpful words to child hearers, lack the sanction of high antiquity in God's church. Long before the days of pulpit

---

[1] " 'Papa, are you going to say anything to-day that I can understand?' asked a little girl of her father—a Massachusetts pastor—as he was setting out for church on a Sabbath morning. This tender appeal touched the loving father's heart, and he could not answer his daughter nay; he could not say to his child that she must sit in penance through all the long service with never a word designed for her instruction and cheer. So, as he preached, he said, 'And now, children, I will say something to you about this.' At once the face of every child in that audience brightened. Sleepy little ones started up; tired ones took fresh heart. Looking first at the minister, then at each other, again back to him, they were all eagerness for his message, as though now there was something else for them than to nod and yawn and ache uncared for; and although the pastor's following sentences to them were few and simple, doubtless many felt as did the child who had pleaded for this attention when, on her return at noon, she said contentedly, 'Papa, I understood all that you said this morning.' Dear children! who wouldn't do as much as this for them in every sermon?—they are gratified so easily." (The Lecturer's *Children in the Temple*, p. 247 f.).

sermonizing, David, in a psalm prepared for public worship, breaks in upon his appeal to the Lord's saints with
the loving appeal to the little ones: "Come, ye *children*,
hearken unto me: I will teach *you* the fear of the Lord."[1]
Similarly, the apostle to the Gentiles stops, as it were, in
his pastoral letter to the churches of his charge, which
was to be read aloud in their pulpits—if indeed they had
any pulpits in those days—to say tenderly to the child
hearers of his message: "*Children*, obey your parents in
the Lord: for this is right. Honour thy father and mother
(which is the first commandment with promise), that it
may be well with thee, and thou mayest live long on the
earth;"[2] and then he resumes his counsel to adults. And
a greater than David or Paul was more than willing to
interrupt the thread of *his* discourse to adults, in order to
minister to the children who were within reach of him.[3]
He was even "moved with indignation" at an objection,
by his chosen disciples, to such an interruption of the
Preacher of preachers; and our Lord made it clear, on
that occasion as on many another, that a loving ministry
to children is never irreverent or undignified, nor is it
out of place, by one who would do most and best for the
honor, and in the service, of the Saviour of the child-like.

It was not an uncommon thing, indeed, in the Early
Church, for the preacher to pause in the middle of a text
of Scripture cited by him, in order that his hearers, young
and old, might take up the text thus begun, and recite it
to its conclusion. St. Augustine mentions, for example,
that when he would cite the words of St. Paul in 1 Tim.
1 : 5, beginning, "'The end of the commandment is'—

---

[1] Psa. 34: 11.   [2] Eph. 6: 1, 2.   [3] Mark 10: 13-16; Luke 18: 15-17.

before he would proceed any farther he called to the people to repeat the remainder of the verse with him; upon which they all cried out immediately, 'charity out of a pure heart,' by which, he says, they showed that they had not been unprofitable hearers."[1] Among the published sermons of Dr. Doddridge, of a century and a half ago, there are illustrations of his method of turning aside from his discourse to adults in order to address his child hearers directly.[2] John Wesley's sermons, also, furnish illustrations of this practice in his day.[3] And so it appears, in this thing as in many another, that what is looked upon by some as a modern innovation is not such a novelty after all.

The preaching of occasional discourses to children is certainly not a thing of recent origin, whatever advance may have been made in the frequency or the quality of such discourses. A sermon of this character, preached by the Rev. Samuel Phillips, of Andover, Massachusetts, in 1739, was published soon after its preaching. It evidently was not a "five-minute sermon," for in its printed form it occupies nearly one hundred pages of an eighteen-mo volume. As an indication of its style it may be noted that it starts out with a careful explanation of the fact that

---

[1] Bingham's *Antiq.*, Bk. xiv., ch. 4, § 26.

[2] See, for example, his *Sermons on the Religious Education of Children*, pp. 59-62. Near the close of his fourth sermon of this series he begins a digression thus: " I would [now] address myself to children. To you, the dear lambs of the flock, whom I look upon as no contemptible part of my charge, I have been speaking for you a great while, and now give me leave to speak to you ; and pray do you endeavor, for a few minutes, to mind every word that I say."

[3] See an illustration of this, in his Sermon on Obedience to Parents (*Works,* VII., 101 f.).   [4] *Children Well Imployed.*

when it is said in the New Testament narrative that Jesus of Nazareth rode into Jerusalem on "an Ass, and a Colt the fole of an Ass, the words do *not* intend that he sat on *both;* sometimes on one and then on the other, as some have imagin'd."[1] Yet only a few years later than this, John Wesley prepared a sermon to children from Psalm 34: 11, in which he used no word having more than two syllables; and this sermon he preached again and again as opportunity offered.[2]

It is, however, within the last three-quarters of a century or so that the importance and the difficulties of preaching to children have come into a recognized prominence in the sphere of the Christian ministry which was quite unknown before. The earliest published volume of brief sermons which had been preached to children, with which I am acquainted, was issued in 1823, by the Rev. Samuel Nott, Jr., one of the first five missionaries of the American Board of Commissioners for Foreign Missions.[3] This volume was followed by another of the same character, a year later;[4] all the sermons in both volumes having been preached by him before their publication. Possibly it was because of his experiences in proclaiming the gospel to the heathen, that Mr. Nott was prompted, and was enabled, to preach in simplicity and

[1] In 1713 the Rev. Matthew Henry preached six sermons to young people, which were published in 1722, or earlier, under the title of *The Pleasantness of a Religious Life Open'd and Prov'd, and Recommended to the Consideration of all, Particularly of Young People.*

[2] Tyerman's *Life of Wesley*, III., 472, 607.

[3] See Sprague's *Annals of the American Pulpit*, II., 192; also, *Memorial Volume of the First Fifty Years of the American Board of Commissioners for Foreign Missions.*

[4] *Sermons for Children, Designed to Promote their Immediate Piety.*

directness to children. About the same time a little volume of expository "Sermons for Children" was published by the Religious Tract Society, of London, for distribution in the Sunday-schools of that day. Indeed, as early as 1819, a collection of seventeen "Sermons to Children" was published in Andover, Massachusetts, by the New England Tract Society; but it is not shown that either of these last two collections was of sermons which had actually been preached before their publication.

The style of none of these sermons was, however, such as to make them peculiarly attractive to children. But this cannot be said of the bright and impressive sermons, or pulpit lectures, to children, given by the Rev. Dr. John Todd[1] at a series of quarterly services for children in his Philadelphia pastorate, and published in 1834, and later. It was in 1840 that the Rev. Dr. F. W. P. Greenwood, of King's Chapel, in Boston, published a volume similar to that of Dr. Todd's as the outcome of a monthly service for the children of his charge.[2] A few years after this, a volume of the same general character, with a corresponding origin, was published in England, by the Rev. Dr. S. G. Green, then pastor of the Silver Street (Baptist) Chapel, Taunton; later, the president of Rawdon College, and now a secretary of the London Religious Tract Society.[3] These volumes marked the beginning of a new state of things, and they helped its developing. The added interest in the religious welfare of children, in England and in America, awakened in and through the Sunday-school, was now being felt in the *pulpit*, as it had

[1] *Lectures to Children.*   [2] *Sermons to Children.*
[3] *Addresses to Children,* and *Pearls for the Little Ones.*

already been felt in the *family ;* and from that day to this the tendency in the Church of Christ, in those lands and beyond, has been more and more toward the intelligent and hearty co-operation of family and school and pulpit, for the right influencing, the right training, and the right impressing, of the young.

It was after this beginning of new interest in sermons to children that the Rev. Dr. Alexander Fletcher, of London,[1] and the Rev. Dr. Richard Newton, of Philadelphia,[2] acquired such prominence as preachers to children — mainly because they were preachers to children when other ministers generally were not; and that the successive volumes of their sermons to children added so largely to the literature of this theme. And now the extent and variety and relative value of published sermons to children command consideration in any proper estimate of the homiletical literature of the day, including, as they do, the work of such men, in addition to those already noted, as Frederick Maurice[3] and Dean Stanley[4] and Bishop How[5] and Bishop Ryle[6] and Drs. Samuel Cox[7] and J. Oswald Dykes[8] and John Edmond[9] and

---

[1] See his *Lectures Adapted to the Capacity of Children.*

[2] See the eighteen volumes of his sermons to children, published by Robert Carter and Brothers. Several of these volumes have been translated into various languages for use among children of other lands.

[3] *The Lord's Prayer, The Creed, and The Commandments.*

[4] *Sermons for Children.*   [5] *Plain Words to Children.*

[6] See *The Child's Preacher,* pp. 278-298, 388-406.

[7] *The Bird's Nest, and Other Sermons, for Children of All Ages.*

[8] See *Outlines of Sermons to Children.*

[9] *The Children's Church at Home.*

Alexander Macleod,[1] of England; Drs. John Cairns[2] and William Arnot[3] and J. R. Macduff[4] and Horatius Bonar[5] and A. A. Bonar[6] and James Stalker,[7] of Scotland; and Drs. William S. Plumer[8] and Andrew P. Peabody[9] and John Hall[10] and William P. Breed[11] and T. T. Eaton[12] and Theodore T. Munger[13] and Robert Boyd[14] and Mortimer Blake[15] and Marcus D. Buell,[16] and many others[17] in America.

But the more there has been done in the line of preaching to children, the more it has been evident that no other kind of preaching is so difficult of right doing as pulpit preaching to children. The few marked successes, and the many wretched failures, in this department of effort, are alike indicative of this difficulty. In order to preach properly to children, a minister needs to be fully qualified to preach properly to adults, as a preliminary to his earliest preparation for his preaching to children. In other words, not until he is already able to preach well to adults, is a man fitted to begin to learn how to preach to children. A good sermon to children must have in it a thought that is worthy of the interest of the maturest mind. When

---

[1] *The Wonderful Lamp*, *The Gentle Heart*, and *The Children's Portion.*

[2] See *Outlines of Sermons to Children.*   [3] *Ibid.*

[4] *Hosannas of the Children.*   [5] See *Outlines of Sermons to Children.*

[6] *Ibid.*   [7] *Ibid.*   [8] *Short Sermons to Little Children.*

[9] *Sermons for Children.*   [10] Special and occasional sermons.

[11] *Grapes from the Great Vine*, and *Under the Oak.*

[12] *Talks to Children.*   [13] *Lamps and Paths.*   [14] *Food for the Lambs.*

[15] *Bible Children.*   [16] See *Outlines of Sermons to Children.*

[17] See McLean's *Food for the Lambs;* Collier's *Little Crowns;* Norton's *Sermons to Children;* Wells's *Bible Echoes;* Ross's *Sermons for Children*, etc.

that thought has control of the preacher's mind, he must go out of his own mind into the mind of a child, in order to think that thought as a child would think it. Then he must choose language which will enable him to present the absorbing thought of his mind to the apprehension of his child hearers' minds. Beyond all this, he must be able to illustrate that truth clearly; to command attention to it, step by step, in the processes of its enforcing; and to make its application evident to the children's personal needs as children. And, obviously, there is here a call for all the elements of successful power in ordinary pulpit preaching—and more. The work of condensing and simplifying presupposes, in fact, the possession of something that is worth condensing and simplifying. Hence the peculiar difficulty there is in preaching to children as children ought to be preached to. As children *ought to be* preached to, I say—not as they *are* preached to; for much of the preaching to children is childish and silly; poorer, if possible, than the poorest preaching to adults.

The testimony of Dr. Todd, as a result of his experience as a children's preacher, is: "That children are a very important class in every congregation, all admit; that ministers owe them some peculiar duties is equally plain; and that they are a difficult part of the flock to feed, the experience of every one, who has ever tried to do his duty to them, will testify."[1] And Dr. Todd cites this yet more explicit testimony of the Rev. Richard Cecil to the same effect: "Nothing is easier than to *talk* to children; but to talk to them as they ought to be talked to, is the very last effort of ability. A man [who does

---

[1] Preface to *Lectures to Children.*

this] must have a vigorous imagination. He must have extensive knowledge, to call in illustration from the four corners of the earth; for he will make but little progress but by illustration. It requires great genius to throw the mind into the habits of children's minds. I aim at this, but I find it the utmost effort of ability."[1] "It is no easy thing to speak effectively to children,"[2] says Dr. S. G. Green. "It is true the difficulty is great," adds the Rev. Alexander Fletcher.[3] Said the Rev. Dr. Newton, years ago, when his preaching was at its best: "My children's sermons cost me more time and labor than any others that I preach."

The Rev. Dr. McKee agrees, at this point, with all other prominent preachers to children. After at least seven years of practice in this field, he said: "I will say that it is the most difficult work, by far, that I have tried to do. I have not half the apprehension in preparing sermons for grown audiences that I have in preparing a sermon for children. If I were going to preach a sermon to the Congress of the United States, I would not have anything like the apprehensions that I would have were I going to preach to the children here in this city."[4] The Rev. Dr. Samuel Cox, whose labors as an expositor have been so prominent and varied, and whose ability as a preacher is so marked, says of his expository sermons to children, "I can honestly say that no sermons have cost me so much."[5] And he adds that, after his best thinking

---

[1] Preface to *Lectures to Children.*
[2] Introduction to *Addresses to Children.*
[3] Preface to *Lectures Adapted to the Capacities of Children.*
[4] *Report of the Fifth National Sunday School Convention* (1872), p. 76.
[5] Preface to *The Bird's Nest and Other Sermons*, p. vi.

over one of these sermons, he has frequently been compelled to write it out two or three times over before he
could at all shape it to his mind. Again, Mr. Spurgeon,
who is not without experience or ability in this field of
pulpit effort, said, in a public address on the subject, that
"for himself he felt that he could preach much more
readily to the low and groveling minds of grown-up
people, than to the purer and sublimer minds of children;
who seemed to be nearer heaven: better and simpler."

It is indeed probably true that one reason for the infre-
quency of sermons to children by preachers of exceptional
power in other fields of pulpit effort, is to be found in the
conscious inability of these preachers, as a result of some
unsuccessful experiments on their part, to meet the peculiar requirements of this higher realm of intellectual performance; as, obviously, another and yet more potent
reason is the undervaluing by such preachers of the importance and advantages of pulpit preaching to children.
And just here I venture to refer to a supposed depreciation
of sermons to children, in a series of lectures delivered in
this place and presence,[1] by a preacher no less honored
and admired, and no less worthy of honor and admira-
tion, than the Rev. Phillips Brooks. And it is because
the opinion of such a man is entitled to have weight in a
matter like this, that I call attention to the wide-spread
popular misinterpreting of Mr. Brooks's words in this connection. He was speaking of the mistakes of ministers,
in their giving undue prominence to any single feature—
however important that feature—of pastoral work. After
noting several special temptations to such overdoing, he

---

[1] In the Marquand Chapel of Yale Divinity School; where the Lyman
Beecher Lectures on Preaching are delivered, year after year.

added: "And so with the children's church; one of the best and purest of the Church's inventions for her work, but by no means enough to make a special, peculiar feature of in any congregation. It almost always weakens the preacher for his preaching to adults."[1]

This statement by Mr. Brooks, which *I*, certainly, should not take exception to just as it stands, has been widely reported as an expression of his opinion that preaching to children tends to impair a minister's power of preaching to adults;[2] whereas he said nothing of the sort. As, therefore, the current *report* of Mr. Brooks's opinion on this subject is a mistake, it is quite unnecessary to show that it would have been a mistake for Mr. Brooks to express an opinion corresponding with that report. He quite properly protested against such a one-sided method of pulpit work for children as would leave the adults unprovided for. He might, indeed, safely have balanced his statement concerning the "children's church," by adding this statement concerning its converse church agency: And so, again, with the *adults'* church; one of the best and purest of the Church's inventions for her work, but by no means enough to make the one peculiar feature of in any congregation. It almost always weakens the preacher for his preaching to children.

In this connection, there is found added force and pertinency in the wise words of Dr. Horace Bushnell, on the entire subject, as he looked back upon it in all its bearings, near the close of his wonderfully fruitful ministerial life. "Is it not our privilege and duty, as preachers of

---

[1] *Lectures on Preaching*, p. 96.

[2] See, *e. g.*, the reference to this by Dr. McLeod, in *Report of Proceedings of the Second General Council of the Presbyterian Alliance*, p. 445.

Christ," he asked of his brother ministers, "to do more preaching to children? I think of nothing in my own ministry with so much regret, and so little respect, as I do of my omissions just here. We get occupied with great and high subjects that require a handling too heavy and deep for children, and become so fooled in our estimate of what we do, that we call it coming down when we undertake to preach to children; whereas it is coming up, rather, out of the subterranean hells, darknesses, intricacies, dungeon-like profundities of grown-up sin, to speak to the bright daylight creatures of trust and sweet affinities and easy convictions. And to speak to these fitly, so as not to thrust in Jesus on them as by force, but have him win his own dear way, by his childhood, waiting for his cross, tenderly, purely, and without art—oh, how fine, how very precious, the soul equipment it will require of us! I think I see it now clearly: we do not preach well to adults, because we do not preach, or learn how to preach, to children. . . . God's world contains grown-up people and children together: our world contains grown-up people only. And preaching only to these, who are scarcely more than half the total number, it is much as if we were to set our ministry to a preaching only to bachelors. We dry up in this manner, and our thought wizens in a certain pomp of pretense that is hollow, and not gospel. The very certain fact is, that our schools of theology will never make qualified preachers till they discover the existence of children."

These latter words of Dr. Bushnell, be it remembered, were spoken before theological seminaries generally had given this phase of homiletics any special prominence. But in their connection these words may still serve to stimulate theological students to avail themselves the more earnestly of all the privileges in this line now set before them in the course of their theological training.

A recognition of the difficulties in the way of learning how to preach to children is in itself a stimulus and an incentive to such attainment on the part of one who is preparing for the ministry, of which this kind of preaching is so important a part. And as to the possibility of learning to preach to children, there can be no reasonable doubt in the mind of one who realizes that the work is divinely commanded, and that the preacher is divinely set to it. The truth on this point was concisely stated by the Rev. Dr. John Cotton Smith, when he said, on this subject: "Jesus would not have imposed upon his ministers a duty which he had not given them the ability to perform."[1] This thought was similarly expressed by the Rev. Alexander Fletcher, when he said of the obvious difficulty of this work: "This is, however, no reason for shrinking from the duty. Is it a duty? Who can deny it? If the ministers of Christ enter upon its discharge, *He* will assuredly impart grace to perform it. He sends none upon a warfare on their own charges."[2]

The Rev. Dr. S. G. Green, writing on this subject nearly forty years ago, said of the difficulty of preaching to children: "But this difficulty, like others, is to be surmounted by study and practice. It is true that the natural gift which we call genius is something; but earnestness and assiduity are at least as much. Few men, whose hearts are set upon the ministry, decline being preachers because they cannot be pulpit orators.

[1] *Report of New York Sunday-school Institute* (1868) p. 112.
[2] Preface to *Lectures Adapted to the Capacity of Children.*

And, in like manner, none need decline being preachers to children because they do not hope to attain eminence [as such]. The excuse 'I have no talent for it' has been made and accepted far too readily; as though success in this department of pastoral toil were not to be attained by the methods which ensure efficiency in others."[1] And much more recently the Rev. Dr. John A. Broadus, in his elaborate Treatise on the Preparation and Delivery of Sermons, has spoken with like effect on the same subject. " Every one notices," he says, " how few persons succeed decidedly well in speaking to children. But many preachers possess greater power in this respect than they have ever exercised, because they have never devoted to the subject much either of reflection, observation, or heedful practice. Examples may be found of men who for years considered that they had no talent for speaking to children, and whose attempts were always comparative failures, and yet who afterwards became very popular and useful in this important department of preaching."[2]

In short, the very fact that proper preaching to children is one of the highest attainments of homiletical power, and that comparatively few preachers have achieved marked success in that line, coupled with the other fact that the duty of preaching to children is inseparable from the mission of the minister of Christ, should incite and stimulate the theological student to prepare himself for the work wherein so many have fallen short, or have lamentably failed. In this direction lies the path of hopeful progress before the young preachers of to-day.

[1] Introduction to *Addresses to Children.*
[2] *A Treatise on the Preparation and Delivery of Sermons*, p. 114 f.

LECTURE X.

PREACHING TO CHILDREN: ITS PRINCIPLES
AND ITS METHODS.

X.

PREACHING TO CHILDREN: ITS PRINCIPLES AND ITS METHODS.

Hints to the Children's Preacher.—A Fresh, Strong Thought Essential in Every Sermon.—A Child's Capacity for Great Thinking.— Need of an Obviously Fitting Text.— Of a Well-Defined Outline Plan.—Of Simplicity of Language.—Of Clearness of Statement.—Of Explicitness of Application.—How to Prepare for this Work.— How to Seat the Hearers.— How to Secure Their Co-work.—How to Guard Against Tiresomeness.—Concluding Thoughts. — Christianity Unique in its Exaltation of Childhood.

It would not be a fair treatment of any practical question, to emphasize the importance and the difficulties of a given line of work, and then to leave it without a proffer of help or suggestion in the direction of its wise methods. Hence, without attempting to cover, in any sense, the ground of this portion of the homiletical field, I am impelled, by a sense of simple fairness, if nothing more, to venture the suggestion of a few primary points which my observations and experiences have led me to deem worthy of consideration by him who would undertake the delicate, the difficult, and the eminently important, work of preaching to children.[1]

[1] The paucity of hints in this line of pulpit effort in the standard works on homiletics, is noteworthy as an indication of its general undervaluing in the minds of preachers and of their trainers.

To begin with, the thought, or theme, or topic of a sermon to children, ought to be, as I have already suggested, one which has value in and of itself, and which is worthy of the preacher's absorbed interest apart from its immediate use in an address to the children of his charge. A very common mistake, and a very serious one, on the part of those who discourse to children, is in supposing that the manner and the phraseology are of chief importance in such a work; that, in fact, the primal thought, or the underlying conception, of an address, is of less importance to children than to adults. An audience of children is a discerning as well as an appreciative audience. It is composed of bright, active minds, not yet trained to indifference or to listless inattention. It is, as a rule, an audience less easily imposed on by unmeaning platitudes, and more intelligently impatient of them, than an audience of grown persons.

A child values a fresh, strong thought; and he is quick to catch it when it is fairly before him. Nor is a child's range of thought so limited, or its channel so shallow, as many would seem to suppose. A child can comprehend the profoundest truths of theology not merely as well as, but better than, an adult of the same native qualities of mind and character.[1] In other words, the great thoughts of God are better apprehended by the human mind in its childhood than in its maturer years; and the preacher who can grasp those thoughts most clearly for himself, and can make them clear to others, will be surer of a hearty welcome to them by an audience of intelligent children than by any other persons to whom he may present them.

---

[1] See pp. 217-219, *ante.*

Hence it is that he who would preach well to children must not think of lowering his plane of thought for their benefit, but must recognize his duty of rising to his best and highest plane of thinking, in order to think a thought which is worthy of their thinking, and which they will perceive to be thus worthy.[1]

Take such a truth, for example, as the immortality of the soul, as the resurrection of our Lord, or as the omnipresence of God; who will doubt that that truth can be more easily grasped in its entirety by a simple-hearted, trustful child, than even by a devout adult whose maturer mind finds rational difficulties in the way of its acceptance, such as the child is yet free from. A Connecticut clergyman gave me an illustration in this line out of his personal experience. Riding along a country road on the borders of his parish, he stopped to speak to a boy whom he saw there. After asking the boy's name, he attempted a little pastoral catechising, after this sort: "Do you know who made you, my boy?" "Yes, sir. God made me." "Where is God?" "In heaven, sir." "Isn't God anywhere else?" "I didn't know that he was, sir." "Well, my boy, God is not only in heaven, but he is everywhere at the same time; and he can see you always, wherever you are." *That* was a new thought to that boy. It impressed him as a new thought. Pointing to a close-faced heavy stone wall, near which he stood, the boy said inquiringly: "Can God see through that stone wall?" "Yes, indeed," answered the pastor, "God can see through that wall. God can go through that wall." "*Go?*" responded the boy, instantly. "*Go?* I

[1] See Bushnell's statement on this point, at p. 341 f., *ante.*

don't see how God can *go* at all, if he's all over to begin
with!"   "Ah!" said that pastor to me, as he told this
story, "that boy had made the truth of God's omnipresence more really his own, in those two minutes, than
I had made it mine in my thirty years in the ministry."
And it was because he was a child that that boy received
the truth of God as a child.   To the minister, God's omnipresence was a doctrine; to the child, it was a reality.

The man who remembers his own childhood's thoughts
knows that he grappled very early with some of the great
problems of theology and of metaphysics that are yet a
bewilderment to him; and he who, as a parent, has attempted to meet the keen questions of his children on
those same problems, and on others which he had never
considered before, has found that his greater difficulties
are in his own limitations of knowledge, rather than in
the inability of his children to receive explanations which
he is competent to proffer them.   When a father's little
child asked him, seriously, "Why did you blow at that
candle, papa?" the father's answer came back quick and
confident: "To put out its light, my dear child."   But
when, as if in instinctive recognition of the imperishable-
ness of matter, the second question came, "Where did
the light *go*, when it went out, papa?" the father was
inclined to realize afresh that it is so much easier to satisfy — with surface statements — grown folks than children, in their search for knowledge.   And this is a truth
which the children's preacher needs always to bear in
mind in his planning a sermon for their benefit.   He is
more likely to fall below their standard of thinking than
to rise above it.

Turn, if you will, to the more striking themes of the

great preachers of the ages, and you will see how rarely one of these themes is in itself beyond the comprehension of a child's mind,—provided only it be stated in words which are fairly within a child's attainments of language. Even as they stand, the themes of many of these master-pieces of homiletical literature are such as a child would grasp quite as quickly as an adult. Thus, for example, Horace Bushnell's sermons on "Unconscious Influence," and "Every Man's Life a Plan of God," and "Living to God in Small Things;"[1] Lyman Beecher's sermon on "The Bible a Code of Laws;"[2] Andrew Melville's, on "The Power of Wickedness and of Righteousness to Re-produce Themselves;" Jeremy Taylor's, on "The Foolish Exchange;" John Calvin's, on "Bearing the Reproach of Christ;" Hugh Latimer's "Sermon of the Plow;" and so all the way back to Cyril of Jerusalem's sermon on "The Creator Seen in the Creations;" and Tertullian's on "The Duty and Rewards of Patience."[3]

This fact of the fitness of great truths to the capacity and the tastes of children, has been recognized, and acted on, by some of the best of modern preachers to children, in their selection of sermon themes for the little ones whom they addressed. Thus, Dr. John Todd gave a chil-dren's sermon on the theme, "Great Events Hang on Little Things," from the text,[4] "A certain man drew a bow at a venture;"[5] and another, on "What Faith is, and what its Use is," from the text,[6] "Without faith it is impossible

---

[1] *Sermons for the New Life*, pp. 9-28, 186-205, 282-303.

[2] *Sermons Delivered on Various Occasions*, pp. 138-181. See, also, Water-bury's *Sketches of Eloquent Preachers*, p. 56.

[3] See Fish's *Masterpieces of Pulpit Eloquence.*   [4] I Kings 22: 34.

[5] *Lectures to Children*, pp. 146-163.   [6] Heb. 11: 6.

to please him;"[1] Dr. Andrew Peabody gave one on " False Shame," from the text,[2] " I am not ashamed of the gospel of Christ; "[3] Dr. William S. Plumer gave one on " The Worth of the Soul," from the text,[4] "Ye are of more value than many sparrows."[5] One of Dean Stanley's sermons to children was on a theme which might practi-cally be stated as The Loving Call of Jesus to Nobler Living. It was from the text *Talitha Cumi*,[6] which he translated as " My little lamb, my pet lamb, rise up."[7] Wellnigh every sermon to children by Dr. Samuel Cox, in his published volume, is based on a Bible theme which is fresh enough and strong enough for hearers of any age. Thus, for a single example, " The Man who was too Busy to do his Duty," from the text,[8] "And as thy servant was busy here and there, he was gone."[9] In a children's ser-mon by Dr. Munger, entitled " The Good, the Better, the Best," the main thought is the essential moral difference between illustrative teachings from Muhammad, Cyrus, and our Lord Jesus; it being *good* to feed our souls as well as our bodies; it being *better* to share our good with others; it being *best* to give as unto God, without a thought of personal gain or return.[10]

And so it ought to be with every sermon to children. Its thought, or theme, or topic, should be worthy of a full man's interest, if it is to be reckoned worthy of a child's keener perceptions and more fastidious tastes. Never, never, never should a preacher to children expect to com-

[1] *Lectures to Children*, pp. 63-80.   [2] Rom. 1: 16.
[3] *Sermons for Children*, pp. 40-57.   [4] Matt. 10: 31.
[5] *Short Sermons to Little Children*, pp. 54-60.   [6] Mark 5: 41.
[7] *Sermons for Children*, pp. 87-94.   [8] 1 Kings 20: 40.
[9] *The Bird's Nest*, pp. 222-237.   [10] *Lamps and Paths*, pp. 109-119.

mand the attention, and hold the interest, and retain the respectful regard, of his young hearers, by calling them his "dear little children," and assuring them that he is "very glad to see" them, and that he wants them to be "good boys and good girls," and telling them pretty little stories. Yet, as Dr. Broadus expresses it, "a good many ministers do, as it were, play the organ in ordinary sermons, and in addressing children play the banjo or the jewsharp;"[1] when, in truth, as he adds, "the two classes of discourses should be on the same gamut, without essential incongruity, and with no difficulty in making the transition from one to the other." Unless, indeed, a preacher has a thought which as a thought fills his own mind fully for the time being, and which he wishes his young hearers to become possessed of, he lacks the first essential of preparedness for preaching to children; however he might succeed in satisfying a congregation of adults with his pleasantries or his platitudes.

A good illustration of the practicability of a preacher's interesting children in a sublime truth which is worthy of his own absorbing interest, has been brought to my notice as occurring since I began the writing of this lecture. In the chapel of the Episcopal Divinity School, in Philadelphia, a small congregation has been newly gathered from its neighborhood in the western suburbs of the city. Naturally, of course, the starting-point of this congregation is a Sunday-school, together with the nucleus of the divinity students, and such families as choose to avail themselves of the privileges of the services there conducted. The Sunday after Christmas Day, the past

[1] Introduction (p. 12) to T. T. Eaton's *Talks to Children.*

23

winter, was a stormy one.   The preacher for the occasion, at this chapel service, was the Rev. Dr. Daniel R. Goodwin; now Professor of Systematic Divinity in that institution; formerly provost of the University of Pennsylvania, president of Trinity College, and a professor in Bowdoin College; an undergraduate in the last-named institution, indeed, so long ago as when the poet Longfellow assumed his professorship there.   He is a man of patriarchal appearance, of wide and varied learning, of pronounced theological convictions, and, withal, of a lovely and winsome Christian spirit.

His sermon for the occasion was a careful and thorough treatment of the doctrine of the Incarnation.   Seeing that his audience was composed largely of boys, he considerately adapted his discourse to their capacities, yet without changing its subject, or the general tenor of its treatment. It was a doctrinal theme, and its treatment involved incidental references to the historic variations in the doctrines of the *kenosis;* but it was a theme in which he had a profound personal interest, and of which he was a master. He presented it in simplicity of speech, and in sympathetic directness.   As the theme possessed him more and more, in his contemplation of it, and in his desire and endeavor to impress it, in all its fullness and preciousness, upon the tender minds of his young hearers, he rose to his loftiest heights of thought and expression in its elaboration; yet he rose to no height whither he might not be followed by the warm hearts and the vivid imaginings of his young hearers, even more easily than by the cooler heads and the more rigid reasonings of adult listeners. He held the attention of those young hearers from first to last.   They comprehended his main thought.   They hung upon his words. Their eyes fairly snapped with delight over some of his keen distinctions. Moreover, it was the testimony of the Dean of the Faculty, and of the students of the Divinity School in this rainy morning audience, that never in his class-room, or in any ordinary pulpit service, had Dr. Goodwin seemed so grand as a preacher, or so effective as a teacher. That sermon, indeed, was more of a sermon for the mind and heart of hearers of any age or any measure of attainment, because it had been raised to the standard of childhood, instead of being kept down on the plane of adults—in its presentation of the sublimest mystery of God's truth. And this is but a single illustration of what might be, and of what ought to be, the state of things in the best preaching by the best preachers to hearers young or old.

When his sermon theme is well defined in a preacher's mind, the Bible *text* which is chosen for its presentation to children should be one which explicitly teaches, or which fairly suggests, that theme; and one, also, which is in a form of words easily apprehended and easily remembered by children. If, indeed, as some would think, the text should be chosen before the theme, it is still important that the text be one which a child can see the meaning of, as well as its bearing on the sermon theme, and one which he can fasten in his mind without difficulty. The texts already cited, as used with good effect by preachers to children, are illustrative of this point. A text which is of involved phraseology, or of obscure meaning, is peculiarly inappropriate to a child's sermon. If, indeed, there is to be a surprise in the use of the text, that use should be one which a keen-eyed child will see the fairness of when it is announced to him.

A child's sermon ought to have a well-defined, clearly-stated, easily-remembered *outline plan*, or skeleton. Not only ought the sermon to be arranged logically,—for a child's mind is a logical mind,—but the logical arrangement of the sermon ought to be announced to the child, as a help to his understanding and to his retention of its main points. Here is where many a preacher to children fails to meet the requirements of his work. He pours out good things loosely before his child hearers, but gives them no basket to carry away the good things in. Just here, on the other hand, is where many a preacher to children has had his chief power as a helpful preacher to children. Good Dr. Tyng was not always felicitous in his choice of texts, nor simple in his language, in this line of pulpit work; but he was pretty sure to make his sermon outline for children one which the children could fasten in their minds. I remember a children's sermon from him, of fifteen years ago, which illustrates this point. His text was the first two verses of the thirty-fourth chapter of Second Chronicles, describing the well-doing of the young king Josiah. In his incisive manner, and with his abrupt tones of voice, Dr. Tyng said: "There are four things told of King Josiah in these verses, which I want you to notice. First, What he did; second, Why he did it; third, When he did it; and fourth, How he did it." Each of these points was then tellingly pressed by the preacher. After showing that *what* Josiah did, was to follow a good example; that *why* he did it, was because it was right in the sight of the Lord; that *when* he did it, was while he was yet young,—the Doctor came to the fourth and closing point of his discourse. "And now," he said, "the question is, *How* did King Josiah do this

good thing? *How* did he do it? Why, *he just did it.*
That is the only way any good thing is ever done. When
you've got a thing to do, *do* it." It was the outline which
made that sermon of Dr. Tyng's. It was the outline
which enabled me to take it away with me, and to carry
it in my mind these fifteen years. And so far I was a
sharer with the children of that congregation in the benefits of a good sermon outline.

Even a very brief sermon to children can have a clearly
defined and helpful outline. In one of Mr. Hill's "five-
minute sermons" on "Walking with God," from the text,[1]
"Enoch walked with God," the outline shows that walking with God involves nearness to God, converse with
God, friendship with God, continuance with God, and that
it results in likeness to God.[2] If, indeed, but a single
point be made for the children's benefit, as a digression
from the preacher's discourse to adult hearers, that point
should be so well defined that the children can make it
their own in the very form in which it has found shape
in the preacher's mind. A sermon skeleton may be *in-
ferred* in a sermon to adults; in a sermon to children, it
ought to be *pointed out*.

So far, a preacher's preparation for a sermon to children is that which would be equally appropriate for many
a sermon to adults. But it is at this point, after his
theme and his text and his sermon outline are ready, that
a preacher's peculiar preparation for preaching to children
as children must begin. Now it is that he must choose
language and illustrations, and must decide on points of
application, that will enable him to transfer the thought

[1] Gen. 5: 24.   [2] *The Children's Sermon*, pp. 50-53.

of his mind to the minds of his children hearers, and that will tend to make the truth, which for the time possesses his entire being, a vital force in their young beings. And here it is that the main difficulty of right preaching to children is found. The preacher has what the children need; but how shall he get it to them? That is the question? "Wherefore let him that speaketh in a tongue, pray that he may interpret."[1]

A great thought loses none of its force by being expressed in simple language, and illustrated in familiar figures; whereas by such expression and illustration it gains a hold on many who would otherwise fail to comprehend it. Take, for example, that great thought of Chalmers's famous sermon, " The Expulsive Power of a New Affection."[2] In its present phrasing it would be obscure to many; but if stated as "A new delight crowds out old worries," or as, "Having something to live for makes one forget petty trifles," and illustrated by the figure of a child forgetting his grief over a broken toy, in the enjoyment of a live pony bought for him by his father, or by the story of a lad lifted above his old interest in pet rabbits by a decision to enlist as a drummer boy in his country's army in war time, then even a child could understand its meaning. And from such a familiar starting-point the thought itself could be expanded to any desirable sweep without carrying it beyond the young hearer's measure of intelligence.

Simplicity of language is by no means babyishness of language. It is important, indeed, in addressing children, not to seem to be talking *down* to them. It is only neces-

[1] 1 Cor. 14: 13.   [2] See Fish's *Masterpieces*, II., 320-335.

sary to employ words which they are accustomed to, and which they know the meaning of. " Our words must be the simplest possible," says Dr. Green. " But," he adds by way of sensible caution, " let us not imagine that we have simplified our language when we have only reduced the size of our words. The measure of simplicity is not *linear measure.*"[1] Yet, as Dr. McKee says in this connection, " there is great power in monosyllables."[2] He ascribes a large measure of his success as a children's preacher to his careful avoidance of Latin derivatives, and to his use of Anglo-Saxon monosyllables, in his sermons to children. Dr. Cox says, similarly : " In rewriting these sermons [to children] for the press, I have been amused to come on clusters of twenty and thirty, or even forty and fifty, words of one syllable."[3] Yet this special feature in his sermons was all unintentional on Dr. Cox's part; his effort being merely to express his thoughts "in the simplest and most colloquial English "[4] he could command; he writing and re-writing his sermons for the little folks until he was measurably satisfied with his effort to be simple and clear in the expression of his thoughts. The Rev. Dr. William S. Plumer had prominence as a theologian and as an exegete, and in those lines of thought and speech his language was that which would naturally be looked for there; but in his published volume of " Short Sermons to Little Children," Dr. Plumer's language is mainly simple Anglo-Saxon; monosyllables predominating without any sign of an effort at their selection. Nor would any one who knew him in the later years of

---

[1] Preface to *Addresses to Children*, p. 12.
[2] *Report of the Fifth National Sunday-school Convention*, p. 77.
[3] Preface to *The Bird's Nest*, p. viii.   [4] *Ibid.*, p. vii,

his life claim that Dr. Plumer's power as a preacher to adults was lessened by his habit of simplifying his language when preaching to children.

Would any one question the high thinking or the strong preaching of Frederick Maurice? It was while he was in the autumnal ripeness of his great powers, and while he was professor of Moral Philosophy in the University of Cambridge, that he was accustomed, on Sundays, to go out into a neighborhood of plain people, and address the children there by way of making clearer to them the all-essential truths which are at the basis of Christian faith and of the Christian life. It is the substance of those addresses to children which are gathered into his little volume on the Lord's Prayer, the Creed, the Commandments, and the Order of the Scriptures,— a volume which, as an example of fresh and vigorous thought in uniform simplicity of language, is as near a faultless model as any volume with which I am acquainted.

Observe, for example, the way in which Maurice begins his explanations of the Lord's Prayer : "A few poor Jews, chiefly fishermen, came to their Master, Jesus Christ, and said, 'Lord, teach us to pray.' He said to them, 'After this manner pray ye.' And then he spoke that prayer which we call 'The Lord's Prayer.' After this manner Englishmen have prayed for more than a thousand years. After this manner Frenchmen, Spaniards, Germans, Russians, pray. They speak in different languages, but the sense is the same. Let us pray."[1] Again, note what he says on the first two words of the Creed: "'I believe.' What is this, I *believe* ? I look into your

---

[1] *The Lord's Prayer, the Creed, and the Commandments*, p. 16 f.

faces. I *see* them. But I do not see what is passing in you. I do not see what you *mean*. I do not see what you *are*. When I say, 'That boy is honest and true,' I speak what I believe, not what I see. When you speak words to me, I say, 'I believe those words,' or 'I believe you who speak those words;' I believe you are telling me what is in you, that you are not speaking one thing with your lips when another is in your hearts. It is much more to you that I should believe you than that I should see you. My belief brings me much nearer to you than my sight. We do not know each other because we see each other. When we believe in each other we begin to know."[1]

And it is in this style that Maurice goes on, with his teachings concerning each clause of the Lord's Prayer, each article of the "Apostles' Creed," each commandment of the Decalogue, and each main group or section of the Holy Scriptures. His thought is such as to command the interest of the profoundest Christian thinker. The expression of his thought is such as to justify his anticipation, when he says, "The language of it, I hope, will be intelligible to any child." That the power thus exhibited is a higher attainment than that shown in any presentation of these same truths to maturer minds in language less simple and clear, would seem obvious. In such an exhibit as this, indeed, it is that we are helped to realize that he who receives the truths of God's kingdom in child-likeness, and who imparts them to children and to the child-like in child-language, the same is greatest in the kingdom of heaven.

---

[1] *The Lord's Prayer, the Creed, and the Commandments*, p. 30.

Stories of any kind should always be a subordinate, and at the best an incidental matter, in a sermon to children; helpful as they may be when used fittingly and with caution. And here is where preaching to children has been belittled, if not actually degraded; while the preacher's preaching power has been lowered, if not lost. So much has been said of the value of story "scrap-books" to the children's preacher, that the idea has gained currency that a sermon to children might be made by stringing together a series of stories from the preacher's scrap-book; and the appearance of not a few of the many published sermons to children would seem to justify the belief that *they* had been made in just that way. The chief aim in preaching to children should be to convey to the children's minds, distinctly and impressively, the thought which the preacher has made the basis of his sermon of the hour. If, indeed, it be the case that a story can make the sermon thought clearer and more impressive to the children,—instead of "diverting" them from that thought,—then it is desirable to use that story; but otherwise a story ought not to be given a place in the sermon. It were better, far better, to give the children a bright, fresh thought in simple language, without a story, than to give them the best story, or the best series of stories, imaginable, without making the thought of the sermon the chief attraction and interest of the preaching. Some very popular and successful preachers to children have rarely, if ever, told a story in their sermons to children. Many preachers to children, on the other hand, have fallen short or have failed in their proper mission through over story-telling.

Illustration as a means of making a truth clearer is of

value in all preaching as in all teaching. Peculiarly is
it helpful in conveying truth to the minds of children.
Hence the preacher who is possessed of a great truth
which he desires to impart to children hearers, is likely
to look about him for illustrations which will aid him in
that endeavor. But this is a very different matter from
story-telling. Better than a scrap-book of stories, and
better than the best available cyclopedia of compiled illustrations, as a help to the gathering of illustrations for use
in a children's sermon, is the study of children themselves. He who would illustrate truth to children must
know the ways of children, and must be familiar with
their methods of thought, of speech, and of action. In
acquiring this familiarity, the preacher to children can be
storing up material for use in his sermons to children.

And as in the matter of *illustrations*, so in the matter
of *applications*, in a sermon to children. The sermon
truth is to be applied by the preacher to children as children, when it has been clearly stated and fittingly illustrated to them by him. Its applications to adult hearers
may be obvious, or it may easily be perceived and made
plain by the preacher, because he is himself an adult,
accustomed to the ways and thoughts and feelings of one
in maturity of life. But these applications may be all
unsuited to children, while the preacher's duty is to show
the application of the truth he has declared to those to
whom he has declared it, in lines and to an extent beyond
their ability to perceive those applications for themselves.
In order to do this effectively, the preacher must be familiar with children as children; and this needful familiarity
with the ways and wants of childhood by the preacher
as a preacher, involves a study of children by the preacher

while a preacher, in addition to his general knowledge of childhood, and to his imperfect memories of his own early years of life.

In short, he who preaches to children must understand children; and no man can understand children unless he studies them. Therefore it is that no set of rules can suffice for the guidance of a children's preacher, any more than a set of rules can meet the necessities of a preacher who goes as a missionary to a people with whose language and whose modes of life and of thought he is unfamiliar. He can indeed be told with emphasis, that it is incumbent upon him to learn that people, and to learn their language; but just how he can do this, it is for himself to ascertain; no man can ascertain it for him. Woe, woe, to him, however, if, because of the difficulties of learning a new language, or of re-learning one which he once knew but has forgotten, the preacher contents himself with preaching to those residents of his missionary field who happen to know the language which he can speak easiest; neglecting, meanwhile, the neediest, the most important, and the most hopeful, natives of that field, to whom he was specifically commissioned as a preacher of God's truth!

Yung Wing, as a Chinese boy, knew the language and the ways of the boys of China. Brought to America, and educated under our best Christian and social influences, he went back to China with the knowledge and the tastes and the modes of thinking of a Yale College graduate. He had forgotten the language of his childhood. He was practically unfamiliar with the life and thought of the Chinese people. His immediate tastes were in the direction of the European and American residents of the Chi-

nese coast. Another man, in his position, might have
been satisfied with Christian work among those foreigners, and even have consoled himself with the belief that
he was on a higher plane of effort than if he were to
accommodate himself to the Chinese, and were to learn
anew to address them in their own language. But, God
be praised! Yung Wing had a higher conception than
this. He saw that the millions of Chinese youth were a
worthier object of his evangelizing endeavors than the
few hundreds of educated European and American adults
who were already within reach of his influence where and
as he was. So Yung Wing set himself to learn anew the
language of his childhood, and to study again those who
were as he was when he was a child. And thus it was
that Yung Wing became a power for good in behalf of
the whole empire of China; as, obviously, he never could
have been, had he not been willing to become as a child
again for their sakes, and for Christ's sake.[1] And herein
is illustrated the duty and the hope of him who would
preach God's truth to children.

The main requisites of a sermon to children are: an
important theme; an obviously fitting text; a well-defined
and easily-remembered outline plan; simplicity in language; clearness of statement, with such helps of illus-

[1] Yung Wing, a native of China, was brought to the United States and educated here. Graduated at Yale College in 1854, he returned to China with a
purpose of doing all in his power for the opening of his native land to the
influences of Christian education. After twenty years of patient watching
and of persistent prayerful endeavor, he induced his government to move in
the matter of sending chosen Chinese lads to America for their elementary
education. Yung Wing was in charge of this undertaking at its inception,
holding at the same time a diplomatic position as a representative of his government at Washington. Yale College conferred on him the degree of LL. D.
in recognition of his important services to the cause of Christian education.

tration as will make that statement yet clearer; and explicit applications of the sermon truth to the needs of children as children.[1]   So far, as to the sermon itself. Now, a few words as to the delivery of the sermon.

If the children who are preached to can be gathered by themselves, immediately before the preacher's eye, the preacher has a decided advantage.   He can be in direct communication with them as a compact body of hearers; and they, on the other hand, can influence and be influenced by each other as a little community by themselves. But, wherever the children are seated, he who preaches to them would do well to make the connection between himself and them a complete and an assured fact, by securing from them the re-statement to him of his text, after he has announced it, before he goes on with his sermon. A preacher who is not accustomed to this method may have difficulty at this point; but, if so, it is important for him to face and overcome this difficulty at the start.   If, indeed, he cannot inspire his young hearers with sufficient confidence to repeat over to him his simple text, a few words at a time, as he makes request for it, he must be at a disadvantage in his effort to transfer the thought of his mind to their minds.   A telegraph operator who fails, after repeated calls, to get a response from the other end

---

[1] While this Lecture is passing through the press, I see for the first time Dr. W. G. Blaikie's manual of homiletical and pastoral theology (*For the Work of the Ministry*), in which there is a chapter on Pastoral Care of the Young, comprising pertinent suggestions to the preacher to children (p. 196 f.), quite in the line of the recommendations made above.   "A good preacher to the young," says Dr. Blaikie, "will be careful to choose a text short, bright, striking; the arrangement will be simple, and the heads as obvious and as easily to be remembered as possible; a large part of his sermon will be illustration; and he will be specially careful to make a specific and not a vague application."

of his wire, understands very well that there is no gain in his going on with his work of transmitting words over a broken circuit. And he who would send a message from the pulpit station to the children's pew has like need, with any other operator, to be sure of a working circuit.

As with the text, so with the successive points of the sermon outline. It is well to state each one of these points distinctly, in its time and order, to the children, and to ask for it back again from the children. The gain of this method is much the same as that of the similar method in vogue in the days of St. Augustine, as already mentioned.[1] It tests and helps the attention of the hearers. And, moreover, it makes the text and the outline, as thus emphasized by the hearers in the repetition, more distinctively their own. With each successive point of the outline, in its order, the preceding point or points should be called for by the preacher and given to him by the hearers. And at the close of the sermon the text itself, together with all of the points of the outline, should be thus called for and repeated. By this method the children are helped to carry in their minds the progress, or movement, of the sermon, and to possess it as an entirety in their memory. This plan, also, has justified itself by the test of experience on the part of successful preachers to children, on both sides of the Atlantic, for now fifty years and more.

It is just here that some preachers to children have had exceptional power as preachers to children, notwithstanding their poorer method in other respects; while others, whose sermons were of a greatly superior grade, have

---

[1] See p. 332 f., *ante.*

had lack. Therefore it is that I give special emphasis to this point. Dr. John Todd ascribed a measure of his success as a children's preacher to his method of questioning his young hearers as he went along with his discourses to them.[1] Dr. Richard Newton did far more, as it seems to me, for his child hearers, by questioning into and out of them his text and his sermon outline, whenever he preached to them, than even by the most attractive of the many stories which he told to them.

Bishop W. Walsham How, of London, in his Plain Words to Children, gives illustration of his questioning method in such preaching, beyond this fastening of the text and outline in mind. Thus, for example, in a sermon on "A Road for God," from the text "A highway for our God," in treating the second point of his discourse, " How is the road to be made?" he says: " Why, here is the very thing described for us. When the prophet Isaiah tells us about the highway to be made for God,[2] he goes on at once, ' Every valley shall be exalted, and every mountain and hill shall be made low: and the crooked shall be made straight, and the rough places plain.' That is exactly the way anybody would make a road anywhere. Did you ever see a new railway being made?" Children who have seen a railroad in process of making, will be prompt to say so. And the questioning and answering goes on: "What did they do with the valleys or hollows? [Filled them up.] Yes; they had to be 'exalted'—lifted up. And the mountains and hills? [Cut them down.] Yes; they were 'made low.' And the crooked places were—? [Made straight.] And the rough —? [Made smooth.]

[1] Todd's *Lectures to Children*, Preface, p. 7.   [2] Isa. 40: 3-5.

To be sure. Now it is just the same when we want a road made in our hearts. Do you think you could tell me what all these things mean? Try and think." And then the preacher goes on to tell them that which they are now all the more interested to know, what is meant by this building of a road in the heart for God.[1]

Questioning in some such familiar way as this tends to make the sermon to children more vividly a matter of co-work between preacher and hearer,[2] according to the primitive idea of the term " homily;" or, as the French call it, to the present day, "conference." In the direction of securing this desirable sense of a personal conference between the preacher and his young hearers, Bishop How says, in the Preface to his published sermons: "I need hardly say that a sermon to children would be a complete failure if read. It must be spoken, and spoken with life and vigor. The sermons in this little book were preached at the Children's Services in Whittington Church; the children on such occasions being ranged in the body of the church, and the sermons being spoken from the chancel step. The sermons were written *after* being preached."[3]

---

[1] *Plain Words to Children*, p. 4.

[2] John Summerfield, the brilliant young English Wesleyan clergyman, who won such laurels as a preacher in New York City from 1821 to 1825, used this power of questioning his young hearers in his sermons to them; for he was great enough to preach frequently to children. The Rev. Dr. Waterbury says on this point, in description of Summerfield (*Sketches of Eloquent Preachers*, p. 28 f.): "His first sermon which the writer heard him preach was addressed to the young. He delighted in preaching to children. He inaugurated almost an entirely new style of preaching to them, that of question and answer, giving him scope, and keeping up the attention of his little auditors."

[3] Here again Dr. Blaikie (*For the Work of the Ministry*, p. 196 f.) emphasizes a point that is pressed in this Lecture. He says: "In his delivery he [the preacher to children] will study to speak in a natural tone of voice. His

24

The preacher should be on the watch against tiring the children by his too long a strain of their attention in one direction, and against losing his hold on them through any restlessness of theirs, or through any special cause of their diversion. Here it is that there is one gain in the calling of fresh attention to the text, or to one of the outline points of the sermon, and asking for its repetition by the children ; or in breaking the sermon delivery by the singing of a hymn. Dr. McKee was accustomed to divide all his sermons to children into three parts, "ordinarily of about equal length," with singing between them. He says: "I found that dividing the sermon into three talks was a great advantage. If any kind of interruption broke the attention during the *first* talk, I made that talk short, and had the children stand up and sing. Then I introduced into the *second* talk most of what I had intended for the first. If interrupted again, I still had a third chance."

This plan, also, has the sanction of antiquity—at least in New England. Many a Puritan preacher, after the first hour or so of his sermon, would rest himself, if not his people, by setting them at singing a psalm or a hymn before he went on with his discourse. Thus it is said of one of the old pastors in Norwich, that " in the summer season, when the heat was oppressive, if he wanted a short recess between the prayer and sermon, he would

performance will be at the furthest possible remove from that of an essay read before an audience; most emphatically it will be a word spoken to them. In preaching to children one can easily get rid of the fear of man which bringeth a snare, and without dread of offense say things which one might shrink from uttering face to face with the old. There is a directness and point in such preaching that often contrasts very favorably with the unnatural tones and vague circumlocutions of ordinary discourses."

give out a long psalm, such as may be found in Watts' version. For example, he would name, perhaps, the 104th Psalm, long metre, beginning at the fourteenth verse :

> 'To cragged hills ascends the goat,
> And at the airy mountain's foot
> The feebler creatures make their cell;
> He gives them wisdom where to dwell,' . . .

While the singing of a dozen verses was going on, in the tune Old Hundred or Hebron, he would retire to a shade in the rear of the church, to catch the breeze that floated up the river; and when singing was ended, he returned to the pulpit, and commenced his sermon."[1] Indeed, the primary idea of a noon intermission between the two services of the day in the New England churches generally, was that of a break in the one long sermon of the day. In a similar spirit, by one means or by another, the preacher to children should feel a responsibility for having and holding the attention and interest of his hearers from the beginning to the close of a sermon to them; and he should avail himself of all proper helps to this end.

As a matter of fact, while children are more likely than adults to show that they are inattentive and uninterested under poor preaching, they are far more likely than adults to be attentive and interested when the preaching to them is such as it should be. No audience in the world is so receptive and so responsive when fitting truth is fittingly presented to it, as an audience of children. Good preaching to children is, it is true, more difficult of attainment than is good preaching to any other class in the com-

---

[1] The Rev. Dr. Bond's *Historical Discourse*, p. 16.

munity, but it is correspondingly remunerative. Testifying to this point, Dr. Cox says of his children audiences, and of his sermons to them: "A more interesting and interested audience than that which sits immediately before me, [at such a time,] no minister could desire. If no sermons I have ever preached have cost me so much labor, none have met with a more immediate response, or have won a more overflowing reward. . . . As long as I live I must remember the rows of bright, intent faces on which I looked down; now attentive and amused, and now attentive and thoughtful, but always attentive, and responding to every note of thought or emotion which happened to be struck."[1] And this could hardly fail to be the testimony of any preacher who, with the scholarship and the preaching power of Dr. Cox, should devote his time and talents so freely and persistently, and with such loving heartiness, to preparing himself to be a preacher to impressible children, instead of only to unimpressible adults.[2]

It is, in fact, in the preacher's sphere as in many another: the easier road is the more alluring to him who would make rapid and pleasing progress, while the more difficult path really opens the way to larger possibilities

---

[1] Preface to *The Bird's Nest*, p. vi f.

[2] A chief reason for the absence, from the ordinary preaching services of the church, of so many children who are in the Sunday-school, is the failure of the pulpit preacher to try to secure their attendance on his preaching, or to address himself to them when they do attend. If their Sunday-school teachers did no more for them than he does, the Sunday-school would not be any more attractive to them than the pulpit is. But if a preacher does his part for the children, the children will do their part for the preacher. This is the testimony of preachers who are readier to preach to the children when they are before them, than to complain of them when they are not there. For example, the Rev. Dr. E. P. Goodwin, pastor of the First Congregational

of high and permanent achieving. Preaching to adults
is the easier; preaching to children is the more hopeful.
The wider and more attractive road is entered and pursued by the many;

> "But wisdom shows a narrower path,
> With here and there a traveler."

And here I rest my suggestions in the line of the principles and the methods of preaching to children; and
here I bring to a close this series of lectures on the mission of the Church of Christ to the young; emphasizing

Church, Chicago, has this to say, in a private letter, of his recent efforts with
the children: "Some years ago I came to know that rather more than half
of the children of our Sunday-school were from families of non-church-goers
[that was a hopeful indication, so far, for the children thus reached by the
church]. In addition to that fact, I had been for some time anxious to see
more of the children of our own people at our church services, especially on
Sunday morning. I determined, therefore, to make an effort to bring a portion at least of these children under the influences and teachings of the Lord's
house. I persuaded my people to change the Sunday-school from the afternoon to the morning—at 9.30, and to put the church service at 11, instead of
10.30. Then I told the children what my desire was, sought to awaken interest among them, and offered three sets of rewards for regular church attendance on their part. . . . In connection with this I have introduced monthly
selections of Scripture, in the Psalms and Gospels and Epistles, which we
learn by heart and repeat together in the Sunday-school and in church service. I have also preached a children's sermon once a month, in the place
of the regular sermon; have introduced into the service more or less of hymns
in which the children could join; have had them repeat with me the Commandments, the Beatitudes, the Apostles' Creed, etc.; seeking to have them
feel that the service is as truly for them as for the old folks. The result has
been, that I have had from three hundred to three hundred and fifty children
very regularly at morning service, and have enjoyed greatly seeing and hearing them. *I* have been helped whether they have or not." In a similar strain
the Rev. A. Hastings Ross, pastor of the First Congregational Church of
Port Huron, Michigan, says (Introduction to *Sermons to Children*, p. ix):
"It was in May, 1881, . . . that I ventured to announce to my people a series
of sermons to children. . . . It still continues, one every Sunday, preceding

once more, as I conclude, the pre-eminent importance of this mission, and the strangeness of its ignoring or its neglect, so generally.

A unique characteristic of the Christian religion as disclosed by its divine Founder, is its exaltation of childhood. Christianity, and only Christianity among the religions of the world, gives the first place in its mission and in its honors to children. Not merely a place, but the first place, is, in its plans, accorded to a child—as its capable recipient and as its typical representative. It was a real flesh-and-blood child that our Lord took and set in the group of his disciples, as a type of the greatest in his kingdom.[1]   It was of that real flesh-and-blood child that he said: "Whosoever shall receive one of such little children in my name, receiveth me."[2]   It was real flesh-and-blood children for whom our Lord insisted on a place in nearness to himself, when his chosen disciples felt that adults were better entitled to such nearness just then.[3] It was to those real flesh-and-blood children, at that very time, that he referred, when he said explicitly: "Whosoever shall not receive the kingdom of God as a little child, he shall in no wise enter therein."[4]   It was real flesh-and-blood children whose praises in the temple courts our Lord commended, when the chief priests were moved

---

the usual sermon, with a short hymn between the two. . . . About the same time we began a roll-call every Sunday in the church-school, embracing [among other things] . . . the number at church services." Mr. Ross says that the average of attendance at the church services shown by the school records was, for the year 1885, seventy-six per cent. If, indeed, Sunday-school scholars do not attend on the pulpit services, it is evident that something ought to be done about it—in the pulpit.

[1] Matt. 18: 1-5; Mark 9: 33-37; Luke 9: 46-48.

[2] Mark 9: 37 (R. V.).   [3] Mark 10: 13-16.   [4] Mark 10: 15 (R. V.).

with indignation against them in their forwardness.[1] It was obviously young children to whom our risen Lord directed the first attention of the leader in the work of his new church, when he asked Peter to evidence his love for him by ministering to the "lambs," before any mention was made of the "sheep" of his flock.[2] Children were clearly included as a main element in the schools of instruction provided for in the latest command of our ascending Lord,[3] as the basis of his Church, which he had already described as made up of children and of the child-like.

This new prominence for children, under the Christian dispensation, was not their prominence in the family as the family; but it was their prominence in the mission and in the ministrations of the Church as the Church. It was an *added* element in God's plans and methods for the uprearing of a holy people; beyond all that was in operation in and through the family, before Christ's Church as a Church was a fact and a force in the active agencies of his kingdom.[4] And because it was a novelty in the world's history this pre-eminence of childhood, as declared by our Lord, was a stumbling-block and an offense

---

[1] Matt. 21: 15-17.   [2] John 21: 15-17.   [3] Matt. 28: 19 (R. V.).

[4] Any careful study of the early years of Christianity will tend to show the new and enlarged interest in children taken by the Church of Christ, as in contrast with the view entertained of them by the ancient heathen and classic world. See, for example, on this point, Uhlhorn's *Conflict of Christianity with Heathenism*, pp. 102, 138, 182 f., 272 f.; also his *Christian Charity in the Ancient Church*, pp. 359, 386-388. There would, indeed, be more prominence given to the facts in this sphere if the subject itself had been a more prominent one in the minds of modern church historians generally. To examine the topical indexes of most of the church histories in current use on both sides of the ocean, would lead one to infer that there were no children in the centuries covered by those histories. But this would be an error!

to proud rabbi and to ambitious apostle.   Nor has it yet
overborne all silent contempt, or all active opposition,
among those who are named by his name.[1]   There are
still Christian rabbis who devote themselves, as preachers
and as teachers, to the elaboration and the discussion of
themes which only the adult mind is competent to, and
is pleased with.   And there are still Christian apostles
who, in the spirit of the ecclesiastical succession *so far*,
stand ready to rebuke any interruption of their own enjoyment of our Lord's teachings, in order that little children may be brought within hearing of him.   But just so
surely as Jesus Christ himself is the same "yesterday and
to-day, yea and forever,"[2] is he "moved with indignation"[3] against this refusal of his followers to recognize the
truth of truths in the plan and methods of his religion.[4]

Those who realize the distinctive character of Christianity as the religion of children and of the child-like

[1] At a large gathering of clergymen in one of the principal cities of the
United States, the presiding officer, who was an eminent minister, of a national reputation, said emphatically that he deemed the preaching to children
a lowering of the dignity of the pulpit!

[2] Heb. 13: 8 (R. V.).   [3] Mark 10: 14 (R. V.).

[4] That there are signs of unmistakable progress in the direction of giving
to children a place in the ministrations of the pulpit is obvious, not alone in
the work of individual preachers here and there, on every side, but in the
action of national and international assemblies of ministers of Christ on both
sides of the ocean.   Thus, for example, the General Assembly of the Free
Church of Scotland recently arranged for a sermon to children, by a prominent clergyman, on one of the Sunday afternoons during its sittings; the
latest Pan-Presbyterian Council, at London, expressed itself in favor of
special sermons to children; and in most of the principal denominations of
Christians, one Sunday in a year is formally recognized as "Children's Day,"
with the understanding that then at least the pulpit will direct its words immediately to children.   It is something to secure one Sunday in fifty-two for
the little ones.   That leaves only fifty-one Sundays in the ordinary year to
be brought into line for their benefit.

should realize, also, the truth that the extension, the up-building, and the establishing of Christ's Church, must, in the plan of God, be done chiefly by means of work among and with and for the children. To them, as they labor in his name, the words of our Lord concerning the reception of his kingdom here on earth have a literal as well as a figurative meaning: "I thank thee, O Father, Lord of heaven and earth, that thou didst hide these things from the wise and understanding, and didst reveal them unto babes: yea, Father; for so it was well-pleasing in thy sight."[1]

[1] Luke 10: 21.

INDEXES.

BIBLIOGRAPHICAL INDEX.

[The following list includes all the works which have been cited at first hand in these Lectures. The edition is in every case that to which reference is made in the footnotes. The following abbreviations are used : n. d. (no date); n. p. (no place); c. (copyright); ed. (edition or edited); tr. (translated). In the citations from the Talmud, made in the text and the notes ot the Lectures, the reference is to the folio and column of the Babylonian Talmud, unless the Jerusalem Talmud is specified; in which case the reference is to chapter and section. The references to the treatise Pirqe Aboth are to the chapter and section of the text as printed in Taylor's *Sayings of the Jewish Fathers*. All references to the Talmud, the Targums, and the Midrash, are at first hand, unless otherwise noted.]

ABBEY, CHARLES J., and OVERTON, JOHN H.—The English Church in the Eighteenth Century. New ed., revised and abridged. London, 1887.

Abridgment of the Acts of the General Assembly of the Church of Scotland. Edinburgh, 1811.

Advance, The. Vol. XXII. Chicago, 1888.

ALEXANDER, ARCHIBALD.—Suggestions in Vindication of Sunday-schools. N. p., 1829.
[The same.] Revised and enlarged by the author. Philadelphia, 1845.

ALFORD, HENRY.—The Greek Testament. With a critical and exegetical commentary. 6th ed., 4 vols. Boston and New York, 1873.

American Board of Commissioners for Foreign Missions, Memorial Volume of the First Fifty Years of the. 4th ed. Boston, 1861.

American Quarterly Register, The. Vol. X. Boston, 1838.

American Sunday School Magazine, The. Vols. I.–V. Philadelphia, 1824-29.

ANDREWES, LANCELOT.—The Pattern of Catechistical Doctrine at Large. London, 1650.

ANDREWS, SAMUEL J.—The Life of our Lord upon the Earth. 4th ed. New York, 1873.

Ante-Nicene Fathers, The. Ed. by Alexander Roberts and James Donaldson : Revised by A. Cleveland Coxe. 8 vols. Buffalo, 1885 f.

ARMSTRONG, WILLIAM.—Five-Minute Sermons to Children. New York and Cincinnati, 1887.

ASCHAM, ROGER.— The Scholemaster. Ed. and reprinted from the 1st and 2d editions, 1570, 71, by Edward Arber. London, 1870.

BACON, FRANCIS.—The Advancement of Learning. Ed. by W. Aldis Wright. 2d ed. Oxford, 1880.

BARNARD, HENRY.— Pestalozzi and Pestalozzianism. Life, educational principles, and methods of John Henry Pestalozzi. 3d ed. New York, n. d. [c. 1862.]

BUXTORF, JOHANNES. — Lexicon Chaldaicum, Talmudicum, et Rabbinicum. Ed. by J. Buxtorf, *filius.* Basel, 1640.

Synagoga Judaica. 4th ed., revised by J. Jacob Buxtorf. Basel, 1680.

CARDWELL, EDWARD.—Synodalia: A collection of articles of religion, canons, and proceedings of conventions in the province of Canterbury, from the year 1547 to the year 1717. 2 vols. Oxford, 1842.

Catechism of the Council of Trent, The. Tr., with notes, by Theodore Alois Buckley. London, 1852.

CHALMERS, THOMAS.—Select Works. Ed. by William Hanna. 12 vols. Edinburgh and London, 1854-57.

CHESEBROUGH, AMOS S.—The Culture of Child-Piety. Boston, n. d. [c. 1886.]

Child's Preacher, The: A series of addresses to the young, founded on Scripture texts. New York, n. d. [c. 1855.]

Christian Spectator, The. Boston, 1819.

Church Cyclopædia, The. See BENTON, A. A.

Church Sunday School Magazine, The. Vols. XX.-XXIII. London, 1884-87.

CLARK, F. E.—The Children and the Church, and the Young People's Society of Christian Endeavor, as a Means of Bringing them Together. With an introduction by C. L. Goodell. Boston, n. d. [c. 1882.]

Young People's Prayer-meetings in Theory and Practice. With fifteen hundred topics. New York, 1887.

COGSWELL, WILLIAM. — The Assistant to Family Religion. 2d ed. Boston, 1828.

COLLIER, JOSEPH A.—Little Crowns and How to Win Them. New York, 1868.

COX, SAMUEL.—The Bird's Nest, and Other Sermons for Children of All Ages. New York, 1887.

CRABB, GEORGE. — English Synonymes Explained in Alphabetical Order. New ed., with additions and corrections. New York, 1879.

CRANZ, DAVID.—The Ancient and Modern History of the Brethren. Tr. and ed. by Benjamin Latrobe. London, 1780.

CURRIE, JAMES.—The Principles and Practice of Early and Infant School-Education. 12th ed. London and Edinburgh, n. d. [1857.]

CURRIER, A. H.—The Life of Constans L. Goodell, D. D. With an introduction by William M. Taylor. New York, n. d. [c. 1887.]

DAVIDS, LOUISA. — The Sunday School: An essay. 4th ed., with an appendix. London, 1855.

DEUTSCH, EMANUEL.—The Literary Remains of the Late Emanuel Deutsch. With a brief memoir. New York, 1874.

DILLMANN, AUGUST.—Die Genesis. 5th ed. Leipsic, 1886.

DODDRIDGE, PHILIP.—Sermons and Religious Tracts. In 3 vols. Vol. I. London, 1761.

Sermons on the Religious Education of Children; Preached at Northampton. A new ed., revised and corrected. Cambridge, 1806.

DOOLITTEL, THOMAS.—A Plain Method of Catechizing. With a prefatory catechism. 4th ed. London, 1700.

DORCHESTER, DANIEL.—The Problem of Religious Progress. New York, n. d. [c. 1881.]

Christianity in the United States. From the first settlement down to the present time. New York, 1888.

DRURY, B. PAXSON.—A Fruitful Life: A narrative of the experiences and missionary labors of Stephen Paxson. By his daughter. Philadelphia, 1882.

DWIGHT, TIMOTHY.— Travels; in New-England and New-York. 4 vols. New Haven, 1821 f.

Theology Explained and Defended in a Series of Sermons. With a Memoir of the life of the author. 12th ed., 4 vols. New York, 1857.

EATON, T. T.—Talks to Children. With an introduction by John A. Broadus. Chicago and New York, n. d. [c. 1887.]

EBERS, G.—Egypt; Descriptive, Historical and Picturesque. 2 vols. London and New York, 1879.

EDERSHEIM, ALFRED.—The Life and Times of Jesus the Messiah. 2d ed., 2 vols. New York and London, n. d.

Sketches of Jewish Social Life in the Days of Christ. London, n. d.

EDMOND, JOHN. — The Children's Church at Home; or, Family Services for the Lord's Day. London, 1861.

[The same.] Second series. London, 1863.

ELLICOTT, CHARLES JOHN.—Historical Lectures on the Life of our Lord Jesus Christ. Hulsean Lectures for 1859. Boston, 1862.

An Old Testament Commentary for English Readers. By various writers. 5 vols. New York, n. d.

A New Testament Commentary for English Readers. By various writers. 2 vols. New York, n. d.

Encyclopædia Britannica, The: A dictionary of arts, sciences and general literature. 9th ed. (American reprint.) Philadelphia, 1875 ff.

EWALD, HEINRICH.— The History of Israel. Vol. VI.: The Life and Times of Christ. Tr. by J. Frederick Smith. London, 1883.

FARRAR, F. W.—The Gospel According to St. Luke. With maps, notes and introduction. [In The Cambridge Bible for Schools.] Cambridge, 1880.

The Life of Christ. 2 vols. New York, n. d.

The Life and Work of St. Paul. 2 vols. New York, n. d.

The Early Days of Christianity. New York, 1883.

FERRIS, ISAAC.—An Appeal to Ministers of the Gospel in Behalf of Sunday-schools. A sermon preached at the request of the Board of Managers of the American Sunday School Union, Philadelphia, May 19, 1834.

FISH, HENRY C.—[Masterpieces of Pulpit Eloquence.] History and Repository of Pulpit Eloquence. 2 vols. New York, 1869.

FISHER, GEORGE PARK.—History of the Christian Church. New York, 1887.

FLETCHER, ALEXANDER.—Lectures, Adapted to the Capacity of Children. Selected from the London ed. of 3 vols., and revised. 2 vols. New York, n. d.

FORSYTH, WILLIAM.—The Novels and Novelists of the Eighteenth Century. In illustration of the manners and morals of the age. New York, 1871.

GEIKIE, CUNNINGHAM.—The Life and Words of Christ. 2 vols. in one. New York, 1880.

Gentleman's Magazine and Historical Chronicle, The. Vol. LIV., Part I. London, 1784.

GESENIUS, WILLIAM. — Thesaurus Philologicus Criticus Linguæ Hebraeæ et Chaldaeæ Veteris Testamenti. 3 vols. Leipsic, 1829-42.

GIBSON, EDMUND.—Codex Juris Ecclesiastici Anglicani. London, 1713.

GIESELER, JOHN C. L.—A Text-Book of Church History. Tr. and ed. by Henry B. Smith. Vol. IV.—A. D. 1517-1648. New York, 1876.

GILBERT, SIMEON.—The Lesson System: The story of its origin and inauguration. New York, 1879.

GILLETT, E. H.—History of the Presbyterian Church in the United States of America. Revised ed., 2 vols. Philadelphia, n. d. [c. 1864.]

GODET, F.— A Commentary on the Gospel of St. Luke. Tr. from the 2d French ed. New York, 1881.

GODWYN, THOMAS.—Moses and Aaron : Civil and ecclesiastical rites used by the ancient Hebrews. London, 1667.

GOODELL, C. L.—How to Build a Church. With an Introduction by E. B. Webb. Boston, n. d. [c. 1883.]

GRAY, GEORGE ZABRISKIE. — The Children's Crusade : An episode of the thirteenth century. New York, 1870.

GREEN, ASHBEL, and JONES, JOSEPH H.—The Life of Ashbel Green, V. D. M. Begun to be written by himself in his eighty-second year and continued to his eighty-fourth. Prepared for the press, at the author's request, by Joseph H. Jones. New York, 1849.

GREEN, JOHN RICHARD.— History of the English People. 4 vols. New York, 1882.

GREEN, SAMUEL G.—Addresses to Children. With introductory suggestions to ministers and teachers. London, n. d. [1849.] Pearls for the Little Ones; or, Lectures on the Bible. Philadelphia, n. d.

GREENWOOD, F. W. P.—Sermons to Children. New ed. Boston, 1868.

GREGORY, ALFRED.—Robert Raikes, Journalist and Philanthropist : A history of the origin of Sunday-schools. New York, n. d.

HAMBURGER, J.—Real-Encyclopädie für Bibel und Talmud. 2 vols. Strelitz, 1870-83.

HARRIS, J. RENDEL.—Fragments of Philo Judaeus. Cambridge, 1887. The Teaching of the Apostles (*Didachē tōn Apostolōn*), newly ed., with facsimile text and a commentary. Baltimore and London, 1887.

HART, JOHN S.— In the School-Room : Chapters in the philosophy of education. Philadelphia, 1868.

Harvard College, Annual Reports of the President and Treasurer of, 1880-81. Cambridge, 1881.

HATCH, EDWIN.—The Organization of the Early Christian Churches. Bampton Lectures for 1880. Oxford and Cambridge, 1881.

HAUSRATH, A.— A History of the New Testament Times. Vols. I., II. : The Time of Jesus. Tr. by C. T. Poynting and P. Quenzer. London, 1878-80.

HENDERSON, E.—The Vaudois. London, 1858.

HENSHAW, J. P. K.—The Usefulness of Sunday-Schools : A sermon preached at the request of the American Sunday School Union, in St. Andrew's Church, Philadelphia, May 20, 1833.

HERBERT, GEORGE.—The Remains of that Sweet Singer of the Temple George Herbert. London, 1848.

HERODOTUS.—Historiarum libri novem. Ed. by H. R. Dietsch. 2 vols. Leipsic, 1864.

HERZOG, J. J., PLITT, G. L., and HAUCK, A.—Real-Encyklopädie für protestantische Theologie und Kirche. Leipsic, 1877 ff.

HESIOD.—Carmina. Ed., with notes, by Carolus Goettlingius. 2d ed. Gotha, 1843.

HETHERINGTON, W. M.—History of the Church of Scotland. From the introduction of Christianity to the period of the Disruption in 1843. 3d American, from the 3d Edinburgh ed. New York, 1844. History of the Westminster Assembly of Divines. New York, 1843.

HILL, JOHN C.—The Children's Sermon. With a selection of five-minute sermons to children. Philadelphia, 1882.

HIRSCH, SAMSON RAPHAEL.—Aus dem rabbinischen Schulleben. [In " Einladungschrift zu der öffentlichen Prüfung der Unterrichtsanstalten der Israelitischen Religions-Gesellschaft zu Frankfurt am Main."] Frankfort-on-the-Main, 1871.

25

Home, the School, and the Church; or, The Presbyterian Educational Repository. Ed. by C. Van Rensselaer. 10 vols. Philadelphia, 1850-60.

HOOD, E. PAXTON.—The Day, the Book, and the Teacher: A centenary memorial. London, n. d. [1880.]

HOW, W. WALSHAM.—Plain Words to Children. 5th ed. London, n. d. [1886.]

HUMPHREY, HEMAN.— The Way to Bless and Save our Country: A sermon preached in Philadelphia, at the request of the American Sunday School Union, May 23, 1831.

JEBB, JOHN.—Pastoral Instructions, on the Character and Principles of the Church of England. Selected from his former publications. New ed. London, 1844.

JESSUP, H. HARRIS.—Syrian Home-Life. Compiled by Isaac Riley. New York, n. d. [c. 1874.]

JONES, WILLIAM.—The Jubilee Memorial of the Religious Tract Society : Containing a record of its origin, proceedings, and results, A. D. 1799, to A. D. 1849. London, 1850.

JOSEPHUS, FLAVIUS.—Opera Omnia. Ed. by Immanuel Bekker. 6 vols. Leipsic, 1855.

JOST, ISAAC MARCUS.—Allgemeine Geschichte des israelitischen Volkes. 2 vols. Berlin, 1832.

JOWETT, B.—The Dialogues of Plato. Tr. into English, with analyses and introductions. 4 vols. Oxford, 1871.

KEIM, THEODOR.—The History of Jesus of Nazara: Considered in its connection with the national life of Israel. Tr. by Arthur Ransom (Vol. II. by E. M. Goldert). 6 vols. London, 1876-81.

KIRK, E. N.—Address to the Convention of Sunday School Teachers, Pittsfield, June 24, 1863. Boston, n. d.

KITTO, JOHN.—A Cyclopaedia of Biblical Literature. 3d ed. Ed. by W. L. Alexander. 3 vols. Edinburgh, 1862.

KÖSTLIN, JULIUS.—Life of Luther. Tr. from the German. New York, 1883.

KRAUSSOLD, L.—Die Katechetik für Schule und Kirche. Erlangen, 1880.

KURTZ, JOHN HENRY.—Text-Book of Church History. [Tr. by J. H. A. Bomberger.] 2 vols. Philadelphia, 1862.

LAGARDE, PAUL D E.— Prophetae Chaldaice. Leipsic, 1872.

LANE, EDWARD WILLIAM.—An Account of the Manners and Customs of the Modern Egyptians. 5th ed. Ed. by Edward Stanley Poole. 2 vols. London, 1871.

LANGE, J. P.—A Commentary on the Holy Scriptures. Critical, doctrinal, and homiletical. Tr. and ed. by Philip Schaff, in connection with American scholars of various evangelical denominations. 25 vols. New York, 1864-80.

The Life of the Lord Jesus Christ. Ed. by Marcus Dods. 4 vols. Philadelphia, 1872.

LAVELEYE, ÉMILE DE.— L'Instruction du Peuple. Paris, 1872.

LEA, HENRY CHARLES.—A History of the Inquisition of the Middle Ages. 3 vols. New York, 1888.

LECKY, WILLIAM EDWARD HARTPOLE.—A History of England in the Eighteenth Century. 6 vols. New York, 1878.

LEVY, JAKOB.—Neuhebräisches und chaldäisches Wörterbuch über die Talmudim und Midraschim. Leipsic, 1876 ff.

LIDDELL, H. G., and SCOTT, R.—A Greek-English Lexicon. 7th ed. New York, 1883.

LIGHTFOOT, JOHN.—Horae Hebraicae et Talmudicae. Ed. by Robert Gandell. 4 vols. Oxford, 1859.

LIGHTFOOT, J. B.—S. Clement of Rome. An Appendix containing the newly recovered portions, with introductions, notes and translations. London, 1877.

Littell's Living Age. Vol. XI. Boston, 1846.

LOCKE, JOHN. — Works. 3 vols. London, 1727.

LOFTIE, W. J.—A Ride in Egypt. London, 1879.

LONGFELLOW, HENRY WADSWORTH.—Poetical Works. Household ed. Boston and New York, 1887.

MACDUFF, J. R.—Hosannas of the Children, and Other Short Sermons for Young Worshippers. New York, 1882.

MACLEOD, ALEXANDER.—The Wonderful Lamp, and Other Talks to Children. New York, n. d.

The Gentle Heart. A second series of "Talking to the Children." New York, n. d.

The Children's Portion. New York, 1885.

MAHAFFY, J. P.—Social Life in Greece from Homer to Menander. 5th ed. London, 1883.

MAHON, LORD [Earl of Stanhope].—History of England from the Peace of Utrecht to the Peace of Versailles, 1713-1783. 5th ed., revised, 7 vols. London, 1858.

MAIMONIDES, MOSES. — Yad Hachazaqa. Part I. [Title-page missing.]

MARCUS, SAMUEL.—Die Pädagogik des israelitischen Volkes, von der Patriarchenzeit bis auf den Talmud. Vienna, 1877.

MASKELL, WILLIAM.—Monumenta Ritualia Ecclesiae Anglicanae. 2 vols. London, 1846.

MAURICE, F. D.—The Lord's Prayer, the Creed, and the Commandments: A manual for parents and schoolmasters. To which is added, The Order of the Scriptures. London, 1870.

MAYER, JOHANN.—Geschichte des Katechumenats und der Katechese in der ersten sechs Jahrhunderten. Gekrönte Preisschrift. Kempten, 1868.

MCCLINTOCK, JOHN, and STRONG, JAMES.—Cyclopædia of Biblical, Theological, and Ecclesiastical Literature. 10 vols. New York, 1870-81.

MCEWEN, ABEL.—Half-Century Sermon on Some Changes which have Occurred in the First Congregational Society in New London; in this City; and in the County to which it Pertains. New London, 1857.

MCLEAN, ALEXANDER.—Food for the Lambs; or, Sermons to Children. New York, 1868.

MEADE, WILLIAM.—Old Churches, Ministers, and Families of Virginia. 2 vols. Philadelphia, 1861.

Menorath Ha-maor. Venice, 1623.

MERRILL, SELAH.—Galilee in the Time of Christ. Boston, n. d. [1881.]

Méthode de Saint-Sulpice, dans la Direction des Catéchismes, avec des plans d'instruction pour les divers catéchismes. 3d ed. Paris and Lyons, 1874.

MEYER, H. A. W.— Critical and Exegetical Handbook to the Gospels of Mark and Luke. Tr. from the 5th German ed., by R. E. Wallis. 2 vols. Edinburgh, 1880.

MICHAUD, JOSEPH FRANCIS.—The History of the Crusades. Tr. by W. Robson. A new ed., with preface and supplementary chapter by Hamilton W. Mabie. 3 vols. New York, 1881.

Midrash Rabba [including the five Megilloth]. [The following treatises are cited: Bereshith Rabba (on Genesis); Wayyiqra Rabba (on Leviticus); Bammidbar Rabba (on Numbers); Midrash Tehillim (on Psalms); Qoheleth Rabba (on Ecclesiastes); Shir Rabba (on Canticles)]. Wilmersdorf, 1673.

REUSS, EDUARD.— Die Geschichte der Heiligen Schriften Alten Testaments. Brunswick, 1881.

RIEHM, EDUARD C. AUG.— Handwörterbuch des biblischen Altertums. 2 vols. Bielefeld and Leipsic, 1884.

ROBERTS, WILLIAM.—Memoirs of the Life and Correspondence of Mrs. Hannah More. 2 vols. New York, 1835.

ROSENMÜLLER, ERNST FRIEDRICH KARL.—Das alte und neue Morgenland. 6 vols. Leipsic, 1818-20.

ROSS, A. HASTINGS.— Sermons for Children. Boston and Chicago, 1887.

RYLE, J. C.—The Christian Leaders of the Last Century ; or, England a Hundred Years Ago. London, 1878.

SCHAFF, PHILIP. — The Creeds of Christendom. With a history and critical notes. 3 vols. New York, 1877.

History of the Christian Church. New ed., 4 vols. New York, 1882-85.

A Religious Encyclopædia. Based on the Real-Encyclopädie of Herzog, Plitt and Hauck. 3 vols. New York, n. d. [c. 1882.]

SCHLEUSNER, J. FRIEDER.—Novum Lexicon Graeco-Latinum in Novum Testamentum. 3d ed., 2 vols. Leipsic and London, 1808.

SCHUMANN, J. CHR. GOTTLOB.— Lehrbuch der Pädagogik. 2 vols. Hanover, 1875.

SCHÜRER, EMIL.—A History of the Jewish People in the Time of Jesus Christ. 2d Division. Tr. by Sophia Taylor and Peter Christie. 3 vols. Edinburgh, 1885.

SEPP, JOHANN NEPOMUK.—Das Leben Jesu Christi. 2d ed., 6 vols. Regensburg, 1865.

SHAW, THOMAS B.—A Complete Manual of English Literature. Ed. by William Smith. With a sketch of American literature, by Henry T. Tuckerman. New York, 1870.

SIMON, JOSEPH. — L'Education et l'Instruction des Enfants chez les anciens Juifs. 3d ed. Leipsic, 1879.

SMITH, WILLIAM, and CHEETHAM, SAMUEL.—A Dictionary of Christian Antiquities. 2 vols. Hartford, 1880.

SMITH, WILLIAM, and WACE, HENRY.—A Dictionary of Christian Biography, Literature, Sects and Doctrines during the First Eight Centuries. 4 vols. London, 1877-87.

SOUTH, ROBERT.—Sermons Preached upon Several Occasions. A new ed. 5 vols. Oxford, 1842.

SPANGENBERG, AUGUST GOTTLIEB.— The Life of Nicholas Lewis Count Zinzendorf. Tr. by Samuel Jackson. London, 1838.

[Speaker's Commentary, The] The Holy Bible according to the Authorized Version: With an explanatory and critical commentary and a revision of the translation, by bishops and other clergy of the Anglican Church. Ed. by F. C. Cook. 10 vols. New York, 1872-81.

SPOONER, EDWARD. — Parson and People; or, Incidents in the Every-day Life of a Clergyman. From the 2d London ed., with an introduction by an American clergyman. New York, 1865.

SPRAGUE, WILLIAM B. — Annals of the American Pulpit. 9 vols. New York, 1857.

STALL, SYLVANUS. — Methods of Church Work, Religious, Social and Financial. New York, 1887.

STANLEY, ARTHUR PENRHYN.— Sermons for Children, including The Beatitudes and The Faithful Servant. New York, 1887.

STAPFER, EDMOND.—Palestine in the Time of Christ. Tr. by Annie Harwood Holmden. 3d ed., with maps and plans. New York, n. d. [1885.]

STEEL, ROBERT.—The Christian Teacher in Sunday Schools. London, 1867.

STEINMETZ, ANDREW.— History of the Jesuits. 3 vols. London, 1848.

STIER, RUDOLF.—The Words of the Lord Jesus. Tr. by W. B. Pope. 8 vols. Edinburgh, 1855.

STRAUSS, DAVID FRIEDRICH.—The Life of Jesus for the People. Authorized translation. 2d ed., 2 vols. London and Edinburgh, 1879.

STRYPE, JOHN.— Memorials of the Most Reverend Father in God Thomas Cranmer, sometime Lord Bishop of Canterbury. 2 vols. Oxford, 1812.

The Life and Acts of Matthew Parker, the first Archbishop of Canterbury in the Reign of Queen Elizabeth. In 4 books. Oxford, 1821.

Annals of the Reformation and Establishment of Religion, and other Various Occurrences in the Church of England, during Queen Elizabeth's Happy Reign. 4 vols. Oxford, 1824.

Sunday School Chronicle, The. Vol. IX. London, 1880.

Sunday School Times, The. Vols. I.-XXIX. Philadelphia, 1859-87.

Sunday School Visitant, The. Vol. I. Utica, 1829.

Talmud Babli. [The following treatises are cited: Baba Bathra; Baba Qamma; Berakhoth; Chagiga; Cheleq; Erubin; Kethuboth; Makkoth; Megilla; Pesachim; Qiddushin; Rosh Ha-shana; Sanhedrin; Shabbath; Succa; Taanith; Yoma.] 12 vols. Sulzbach, 1755.

Talmud Yerushalmi. [The following treatises are cited: Chagiga; Kethuboth; Megilla; Shabbath.] 5 vols. Zhitomir, 1860-67.

Targum of Jonathan on the Pentateuch. [See WALTON, BRIAN.]

Targum of Jonathan on the Prophets. [See LAGARDE, PAUL DE.]

TAYLOR, CHARLES.—Sayings of the Jewish Fathers [Pirqe Aboth]. In Hebrew and English, with notes. Cambridge, 1877.

TAYLOR, JEREMY.—The History of the Life and Death of Jesus Christ. New ed., revised by J. A. Buckley. London, 1860.

THAYER, JOSEPH H.— A Greek-English Lexicon of the New Testament: Being Grimm's Wilke's Clavis Novi Testamenti, tr., revised and enlarged. New York, 1887.

TODD, JOHN.—Lectures to Children, Familiarly Illustrating Important Truth. 2d ed. Northampton, 1834.

TREMELLIUS, IMMANUEL, and JUNIUS, FRANCISCUS.— Testamenti Veteris Biblia Sacra. Geneva, 1630.

TRUMBULL, H. CLAY.—Children in the Temple: A hand-book for the Sunday-school concert, and a guide for the children's preacher. Springfield, 1869.

A Model Superintendent: A sketch of the life, character and methods of work of Henry P. Haven of the International Lesson Committee. New York, 1880.

Teaching and Teachers; or, The Sunday-school Teacher's Teaching Work, and the Other Work of the Sunday-school Teacher. Philadelphia, 1885.

TURNER, WILLIAM, JUN.—Sunday-Schools Recommended: In a Sermon preached before the Associated Dissenting Ministers in the Northern Counties, at their annual meeting, at Morpeth, June 13, 1786, and published at their request. To which is added, an appendix, concerning the formation, conduct, and expence of these schools. Newcastle, 1786.

TYERMAN, L.—The Life and Times of the Rev. John Wesley, M.A., Founder of the Methodists. 3 vols. New York, 1872.

TYNG, STEPHEN H.— Forty Years' Experience in Sunday-schools, New York, 1860,

SCRIPTURAL INDEX.

TOPICAL INDEX.

AARON, learning and teaching, 25 f.
Abbey and Overton's history, 99 f., 104.
Abooyah, Elisha b., his maxim, 27.
Abraham at school, 5; his trained servants, 6 f., 151, 280 f., 285.
Accommodations for the Sunday-school to be provided by the church, 209 f.
Admission of new scholars, 240 f., 258 f.
Adults: included in Sunday-school membership, 188 f., 191-196; preaching to, does not reach the children, 256 f., 312-315.
Advance study of the lesson, 230.
Ahaz, the enemy of Bible schools, 6.
Albigenses, as Bible students, 65.
Alexander, Archibald: on Sunday-school membership, 192, 194; on the family and the Sunday-school, 148 f., 171 f., 179.
Alexandria, the great school at, 56-58, 220, 250.
Alford, Dean, on the word "teaching," 36.
Alleine, Joseph, the school of, 112.
Allen, Franklin, the Sunday-school methods of, 240 f.
Alpine shepherd, the, example of, 190.
America: family religion in, 165-176, 179-182; introduction of the Sunday-school into, 122 f., 165; Sunday-school progress in, 122-142, 188-190.
American Board of Commissioners for Foreign Missions: its early missionaries, 334.
American observer, an, on family religion in England, 155 f.

American Sunday-school, the: differs from the English school, 127, 156 f., 187 f., 304 f; foreign opinions concerning, 132 f.; its founders, 122 f.; its introduction into Europe, 134-136; its work for Christianity, 122 f.; progress of, 122-142, 188-190.
American Sunday School Union, the, 123-125, 131, 189, 305.
Amoraim, in synagogue schools, 19.
Analogies to the influence of the Sunday-school on the family, 176 f.
Andrew, the apostle, 219 f.
Andrewes, Lancelot, on Julian the Apostate, 49, 73.
Anniversary of the Pomfret Church, 129 f.
Apollos, the preacher, instructed, 41, 220.
Apostles' Creed, the, 259, 361, 373.
Apostolic Church, the: teaching in, 37-44, 47-49.
Appliances, Sunday-school, to be paid for by the church, 210 f.
Application of a children's sermon should be specific, 363-366.
Aquaviva, the Jesuit, 69.
Architecture, Sunday-school, 51, 209 f.
Armenia, early Sunday-schools in, 62, 111.
Arminian Magazine, 113.
Armstrong, Wm., sermons of, 329.
Arnot, Wm., sermons of, 337.
Asbury, Bp., Sunday-school organized by, 122.
Asbury, England, a Sunday-school in, 112.
Ascham, Roger, his protest against rote learning, 83.

396

Blair, David, Sunday-school started by, 112.
Blake, Mortimer, children's sermons of, 337.
Blowing out the light, a child's question concerning, 350.
Blue Ribbon Army, 291.
Boehler, Peter: his impress on John Wesley, 107.
Bohemian Brethren, Bible-school idea among the, 65.
Bolton : James Heys's Sunday-school at, 112; voluntary teaching at, 119.
Bonar, A. A., children's sermons of, 337.
Bonar, Horatius, children's sermons of, 337.
Borromeo, St. Carlo, Sunday-school work of, 71 f.
Boston, children's services in, 322; preaching to children in, 335.
Bowdoin College: D. R. Goodwin and Longfellow in, 354; religion in, 166.
Boyd, Robert, children's sermons of, 337.
Boys' Brigade, 291.
Boys' Circles, 294 f.
Boys, lady teachers for, 223.
Bradley, Dean: his sermons to children, 324.
Breath of the children, Jewish estimate of, 26 f.
Brechin, Scotland, Sunday-school beginnings in, 112.
Breed, Wm. P., children's sermons of, 337.
Brethren of the Common Life, Bible-school idea among the, 65.
Bright, Ireland, Sunday-school beginnings in, 112.
Bright, John: his tribute to Sunday-schools, 121.
Brighton, Church Congress at, 323.
British and Foreign Bible Society, the: owed its origin to the Sunday-school, 120.
Broadus, John A., on preaching to children, 325 f., 344, 353.
Brooklyn, Sunday-school convention at, 256.
Brooks, Phillips: his estimate of the children's church, 340 f.
Brown, G. Baldwin: his view of early church methods, 47.

Buell, Marcus D., children's sermons of, 337.
Buisson, F.: his tribute to the American Sunday-school, 132 f.
Bullard, Asa: tells of large Sunday-school attendance, 195.
Bunsen, Baron: his estimate of the school in early church plans, 48.
Burns, Robert: his "Cotter's Saturday Night," 168.
Bushnell, Horace: his sermon-titles, 86, 351; on a child's capacity for great truths, 219, 341 f ; on song-worship for children, 197 f.

CAIRNS, John: his sermons to children, 337.
Calvin, John: his catechisms, 68 ; his estimate of work for children, 106; his sermon on "Bearing the Reproach of Christ," 351.
Capacity of a child to comprehend great truths, 218 f.
Cappadocia, Bible schools in, 62.
Catechetical teaching: a necessary condition of the Church's progress, 49, 64, 66-68, 73, 89, 104; approved in the divine plan of religious instruction, 4-7, 20-28; 30-39; decline of: before the Dark Ages, 63-65; after the Reformation, 73-76, 87, 94, 104 f.; in New England, 88 f.; essential to a Sunday-school, 3 f.; Jesus' part in, 29-31; the method of the Jewish Bible-schools, 20-26; use of, by Jesus, 32-36 ; by the apostles, 37-41; by the Early Church, 48-63; by the Waldenses and others, 64-66; by the Reformers, 68, 74 f.; by the Church of Rome, 69-72; by the Moravians and others, 94; was by form of question and answer, 20-24, 29, 32-41, 43, 52-61, 75, 78.
Catechismal service: its place in church plans, 3 f., 48.
Catechisms: early, 64 f.; intended as aids to interlocutory teaching, 68, 72, 75–88; prepared by Luther and his co-workers, 68, 77 f.; by Calvin, 68; by the Council of Trent, 70 f.; by Bellarmine, 72; by Protestant Church leaders, 75; by the Church of England, 78-80; by the West-